To
Klaus + Irma Wagenbach
with thanks for listening

Norma H Lloyd

W9-AEM-149

The View From Olympus

A New Gnostic Gospel

Pluto In Sagittarius (2000 -   )

Pluto will enter Sagittarius around the year 2000, marking a period of spiritual regeneration at the beginning of the Aquarian age. At this time there will be a fundamental understanding of deeper spiritual values among all people. Religions as they are known at present will be completely transformed. There will be one world religion based on man's direct intuitive communion with the One Creator. New spiritual leaders will arise to teach the fundamental laws governing all life in the universe. The new world religion will combine all the highest expressions of the great religions of the past, with a more comprehensive scientific understanding of the underlying forces of life.

The Astrologer's Handbook
Frances Sakoian & Louis S. Acker

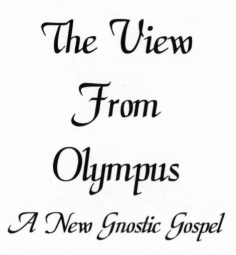

The View From Olympus

A New Gnostic Gospel

By
Donna H. Lloyd, PhD

Deltaran Publishing Co., 2675 W. Hwy. 89A, Suite 410
Sedona, Arizona 86336

Published by Deltaran Publishing Co. Sedona, Arizona

Copyright ©1991 Deltaran Publishing Co.

All rights reserved. Except for brief excerpts quoted in
reviews, no part of this publication may be reproduced,
stored in a retrieval system or transmitted in any form or by
any means without written permission of the publisher.

Library of Congress Cataloging in Publication Data: Lloyd,
Donna H. Ph.D. The View From Olympus 1, Mystic
Philosophy. 2, Religious History. 3, New Age
Library of Congress Catalog Card Number: 90-084184
ISBN: 0-9627291-0-8 hardcover
ISBN: 0-9627291-1-6 paperback

Excerpt from THE ASTROLOGER'S HANDBOOK by
Frances Sakoian & Louis S. Acker. Copyright ©1973
by Frances Sakoian.
Reprinted by permission of Harper & Row, Publishers, Inc.

Cover design and drawings by Arthur C. Newhall

Printed in the United States of America

Acknowledgements

I wish to thank the friends who have supported me through good times and bad while I researched and wrote this book. Special thanks are due to my friends Deama Bowles, Margaret Schiffel, Klaus and Irma Wagenbach, and my artist and his wife, my good friends, Arthur and Emma Newhall. Finally, I must express my great appreciation to my editor, Kathy Dame-Glerum, whose assistance has been invaluable.

In
Memory
Of
David Edward
For
Todd Allan and Randall David

Table Of Contents

Illustrations

Preface

Everyone, at some time in his or her life, has wondered about the meaning of life, about the universe and mankind's place in its scheme. To answer these questions has been the goal of both science and religion, but, so far, both have fallen short of the mark. Consequently, we have been left with nagging, unanswered questions.

I was born into the fourth generation of a family of Protestant ministers and teachers and was saturated with Fundamentalist/Evangelical Christianity at an early age. But, being endowed with a logical turn of mind, I soon concluded that something was lacking in the dogma of the Church. It did not equate with my sense of reason. While wandering about the fields of our farm one day, it suddenly came to me that I would devote my life to the task of finding the truth about the nature of the universe and our place in it.

After many years of searching for the causes of the problems which plague us, both as individuals and as a society as a whole, some very interesting facts have come to light which seem to provide keys to the answers which we seek. It has been found that mankind was once privy to a body of highly sophisticated knowledge which became lost several thousand years ago. I believe, as do others, that the answers to our questions may be contained in this ancient and forgotten wisdom.

The purpose of this book is to try to identify the causes of our present dilemma and to suggest some cures based upon this Ancient Wisdom. In so doing, it will be necessary to point out some of the errors which have been made by our established institutions. But, where certain beliefs and practices are called into question, the purpose is not to condemn but rather to diagnose the illness in order to effect a cure. Many modern institutions have made valuable contributions to our goal of enlightenment. Nevertheless, because they have based their premises upon the faulty reasoning of older institutions, they have failed to see the picture in its true perspective.

One of the major principles which has been overlooked is that of the Universal Laws to which mankind is subject just as is the rest of the natural world. We must, therefore, learn to understand and abide by these Laws if we wish to have an orderly world in which to live.

All of us have known for a long time that our society is dis-eased. But, so far, the remedies which have been applied have not worked. They have failed because they treat only symptoms, not causes.

Even the worst of us has a picture in mind of the ideal society in which we would like to live. This is the reason we are so easily fooled by high-sounding phrases coming from the lips and/or pens of those who claim to have the key to the answers we seek. But it is obvious that it takes more than lofty platitudes to effect the desired results.

To realize the desired changes, we must first recognize that this is not just a societal concern, it is the problem and responsibility of every individual and requires that each of us become aware of the causes behind the dis-ease from which we suffer. Furthermore, we must be willing to expend the necessary effort to make the difference. Society did not create the problem. The causes lie in the attitudes and behavior of the individuals who make up the society. Consequently, the cure must begin with us as individuals.

Although there is a small segment of our society which has already begun to show a readiness to be responsible for making changes, they are in the minority. There will be no meaningful changes made until greater numbers accept the challenge to make a difference by taking responsibility for their own lives.

In this book a study is made of the ancient, prehistoric past in search of the causes of our modern problems. The answers revealed will, hopefully, provide a foundation of truth upon which each individual can build his or her own new and harmonious world.

✦

Introduction

The theme frequently heard today is that of a coming "New Age" in which, it is anticipated, there will be many changes. However, few seem to understand the fundamental meaning of such an event. They simply accept it on faith, if they accept it at all. The purpose of this book is to attempt to clarify the confusion surrounding the issue. The best way to accomplish this seems to be to try to establish a continuity between the past, present and future within the framework of the astrological ages and see what sense can be made.

In modern times both science and religion deny that the astrological ages have any meaning for the modern world. But, the fact that it has been a belief for a very long time leads one to wonder if, perhaps, there was a time when the subject was better understood than it is today. If so, one might also wonder if it might have some significance for us.

The answer to these questions can only be found by going back in time to where the idea of the astrological ages began. The first obstacle one confronts in the search is the fact that written records do not go back far enough. But, when one dares to go outside the established, accepted sources for information, it is found that there is evidence available which indicates that the system of knowledge which contains the secret of the Ages goes back into prehistory. It goes back many thousands of years beyond written history which began less than 6,000 years ago.

It has been discovered that the body of knowledge which has been passed down to us through myth, legend and various ancient records contained information regarding the construct of the universe of which modern science has become aware only since the relativity and quantum theories have been known, or, in the twentieth century. This fact alone is a testimony to its validity.

Modern scholars call this body of knowledge "The Ancient Wisdom" or "The Perennial Philosophy." It was preserved not only in myth and legend but in the ancient literature of Persia, Egypt, India and other cultures by the educated few. Sometime around the 6th century B.C.E. it began to be revived in Greece, China and India but was lost to the masses again during the major part of the "Christian Era" or the Piscean age.

Knowledge of the nature of the universe and our relationship to it constituted a large body of information which was in the possession of a great prehistoric civilization. Fortunately, it was not totally lost during the period of decline which was apparently experienced. While it is not understood by theologians, some of this knowledge is contained in the literature of the major religions today. Additional information has been found in records which archaeologists have unearthed in the last two hundred years.

In recent years, archaeology has done much to remove the curtain which separates us from the prehistoric past. By following the rules of proportion, it has developed the art of reconstructing the forms of ancient animals guided by only a few recovered bones.

More recently, this art form has been used in forensic medicine to determine not only the cause of death but to recreate the facial features as an aid to the identification of a recently deceased person when bones are all that remain. Because of the success of the latter, the validity of the recreations of prehistoric creatures seems more likely as well.

In a similar manner, based upon what is known about the past five or six thousand years as found in the study of history, an attempt is made in this book to recreate the cycles of the devolution and evolution of our race through the astrological ages, including those which occurred in the prehistoric past. It is hoped that, in a manner similar to that of archaeology, by fleshing out the prehistoric past in the context of our evolution through the ages, we can acquire a new perspective on the present and, perhaps, even the future.

Archaeological finds confirm the picture, as will be described in the context of the cycle of the astrological ages, that the consciousness of mankind was on a decline when written history began. This trend continued until about 2,600 years ago when the consciousness of the Piscean age first began to be felt.

Academicians, as well as theologians, tend to judge mankind and its potential according to the period of time which falls within the bounds of written history. History, they say, shows that the race has always been perverse. Since there has been little evidence of change in our behavior in the historical past, they argue, there is no reason to expect change to occur in the future.

But the view, seen from the vantage point of our knowledge of the astrological ages, provides us with a panoramic picture which greatly enhances our perspective. With this new view, it becomes clear that what has been experienced in the past five or six thousand years is only a phase through which we have passed as part of the cycle of the ages. What is to come in the future will be drastically different from that which has been experienced in the past phase.

The view from Olympus reveals that the influence of Uranus, the planet of creativity, is already creating changes by destroying the old, outdated attitudes and the institutions which foster them. Because these institutions are unable to adjust to the new ways, there will be no place for them in the New Age.

Under the influence of Saturn, the co-ruler of Aquarius, modern people are becoming more serious and more reasonable in their approach to life. The movement of the new consciousness onto the stage of life can no longer be deterred. Although organized religion and other established institutions are hard at work attempting to stem the tide, it is only a matter of time before the new consciousness prevails.

The greatest changes will be realized in the department of life now controlled by organized religion. Religion, which is based upon emotional interpretations of the phenomena of nature, will be replaced by a New Philosophy. In the new philosophy the separation between science and religion will be eliminated. The fundamentals of science, representing the objective side of life, will combine with mysticism on the subjective side. Once again mankind will understand that each individual is a meaningful part of creation and is, as a god in the making, responsible for his or her own salvation. By rediscovering the Universal Law which governs both the objective and subjective sides of life, we will become equipped with the knowledge necessary for the final attainment of our personal salvation or enlightenment.

As the vibrations of the new age are felt more strongly, many thinking people are not only unwilling to accept the limitations imposed by science and religion in the area of exploration but also find it impossible to reconcile the difference between the facts revealed by science and superstitious beliefs still embraced by organized religion. Although science has rediscovered much of the knowledge of the objective/material universe which was a part of the Ancient Wisdom, modern religions, which profess to be the keepers of the truth about the subjective/spiritual/mental universe, have failed to keep pace.

Consequently, our understanding of the subjective side of life is still governed by our emotions. Reason plays only a small part in our personal lives. The result has been that we have a poor understanding of the psycho/mental aspects of ourselves. Without this knowledge we can have little understanding of how to relate to one another or the environment in which we "live and move and have our being."

While other religions may have played a prominent role during the past two thousand years, it is clear that the Christian religion has dominated the age of Pisces. Although Islam is equal to Christianity in number of members, the greatest power has been concentrated in the part of the world dominated by Christianity. It is here that business, industry and technology have excelled.

Still, both religions are closely related since they have their origins in the Hebrew religion. Both were strongly influenced by the Father-God concept from their very beginnings and have used it as a guide for their moral and social conduct. It is the coercive attitude, derived from their God-dominated religions, that has most fully characterized Islam and Christianity. Both deny the individual the right to take responsibility for him or herself when it brings them into conflict with their religious dogma. And, when they have the power at their disposal to do so, both exercise extreme measures to deal with those who resist their authority. For the greater part of the past two thousand years, most of the human blood which has been shed has been in connection with acts of war and the persecution of "heretics" at the hands of these two powerful institutions.

While both claim their purpose to be for the peace, tranquility and general welfare of the people, they have in fact been the major perpetrators of violence against the people they have sworn to nurture and protect. For this reason, it can hardly be wrong to blame them for the violent, antisocial behavior of individuals which runs rampant today. Although Judaism, the Father of modern Christianity and Islam, has been a minority religion for the past two thousand years, in recent times it too has been a major cause of bloodshed in the "name of God," or, their religion.

There is another picture emerging, however, which forms a contrast to the selfish, anti-social behavior which seems on the rise. But it is occurring outside and in spite of the organized institutions of religion, politics and commerce. This new surge of interest in higher awareness is accompanied by a greater concern for the welfare of others. It is based upon rational, psycho/mental self-understanding instead of upon either faith in the emotional, superstitious beliefs of organized religion or the materialistic view of science.

Throughout written history, religion and politics (which have walked hand in hand) have been based upon the concept of power of the few over the lives of many. But, as we move into the new age of Brother and Sisterhood, regardless of how it may appear at the present, conditions are changing as the demand for individual freedom and a society governed by reason and the true welfare of the people grows.

As the vibrations of the new age of Aquarius grow stronger, the consciousness of forward looking people is being stirred. More and more leave organized religions each day to seek meaning in the new philosophy which encourages them to take responsibility for their own salvation.

Although many have gone the way of drug abuse and an excess of sex and violence as a means of revolt against the hypocracy of religion and politics with their corrupted ethics and morality, many are finding freedom in the teachings of the Ancient Wisdom which is once more being awakened in the hearts and minds of mankind.

✦

The Ancient Past

I

The Ancient Past

Humankind seems to be a collection of contradictions. Perhaps the reason our evolution is slow is because we tend to allow one part of our nature to cancel out the other. Often we appear to move forward two steps only to take a step and a half backward. It is as though two conflicting sides of ourselves are pushing against one another. Just as our curiosity is about to lead us into exploration and discovery, our fear of change pulls us back.

As we look at our scientific accomplishments, it appears that we have come a long way from our primitive past in which we were terrified of the unknown forces of nature. But, in spite of the fact that the forces of nature no longer hold us in their thrall, there is still a part of us that recoils from anything that appears to stray too far from the accepted norm.

This fear of the unknown was, no doubt, inherited from unsophisticated ancestors who had little understanding of the nature of the universe or of themselves. As will be shown, the people who lived during the early part of written history were the tag end of a once high civilization. What knowledge was retained was distorted and became incorporated into a system of superstitious beliefs. Because the knowledge of the construct of the universe and their relationship to it was no longer understood, they did not know how to control their own destiny and, consequently, lived in constant fear of the environment.

Since these people had no understanding of the laws which governed their world, like small children who believe in Santa Claus, they interpreted literally the allegories which personified the elements of nature. From this distorted view point, they invented a fantasy world in which the elements became superior beings, like the gods who lived among them, to whom they could appeal for protection.

Despite our enlightened state today, some of the characteristics of our unenlightened ancestors linger on in our unconscious minds. One of these is the fear of change. The fear of change no doubt had its roots in the fear of death by unknown forces.

Regardless of all of the advances we have made through scientific discovery, when it comes to understanding the scheme of the universe and our place in it, the key to full understanding seems to be lacking. However, conditions appear to be changing as a discontent with the old superstitious beliefs grows. Many are beginning to see that these answers, which reflect the fears of our ignorant ancestors, do not apply to the circumstances of the present. But, in order to understand how to free ourselves from the fears of past ages, it is necessary to know more about the past.

In recent years there has been a growing feeling of a

need for continuity. This is revealed in the interest shown in tracing one's personal or biological heritage. We seem to have a restless desire to understand our ancestry as though it holds the secret to our future destiny. Perhaps, buried deep in our collective psyche, is the need to trace the roots of our racial heritage as well.

Psychology has come to a point in its evolution at which it recognizes the need for the individual to become integrated by being able to see him or herself in perspective. Part of the process of gaining this state is to examine one's personal past. This aids one in understanding why one has certain personality traits in the present. This being true for the individual, it would seem equally important for the race. Perhaps the madness which has overtaken people around the world could be cured were we to gain a perspective on our collective selves as well. If so, by what means can this objective be met?

Reason would seem to dictate that the best way would be to start at the beginning, wherever that may be. However, attempts to go back to the beginning seem to be met with blocks which make the task difficult. Common sense tells us that, if the slowness of our evolution during written history is an indication of our rate of progress, our past must extend far back into prehistory. Yet this idea, when voiced, immediately brings one into conflict with the established beliefs of both science and religion. These must be confronted before it is possible to proceed.

Our education has led us to believe that we are enlightened beings. Not only do we take pride in our enlightenment but in being the most enlightened civilization that has ever graced this planet. This belief in our superiority is important to our sense of well-being. Therefore, any threat to this belief cannot be tolerated. But one wonders what Mother Nature would have to say about the state of our enlightenment when one considers the havoc the race has inflicted upon itself as well as the environment upon which it depends for its existence.

We have been aided and abetted in our delusion by the two major institutions that control our thinking. For the past two to four hundred years, tradition has led us to look to science and religion for an understanding of ourselves and the universe. For several thousand years before that, religion had a monopoly on the control of the human mind.

Unfortunately, both institutions have a tendency to manipulate the facts in order to make them fit into sets of beliefs to which they have previously committed themselves. For this reason, they are often reluctant to conduct a serious research into areas which fail to conform to their established beliefs. Even worse than the avoidance of certain subjects is what often appears to be direct attempts to cover up pertinent evidence which, if revealed, might lead to changes in our perception of reality.

The conflict begins within the two institutions themselves where there is always a struggle to maintain the status quo. Change, it seems, is perceived by the hierarchy of each to be a threat to its position of authority. Therefore, once a commitment has been made to a particular set of beliefs, those in control frequently use the power of their positions to maintain the present position regardless of the consequences. Thomas Kuhn[1] makes the point that this struggle within the ranks of the scientific community causes a delay in the evolution of scientific knowledge. Clearly, the same results occur within the religious community as well.

Even more disruptive is the contest which has ensued between science and religion since the sixteenth century when Copernicus rediscovered the heliocentricity of our solar system. From that time forward a struggle has raged between them to supplant one another as the final authority regarding the order of the universe.

Western science has held aloof from religion in the belief that it is superior to the superstitious and idolatrous priesthood. But it is not altogether free from this condition itself. Like a child who clings to his blanket for security, it, as Roger Jones points out, is guilty of its own form of idol worship.[2] One might say that matter has become its idol and the belief in a mechanistic, segmented universe its dogma.

When pressed to justify their positions, both science and religion often resort to subterfuge or denial in order to maintain their standing of authority. It has been reported that, for twenty years after publishing his General Theory of Relativity, Albert Einstein refused to accept the idea that it laid the foundation for the Theory of the Expanding Universe. It is believed that he held this position because he was afraid the creationists would use it to support their theory of creation.[3]

On the part of religion, several references in the Bible clearly indicate a belief in reincarnation. For instance, it is clear that Daniel is told that, although he is an old man soon to die, he will be alive at the end of the age of Aries some five hundred years in the future.[4]

The View From Olympus

In the New Testament, Jesus makes reference to reincarnation when he asks his disciples who the people say he is. The names suggested by them, with the exception of John the Baptist, who had recently been beheaded, were all prophets who had long been dead.[5] However, ever since the Emperor Justinian (483-565 A.C.E.) decreed that a belief in reincarnation should no longer be taught, the Church has denied that certain passages mean what they say.

So, it seems both science and religion are inclined to select the facts which support their particular beliefs and to disregard or disparage other evidence. The pressures brought to bear upon the general lay population to conform to their separate dogmas vary only slightly.

Because of the battle between the two institutions, we find that we live in a world of conflicting signals. Lay people are expected to accept the authority of each without question. Yet, if we accept the authority of one, we are condemned by the other. In the end we find that we are left with a large body of evidence which has not been explained by either, yet is condemned by both.

It is, therefore, important that we all become aware that there is an alternative source which goes beyond the knowledge that present day science and religion offer us. It is an old paradigm, or model of the universe that has been hidden for thousands of years. But, because the facts it contains have been missed or denied by science and religion, it seems new to us now. This new/old model allows us to go back into prehistory and dares to include the people and events which myth and legend have preserved for us. Included are also many archaeological discoveries which confirm the myths and legends by providing physical evidence to support them.

Scholars have long viewed the myths and legends of Egypt, Greece, Rome and other civilizations as the mere childish imagination of a primitive people. But, when confronted with findings such as appear in the *Chaldean Account of Genesis* of George Smith and the tradition of the Dogon Society along with the many ancient monuments found around the world, another picture begins to surface which makes it difficult to wave them aside. In these findings we discover evidence of knowledge held many thousands of years ago which modern science has only recently discovered.

Scholars now agree that the history of Western Civilization had its beginnings in Mesopotamia in the area presently occupied by Iraq. It is, therefore, to that region we must look for our roots – in the ancient civilizations of Sumer and Akkad, Babylon and Chaldea.

When Alexander the Great conquered the area in the 4th century B.C.E., he commissioned a local priest to compile a history of the region lying between the Tigris and Euphrates Rivers. Until the excavation and translation of the texts found in the ruins of Assyria in the 1st century, much of our information regarding the civilization which had flourished there in the ancient past came from references to the report which Berosus wrote at Alexander's request. In his history, Berosus gives an account which agrees with the Chaldean Account. He lists ten kings who reigned before the Flood and eighty-six who reigned after the Flood down to the Median Conquests of the 7th century B.C.E.

The View From Olympus

In general, scholars have disregarded the lengths of time given in the legendary history of the area as too far fetched to be taken seriously. The enormous periods of time ascribed to the various reigns of the kings make a total of 432,000 years.[6] However, Ignatius Donnely, the famous Atlantologist,[7] points out that other "histories" have been disbelieved and later proved to be true. For a thousand years the folk tales about the buried cities of Pompeii and Herculaneum were regarded as fables. These two cities, which were buried by an eruption of Mt. Vesuvius in 79 A.C.E., were rediscovered in the first half of the 18th century.

Herodotus (484-425 B.C.E.), who is now regarded as the "Father of History," was called the "Father of Liars" for more than a thousand years because his accounts of the wonders of the ancient civilizations of Egypt and Chaldea were not believed by the educated world.[8] This attitude was changed around the middle of the 19th century when Sir Austen Henry Layard, an English archaeologist, excavated in Mesopotamia and Babylon, especially in Ninevah. At the same time Sir Henry Rawlinson, serving in the Persian army, began to decipher the cuneiform inscription of Darius I at Behistun. It was after the British occupation of Egypt in 1882-83 that excavations were begun in that country.

The city of Troy, described in Homer's Illiad and Oddessey, was regarded as fabulous until it was unearthed by Heinrich Schliemann in the late 19th century. And the Hittite Empire, described in the Old Testament, was thought to be nonexistent until scholars began to piece together the ancient history of the whole region separate from the Hebrew records.

Although the cities and nations just discussed existed within the time frame of between 2,000 and

The Ancient Past

4,000 years ago, there is evidence of higher civilizations which are dated much further back in time. Sir Leonard Wolley, the British archaeologist, states that his findings at the excavations around many of the ancient Sumerian cities have done much to confirm the long period of time of more than 30,000 years between the Flood and the first dynasty given in the Chaldean Account.[9]

While the oldest of the Chaldean records in existence today were not compiled until 2,000 B.C.E., they appear to scholars to have been derived from a large store of documents which were at their disposal. Or, perhaps, as George Smith[10] suggests, they may have been long-held oral traditions before they were recommitted to writing.

If they were derived from oral traditions, it is quite possible that they had their beginnings in more ancient writings which were lost in the interim. For, as the Chaldean tablets state, the superior beings who came to teach mankind and to humanize them also taught them to write. They were given a written account of the creation of the universe, the planets and mankind along with the history of the ten antediluvial kings.[11]

Furthermore, it is stated that Xisuthrus, the Sumerian Noah, was instructed by the god Cronos to "write a history of the beginning, procedure and conclusion of all things," and to bury them in the city of Sippara.[12] This, of course, is an indication that writing was a skill known before the Flood.

The Egyptians did not take credit for the development of writing. They attributed it to the "gods" who were, perhaps, their ancient and highly civilized ancestors. Nor did the Phoenecians take credit for the authorship of writing, although scholars have credited them with this invention for many years. Sanchuniathon, the Phoenician historian, says that the art of writing was invented by Hermes, whom the Egyptians called "Thoth."[13]

If the Flood legends can be believed, then we must accept that writing predated the deluge. Plato says that the people of Atlantis inscribed their laws on bronze columns and gold plates. The Druids believed in books which existed before the Flood. Hebrew commentators on Genesis assert that Adam was given a book by God which was passed down to Noah and finally lost. The Chinese also have traditions which state that the earliest race of their nation taught rules of living and "wrote books."[14] These and many more traditions of antediluvian people indicate that they had a written language.

Another piece of the puzzle of our past, which both science and religion choose to ignore, is the body of legend which indicates that two races co-existed on the planet in ancient times. The Babylonians described them as the "Adamu," or dark race, and the "Sarku," or light race.[15] The latter were the superior beings to whom the Adamic race referred as "gods." The Revised Standard Bible says, "The Nephilim were in the earth in those days, and also afterward, (referring to the Flood) when the sons of God came in to the daughters of men, and they bore children. These were the mighty men of old, the men of renown."[16]

It is evident that the Sumerian Flood story is parallel to that of Noah and the Ark in the Old Testament, except that there were people other than the family of Xisuthrus who were saved. After the Flood, the gods, it is reported, repented of their harsh treatment of mankind and began to educate them and to teach them to be more human. The same story is found in the Old Testament with the exception that the gods have been singularized.

It was at this time, the records indicate, that mankind was taught to till the ground for crop production, to build cities, and to develop arts and crafts. The book of Genesis tells very much the same story when it says that, "Noah became the first tiller of the soil,"[17] and others of his family are mentioned as craftsmen and builders of cities.

According to the Sumerians, it was at this time that kingship was removed from the heavens (the gods) to earth (mankind). When the gods set mankind up to rule themselves, they were installed as servants of the gods and not as sovereigns. It was not until early in the fourth millennium B.C.E. that the kingdoms of Ur and Egypt are said to have been ruled by a human as a sovereign and not by a demi-god under the tutelage of the gods. This is also the period from which scholars date the first dynasties of written history.

The question of whether or not the legends of Atlantis fit into the picture of the Sumerian history must not be overlooked. Lewis Spence[18] says that Diodorus, a historian and contemporary of Julius Caesar and Augustus, learned about the history of Atlantis from the people of Atlas in North Africa who were, presumably, colonists from that island country.

They are said to have boasted that the gods were born and lived among them. They also claimed that Uranus was their first king and that he civilized them and taught them to till the soil and to build cities. He was also said to have been an astrologer who prophesied many future events and who installed the solar year and lunar month as measurements of time.

The View From Olympus

The Egyptians, too, asserted that their earliest kings were gods who dained to live on the earth among men. From the very beginning, their worship of the gods was accompanied by the deification of dead kings and other royal persons. When the physical body of the king died, it was thought that the divine portion returned to its original home with the gods in the heavens.[19] The people paid honor to the gods by calling the starry heavens after their names.

This last fact seems to clear up the confusion over how the heavenly bodies (the stars, constellations and planets) were called by the names of the gods who had lived on earth and appear to have been quite human in their behavior.

Evidence to confirm the source and content of some of the science of the ancient past has been located in a most unlikely place: the jungles of North Western Africa. The information has been garnered from tribes living on the Niger River in Mali, the former French territory of Sudan. We are indebted to Professor Marcel Griaule, the director of the French ethnographic field studies in Africa for more than twenty-five years, for information which puts new light on the scientific knowledge of the ancient past.

The research reveals that the Africans have systems of their own in the fields of astronomy and time measurements as well as other sciences, in the form of calendars, mathematics, physiology, and pharmacopia. They too, like many other tribes and nations around the world, claim to have come by their knowledge through contact with superior beings whom they believe to have come from somewhere in the heavens.

It is, however, their understanding of cosmology which is of present concern. For the evidence reveals that they have knowledge about the movements and characteristics of certain stars that has become known to modern scientists only by the aid of complex instruments developed in modern times.

It is the tribe known as the Dogon who appear to have the most complete knowledge of the cosmos and is the one which Professor Griaule studied most thoroughly. By tracing their origins, Robert K.G. Temple[20] has placed them back in Egypt and Greece. Thus it is shown that the knowledge now held by the Dogon was probably derived from the cosmology of those civilizations. In this way we are also able to determine the true nature of the knowledge once held by the Mediterranean and Mesopotamian civilizations. If this connection is valid, then it must have been the same "Wisdom of Egypt" in which Moses was schooled.

The primary focus of the Dogons is Sirius, which is located in the constellation Canis Major and the brightest star seen from the earth. Their special interest in this part of the heavens stems from their belief that the superior beings from whom they acquired their knowledge came from this area of the heavens. They, therefore, consider that part of the heavens to be of the greatest significance.

But the most important star in the sky to them is one that is invisible to the naked eye.[21] It has been demonstrated that they have an accurate knowledge of the nature and position of Sirius B, a white dwarf which they have long known to have an orbit around Sirius A which lasts fifty years. The fact that it is very small and compact has also been noted by them.

It is interesting to note that Sirius B was the first of its kind to be discovered by modern scientists.

Although its existence was suspected in 1814, it was not actually seen until 1862. Its extremely compact nature was not recognized until 1915.[22] While white dwarfs are familiar objects to astronomers today, they have been studied only since 1914. It is now known that a white dwarf is one of the stages in the life of a star. It is, in fact, the first step in the death of a star, the last two stages being the neutron star and the black hole.

Another bit of obscure information the Dogons have preserved is the fact that Sirius A is not the center of the orbit of Sirius B but one of the two focal points of its elliptical orbit. They are also aware of the nature of the Milky Way and our place in it.[23] Even more surprising is the fact that they have a knowledge of the motions of the heavenly bodies which they compare with the circulation of the blood,[24] a fact not known in Europe until Harvey made the discovery in 1619.

A further point of interest is that the ancients seem to have been aware of the interchange of matter between ourselves and the heavenly bodies. Wallis Budge quotes an Egyptian source which says that a holy emanation pours forth from Osiris (identified with both the Moon and Orion) and "vivifies gods, men, cattle and creeping things."[25] This same idea is expressed by modern scientists. William J. Kaufmann III[26] says that white dwarfs cool gradually, radiating energy into space. He further states that every atom in our bodies as well as every atom we touch or breathe had its origins in the dust of stars.

As in most every other ancient civilization which has any knowledge of the cosmos, the Dogons also have some knowledge of the signs of the zodiac. But, at present, there is no indication that astrology plays a large part in their lives.[27]

The Dogon knew of the four main moons of Jupiter, of the rings of Saturn, and that the earth rotates on its axis. In addition to a solar and lunar calendar, they also have calendars based upon the cycles of Sirius and Venus.[28] It is well known that the Egyptians used a calender based upon the rising of Sirius with the Sun on the 19th day of July, the date that also coincided with the flooding of the Nile River, which signalled the time for planting. In fact, it is now clear that Sirius was the focus of the Egyptian religion.[29]

In a translation of an Egyptian text made by G.R.S. Meade, it is found that Sirius A relates to Isis, while Sirius B has a relationship to Osiris. We also learn from this work that the great wise teacher, Thoth, was one of the race of gods who taught mankind the arts and sciences of civilization. When he left Earth to return to his home in the heavens, it is said, he left a person (or persons) designated as "Tat" (or Thoth) who had been initiated into the mysteries of the cosmos to carry on the work of teaching these truths to mankind.[30]

Wherever the remains of an ancient civilization with a well developed system of cosmology are found, the legend that the knowledge was given to man by gods is also prevalent. In addition, it is found that the gods have become intertwined with the cosmos itself (with the planets, stars and constellations).

It seems the fact that primitive mankind identified the gods with the various parts of the heavens has caused many scholars to miss the sophisticated knowledge buried in their myths and legends. This may also be one of the reasons why they fail to give the ancients credit for an advanced body of scientific knowledge. But it would seem that the naivete of the tellers of these tales should be a clue that what they say is based upon fact, for it is on the whole beyond their present comprehension. Thus, it seems logical to conclude that there must have been an advanced race who interacted with primitive mankind at some time in the ancient past as is reported. Whether or not they came from another planet is another question upon which we will not speculate further.

It appears that the knowledge which has been preserved by these tribes, in the monuments found around the world and in the literature of many religions, is the kind that only a technologically advanced society could have developed. This is further borne out by the fact that archaeologists have found the older civilizations to have been superior to the more recent cultures. These finds also confirm the idea of the declining nature of our civilization at the beginning of written history.

By establishing the possibility of at least one high, technologically advanced society in the ancient past, it becomes feasible to contemplate the possibility that the science of Astrology was invented by a highly advanced society in the prehistoric past. Furthermore, it makes legitimate the speculation that the ages, as described in the Ancient Wisdom, are a valid part of the science of the ancient past. And, when properly studied, the science of the astrological ages can also reveal some interesting things about the nature of the evolution of our consciousness.

✦

II

Evidence Of The Ancient Science

A serious effort to trace our origins and the origins of our civilization inevitably draws one back to the Ancient Mysteries which contain the archaic science and legends of a past high civilization. Modern scientists look to Copernicus as the Father of Modern Science and to Euclid for the basis of modern mathematics. Yet, each of them stands on the shoulders of others who can be traced directly to the Ancient Wisdom.

In his writings, Copernicus, who is credited with being the first modern scientist to discover the heliocentricity of our solar system, clearly indicates his indebtedness to Aristarchus, a third century B.C.E. astronomer, whose own writings indicate a belief in the heliocentric system seventeen or eighteen hundred years before the birth of Copernicus. It is known that Aristarchus was a student of the university attached to the museum at Alexandria that housed a library containing the ancient records of past civilizations.

Included was the ancient science of both Sumeria and Egypt. These, along with the material which had been collected by Ptolemy Philadelphus (304-346 B.C.E.) from all over the known world, were later destroyed by orders of the Christian Fathers.

While Euclid (cir. 300 B.C.E.) also attended the university at Alexandria, it is commonly agreed that he got his inspiration for the first part of his geometry from the Pythagoreans who were in possession of the knowledge at least two hundred years prior to his birth. They were the first in written history to reject the theory of a geocentric system and to reduce the earth to a planetary status in orbit around the sun.

Although little is known of Pythagoras himself, it has been established that he was tutored by both Anaximander and his teacher, Thales.[1] Thales was the first Greek philosopher to substitute scientific for mythological interpretations of the natural/physical world. He, as well as the other six "Wise Men of Greece," is said to have studied in Egypt, Babylonia, and Arabia, and was initiated into each of the respective "Mysteries."

Kepler (1571-1630), the German astronomer and author of the Three Laws of Planetary Motion, was influenced by the teachings of Copernicus, who, as stated, was influenced by Aristarchus. But, he is also known to have had contact with the writings of Proculus (410-485 A.C.E.), a Neoplatonist philosopher who had been initiated into the Egyptian Mysteries.[2]

A further indication of the reliance of the founders of modern science upon the ancient science is found in the case of Newton, who is noted for his work in rediscovering the law of gravity. Newton (1642-1727 A.C.E.), an English physicist, turned to the Temple of

Jerusalem and the Egyptian pyramids for accurate measurements of the earth's dimensions and used them as a basis for his calculations. As we shall see, the Temple of Jerusalem was laid out according to a plan which duplicated the astrological zodiac of ancient times.

Both Kepler and Pythagoras, who were important contributors to modern science, recognized the superiority of the ancient science and sought inspiration from it for their own work.[3] Thus, it is seen that modern science is not new but, instead, has borrowed the knowledge which forms the foundation of its understanding of the universe from the ancient prehistoric past.

Throughout the world, whenever the knowledge found in the Ancient Wisdom has surfaced – in Egypt, Greece, Sumer, India, China, and the Americas, as well as other cultures – the story is the same. Without exception, each points to the gods as the source of their information. It seems foolish to deny the possible existence of such beings in the light of persistent claims. Clearly, this knowledge is far too sophisticated to have been invented by the superstitious people of a declining civilization five or six thousand years ago.

As is shown by recorded history, which began six thousand years ago, whatever knowledge had been known of the construct of the universe before then had degenerated into ritualistic and superstitious beliefs. These rituals and beliefs included animal and human sacrifice to placate the anger of the gods of the forces of nature. But the true knowledge of the gods, the Ancient Science, was preserved in the great centers previously mentioned. The gods to whom they referred were not the elements of nature but real people who were the creators of a past, lost, high civilization.

The View From Olympus

When the cycle of the ages is discussed in the next chapter, it will be seen that the possibility exists for other high civilizations to have existed on earth in the past. And that their rise and fall are a natural result of the cycle. The lesson to be learned from the study of the cycles of nature is that, without devolution, there can be no evolution.

The Ancient Wisdom teaches that the earth is like a school for gods. Each of us is a god in the making just as a child is an adult in the making. And, just as a child must learn the lessons of each age through which it passes on the way to adulthood, so the race must also learn the lessons of the universal, or Astrological Ages. Not everyone goes on to graduate school to become fully educated regarding the objective/material world. By the same token, only a few go on to become fully enlightened regarding the subjective/spiritual or mental world.

At points in the cycle of the ages when technology is at a peak, such as in the present age, the ranks of graduate students grow and large numbers of people learn to comprehend the objective/material world of science. Many come to understand the subjective/mental side as well. It is at this point that science and religion merge into an enlightened philosophy. The childish, superstitious beliefs of religion are replaced by the reasoned understanding of adults.

Those who become fully enlightened on the earth plane are graduated and go on to higher schools of learning in other realms of the universe. On the other hand, the laggards are required to repeat the course through many more incarnations until they too have become awakened to a full understanding of the relationship between the objective/physical and the subjective/mental worlds.

As we follow the story found in legends regarding the last solar cycle, we find that the people of the past high civilization lived and interacted with mankind for several thousand years before the Flood. But, after the Flood, they withdrew and lived apart from the primitive-minded people. However, they continued to return to teach and guide them in the process of their evolution. We, of course, are the laggards who were taught by the gods after the Flood.

The legends of many people of the earth tell that after the Flood their ancestors were transported to different parts of the world by the gods. One of these stories is found in the Judeo/Christian Bible in the story of the Tower of Babel. Some South American Indian tribes have a legend which states that the gods moved their ancestors with airships and deposited them in areas remote from their own places of abode. After giving them basic instructions on survival and the civilizing arts and sciences, the gods left them to fend for themselves.

Prior to the Flood the gods ruled the earth, but afterward they set up kingdoms which were ruled by demi-gods (persons who were educated in the Mysteries of the universe and the technology of the super race). They ruled for several thousand years until the middle of the 4th millennium B.C.E. when they fought among themselves and devastated the earth with the sophisticated weapons they had inherited from the super race, their ancestors.[4]

After some time, when these areas were habitable once more, the first modern dynasties were founded. It was at this point that our written history began. When the dynastic, mortal kings began to rule, they started a tradition of keeping records of their activities. But, henceforth, there was a gradual decline in the level of civilization until the people were mired down with superstitious beliefs and barbarous behavior. The wisdom of the super race was hidden and preserved in the literature of the religions, myths, and legends, to await the dawning of a new day.

The dawn began in the last quarter of the Arien age (6th century B.C.E.). But it was not until the last quarter of the Piscean age, which we are now leaving, that science began to free itself from the tyranny and superstition of organized religion. In the process, however, as a reaction to the repression of religion, it rejected all forms of mysticism (the subjective/mental side of life). In so doing, it also rejected the genuine scientific information hidden behind the superstitious beliefs along with everything else that could not be tested in a laboratory setting. The scientific view of life can be summed up in the simple statement that nature, including mankind, can be reduced to "physio/chemical machines." [5]

This has resulted in a serious imbalance. There is no question that we have made great strides in harnessing the objective/physical energy of nature, but, without the understanding of the subjective/mental side, we lack the wisdom to use it properly. This, in turn, has brought us to the brink of self-destruction.

However, we may yet be saved. For, since early in the twentieth century with the introduction of the relativity and quantum theories, various physicists have found interesting parallels between these theories and the mystical transcendental religions of the East whose origins are found in the Ancient Wisdom.

Among the many points of agreement between

Evidence Of The Ancient Science

Western Science and the Ancient Mysteries as found in the Eastern religions are: 1. The oneness of the universe; 2. The changing nature of the universe – constant movement and flow; 3. The cyclic character of nature – on both the microcosmic and macrocosmic levels; 4. The vibratory connection between bodies in space; and 5. The holographic nature of the universe.

One of the major points at which the new and old science meet is in the concept of the "holistic" view of the universe. David Bohm affirms this parallel in his statement that science, like mysticism, is now demanding a "non-fragmentary world view."[6] He explains that the undivided wholeness of the universe, as implied by the relativity/quantum theories, provides a more orderly way to consider the nature of reality than the old fragmented, mechanistic mode. James Jeans goes a step further to suggest that the universe is not only holistic but beginning to seem more like a "great thought than a great machine."[7]

It is also said by the new scientists that the universe is now seen as something which is experienced rather than observed. Bohm believes that we can no longer accept the idea of a division between the observer and the observed. Instead, both appear to merge into one indivisible reality. With the new perception it is reasoned that the mystical experience of oneness may in fact be a valid experience of the "implicate and universal ground" as it is described by Bohm.[8]

So, it seems we have come full circle back to the source of our knowledge – the ancient, prehistoric knowledge. This knowledge is not only preserved in the ancient religions, myths and legends but may also be found in the form of physical evidence scattered all over the world on every continent and the islands of the sea. Straight lines, mounds, giant figures, and monuments are now thought to have been put in place by a civilization which was global in scope, as ours is today. They form, as John Michell says, a colossal scientific instrument.[9] During the past four hundred years, men have occasionally taken time to examine these prehistoric remains in various parts of the world, but there had been no sustained interest in them until this century.

In England, in the late 16th century, Dr. Dee, the famous scientist/occultist, found in the Glastonbury area what he believed to be Merlin's secret. As he examined the arrangement of these prehistoric figures and markings, he determined that they represented the configurations of the constellations of the zodiac. He, therefore, concluded that astrology and astronomy were combined by scientific measurements to reproduce the pattern of the heavens.

During the 1920's, a young artist, Kathryn Maltwood,[10] became interested in the enormous figures which Dee had found etched on the landscape between Glastonbury Tor and Cadbury Hill. After studying aerial photographs of the area, Maltwood detected a circle of figures more than ten miles in diameter. She found that the natural folds of the earth and the course of streams had been altered to allow the figures to represent the various signs of the zodiac. Each figure, it seems, was located so as to correspond with the position of the appropriate constellation.

In 1921, Alfred Watkins,[11] a member of the Antiquarian Society of Britain, announced that the ancient monuments and sacred sites found all over Britain had been originally laid out in patterns of straight lines which he called "leys." But professional archaeologists were not impressed with this view. They persistently denied the existence of the leys or their connection to a prehistoric society. To accept them would have required them to agree that the ancients were very skillful in surveying and in the knowledge of astronomy and other sciences as well.

The idea that these markings were related to some form of ancient science had been suggested for many years, but it was not confirmed until 1967 when Alexander Thom,[12] a retired Scottish Professor of engineering, announced his findings. In twenty-five years of surveying many of the more than five hundred stone circles and other markings, he found them to be part of an elaborate system drawn in the form of geometrical figures. They are so precisely drawn that they are found to be accurate to one part in a thousand. Furthermore, they are based upon Pythagorean triangles. But, since the figures were placed there long before Pythagoras was born, it seems likely that they are a physical expression of the ancient science from which Pythagoras gleaned his knowledge.

With Thom's discovery of the geometry of the stone circles, the old ideas of the primitive status of prehistoric peoples seems less certain and, perhaps, makes it more acceptable to speculate on the existence of a more advanced civilization in the ancient past with a knowledge of science comparable to our own. As previously suggested, this high civilization may have existed side by side with the more primitive society whose clay and stone gods and other symbols indicate a lack of such scientific understanding of the universe.

The View From Olympus

In speaking of the mounds and treasures of Silbury, England (another segment of the world-wide system), Michael Dames[13] concludes that, as we learn to decipher their meaning, the wisdom found in these monuments is becoming available to us once again. It seems that the people who developed this system were the ancient sages who saw the earth as a living creature interacting on the universal stage with all of the other heavenly bodies. It was upon this understanding that they based their code of science, designed to foster harmony between human society and the living earth as well as the cosmos itself.[14]

Not only is great skill displayed in the construction of these ancient figures and monuments but, when properly interpreted, they reveal a grand prehistoric philosophy which has meaning for the present. This philosophy is an expression of an understanding of the unity of all things through the recognition of the correspondence between the individual and the universal as well as the indivisibility of Mind and Matter. This is the very substance of the esoteric side of the religions of the world. It is what various religious traditions claim was conveyed to their ancestors by the gods.

Evidence suggests that thousands of years ago mankind not only knew about the earth's magnetic fields but was able to utilize them in daily living. Those early people, tradition says, viewed the earth as a living being whose magnetic fields corresponded to the nervous system in the human body. The vortexes or power centers which are of such importance to many of the so-called "New Age" people today are the points on the earth in which the flow of energy converges.

Evidence Of The Ancient Science

These magnetic centers of the earth correspond to the acupuncture points of the human body and, because of the concentration of energy, were regarded in the past as sacred or of special importance. It was for this reason they were chosen as places upon which to build important structures such as public buildings and religious temples. The ancients apparently believed that the energy from these centers could be absorbed by the human nervous system.

All of the stone circles and monuments, including England's Stonehenge, are now known to be situated on one of these energy points. Furthermore, it has been established that the pattern in which the stone monuments have been laid out reflects the pattern of the heavens or the "body of God." [15]

Nigel Pennick, an acknowledged authority in the field of ancient geomancy (the science of architecture based upon these energy centers), says that the inhabitants of Britain used advanced science and mathematics to build their megalithic monuments before the First Dynasty of ancient Egypt. [16]

When the Christian religion reached England, the system of geomancy was in full use. Documented evidence shows that the early Church had a policy of appropriating the ancient temples which were already situated on these centers and searching out these points upon which to build new Churches. [17]

Evidence further indicates that geomancy was retained in England until the Middle Ages. With the Protestant reformation and the destruction of the monastic libraries, the ancient records were destroyed as worthless. Persons who continued in the practice were "hounded and punished for practicing witchcraft." [18]

The View From Olympus

Later, in the late 17th century, Jesuit missionaries went to China and, after gaining the confidence of the emperor, set about to destroy the major books on the subject of "Feng-Shui," the Chinese term for geomancy. By this means they succeeded in bringing the practice to an end in that country as well.[19] But, although the knowledge has become degenerate in this modern world of advanced technology, geomancy is still practiced in Hong Kong, Taiwan, Nepal, Indonesia and in some parts of Africa.[20]

Many modern scholars treat stories of dragons and the heroes who slew them as entertaining myths of no substance. But Michell[21] speculates that the term applies not only to the slaying of the monsters within ourselves but may also have significance as part of the history of the cycle of the astrological ages. On this level, these myths represent the struggle between those who hold on to the attitudes of the old age and those who wish to move forward into the new. The Christian Fathers regarded the Church as the dragon slayer of the Piscean age. But, instead of destroying the old gods, they gave them new names and adopted most of the old rituals and dogma of the past age.

Sacred places, which had been laid out according to the zodiac and dedicated to the god associated with a particular planet or constellation, were redesignated by the name of a Christian saint or angel and assigned the attributes of the former god. In this manner, it seems, St. Michael and St. George replaced Castor and Pollux.[22] So, although the symbols of the past ages remain prominently visible in the Judeo/Christian Bible, the Church has lost the understanding of the meaning found in astrological symbology because of its practice of altering the meaning of old symbols to suit its own purpose.

In those few places in Britain where no substitutions were made, some localities still reflect the names of gods associated with the Egyptian Pantheon. The names of Thoth, the Egyptian Mercury, and Baal, the Sun god, are still found in many places. One old deserted village near Loch Ness, for instance, is still known as Baalbeg or Baal's Town.

Sacred sites known to be situated on power centers are found around the world. China is one place in which these centers are still quite evident since the Chinese continued to retain the knowledge and to preserve the ancient architecture into modern times. It did not suffer the destruction which the British architecture suffered at the hands of the fanatic Puritans. So, by examining the Chinese system of Feng-Shui it is possible to gain an insight into the hows and whys of Britain's ancient system of architecture.

The geomancers of China were charged with the responsibility of determining how and where to lay out new buildings and landscaping. They read the hidden meaning in the contour of the countryside as it related to the cosmos. the topography of the earth was interpreted astrologically according to certain celestial influences.[23]

According to evidence now available, indications are that the ancients studied both the science of astronomy (the physical nature of the cosmos) and astrology (the interrelationship between the cosmos and the earth and her inhabitants). From the time that modern people first took notice of the ancient markings there has been speculation that they were astrological and/or astronomical in nature and that they were regarded by the builders as being of sacred importance. Now, it seems certain that they do, in fact, pertain to the oneness of the universe.

In her book, *The Glastonbury Zodiac*, Mary Caine[24] picks up the search from Maltwood and Watkins and carries it back into the history of both British and Greek Mythology. In so doing, she makes a strong case for Britain as the location of the Hyperborea of the Greeks. The meaning of the myths are thereby demystified since it appears that they make reference to the Glastonbury Zodiac in Somerset, England.

The conclusion to be drawn from Caine's research is that the folklore of Britain makes it a remnant of Atlantis, the legendary land which it looks to as a lost homeland. The Glastonbury Zodiac is said to be one of the remnants of the ancient Atlantean science/philosophy.

The stories told in the myths of the Sumerian Gilgamesh and the Greek Hercules and Odysseus are of the quest for the knowledge contained in the secret mysteries of the ancients whose symbols are contained in the monuments and markings of Britain. Apollo was also said to have visited the land of Hyperborea. The legend of Camelot is thought to be directly tied to the Glastonbury Zodiac. Although Arthur appears to have actually lived and ruled a small kingdom on the coast of Wales in the 6th century A.C.E., his legendary kingdom was later associated with the zodiac in Somerset. As the myth surrounding him grew, he became equated with Osiris, Krishna and Christ.

From our present knowledge of the meaning of the astrological ages, it becomes clear that the zodiac is a physical representation of the path which mankind must take in the quest for self-realization or enlightenment. The twelve houses of the zodiac, as a reflection of the twelve constellations, represent the twelve basic aspects of our nature which must be mastered before we can become perfected gods and, as such, co-creators with the creative source.

Thus it is seen that astrology/astronomy was the basis of the ancient science/philosophy. By showing the correspondence between mankind and the cosmos, it provided a guide to an awareness of our godhood and, thus, to our latent creative powers. As the legends indicate, those who discover their creative powers and develop them and learn to use them to control the powers of nature within themselves are truly enlightened. When the powers of nature in the environment are controlled by enlightened people, they are used in constructive, cooperative ways.

Modern science has made great strides in rediscovering the secrets of nature and in learning to utilize her forces. But, at the same time, it lacks the wisdom to know how to use those forces constructively. As a consequence, we are on the verge of destroying the earth and ourselves along with her.

In their arrogance, both science and religion have downgraded the ancient science of astrology and ridiculed it as a superstition. But, today, it seems clear that we must once again learn to understand the lessons which astrology has to teach if we are going to save ourselves from our own foolishness, born of our ignorance of the true facts of life.

◆

The View From Olympus

III

The Astrological Ages

Although there is little understanding of what it means, the idea that we are entering a "New Age" has been mentioned so often in recent years that many have accepted it as fact. Others refuse to accept the idea because it does not fit into their mental picture, or paradigm, of the universe.

The concept of the ages is derived from the ancient science of astrology which we now know is an integral part of the "Ancient Wisdom" of the prehistoric past. Astrology is the system by which one of the major concepts of the ancient philosophy is explained. It deals with both the macrocosmic (universal) and microcosmic (individual) levels of existence.

In astrology, a chart called a "horoscope" (Greek meaning "observer of the hour of birth") is used to explain the interrelatedness between mankind and the rest of the universe. The horoscope is divided into twelve houses or departments which are said to be governed, or influenced, by the constellations in the zodiac. The zodiac (from the Greek word "zodiakos" meaning "a circle of animals") is composed of the twelve constellations which circle the earth's equator.

While the planets of our solar system move through the constellations as they circle around the sun, the sun circles around the zodiac in an orbit of its own, circling around the "Central Sun," the source of creation. The period of time the sun spends in each constellation is called an "age." It has been established that an age is approximately 2,160 years in length. It takes twelve ages for the sun to complete a cycle, or solar year, of nearly 26,000 years.

The last two thousand plus years has been spent under the influence of the constellation Pisces. The age into which we are moving is called "Aquarius." In this chapter we will explore the meaning of the influences of the ages on the affairs of mankind.

Modern historians have arbitrarily placed the invention of the science of astrology at the beginning of written history. However, this places it, as archaeologists indicate, in a period of decline from a much higher civilization. Furthermore, evidence places it at a period several thousand years earlier. Or, in prehistory.

Newton (1642-1727 A.C.E.) was the last scientist who openly recognized the validity of astrology and accepted it as a part of the ancient science to which he was indebted for his own knowledge. However, modern science disregards this part of his work while, at the same time, giving him credit for major contributions to their field.

It is believed in scientific circles that, while Newton was clear headed enough to have formulated the **Law** of **Gravitation**, to have invented the **Reflecting Telescope**, and to have made a major contribution to the understanding of the **Nature of Light**, he must have been addlepated to have believed in the validity of astrology. While Edmund Halley, the discoverer of the comet known by his name, was indebted to Newton for the theories which made his discovery possible, he, nevertheless, chided him for his involvement in astrology. Newton's reply is reported to have been, "Sir, I have studied it, you have not."

The same reply could be made to the criticism made by modern science. There seems to be a common belief among scientists that it is not necessary to study the subject in order to pass judgment upon it. However, had Newton's other contributions been treated with a similar cavalier attitude, our present day technology might still be only a dream for the future.

Because of the bastardized status to which it has long been relegated, the meaningful side of astrology is only now beginning to be rediscovered. Recently, it has been adopted by a few pioneers in the field of psychotherapy as a adjunct to psychology. This will be discussed further in Chapter XII.

Most legitimate astrologers would resent being called fortune tellers since they do not believe the stars control our lives. When they say "the stars impel, they do not compel," that is exactly what they mean. We are influenced by the stars just as we are influenced by the people with whom we associate. We are not controlled by them unless we are in an unhealthy relationship. We are stars (or gods) in our own right and, therefore, have the power to control our own destinies.

The famous astrologer, Llewellyn George[1] has explained the difference between science and astrology by defining the science of astronomy as purely objective, concerned with the outer expression of the physical universe. By contrast, astrology is a subjective science which deals with the life within physical forms and with the effects the various forms or bodies have upon one another.

Another way of making a comparison is by the statement that astrology is to astronomy what psychology is to physiology.[2] One deals with the tangible, physical world while the other deals with the intangible, mental side of life. The latter cannot be measured in a laboratory setting. Since it is subjective in nature, it can only be verified experientially.

Nevertheless, the two do have something in common. They both rely upon experiment (or experience) and observation, and both believe there is some kind of order in the universe. One might say that they are two sides of the same coin. But, while science is still searching for an understanding of the nature of the order, astrology has already developed a system by which it can be described.[3]

This system is based upon an awareness that the universe is both holistic and cyclic. While science has begun to recognize the truth of this condition, it has yet to understand how it functions. The reason for this failure is, no doubt, to be found in the fact that science denies the subjective side of nature.

The knowledge of the Ancient Wisdom was lost to the masses long before our written history began. It was preserved in special learning centers in Mesopotamia, Greece, Egypt and India until it began to be revived around the 6th century B.C.E. But, soon after the Christian Church rose to power, it was once again forced underground where it has been saved in the religious centers of the East and by certain secret societies in the West.

The Magi of ancient Persia and the priests of Egypt, Greece and India were scientists first and foremost. They were the true seers of their times. While they were well educated in both astronomy and astrology, they were also adept in music, the arts, mathematics, and all the fundamentals of the other physical sciences. As legend indicates, they were adept in the use and control of some of the forces of nature. This was demonstrated in the life of Pythagoras, whose purpose in life was to revive the Ancient Wisdom of the past ages.

But, in our times, the credibility of astrology is strained by the fact that many of its practitioners lean toward the phenomenal aspects of predictive astrology. They are neither experts in the fields in which they make predictions, nor are they sufficiently enlightened to function without inserting their personal prejudices. Their accuracy is, therefore, distorted by both a lack of background knowledge and by their own preconceptions.

Among other things, astrology, when properly understood, is the study of the changing attitudes of human society in general. Contained within it is the knowledge not only of the aspects which affect the relationship between the earth and other heavenly bodies, but of the cycle of the ages and the changing patterns unique to each as they concern humanity.

Because the study of astrology is many faceted, it may be approached from many points of view. It may be studied from the angle of the race as a whole or from that of the individual. It may be studied from social, mental, spiritual, and/or physical perspectives. But, at all times, it must be understood that all these function within the context of the whole.

Whether an entity is composed of one or many segments, it makes no difference. A person, a marriage, a family, a clan, nation or race, is each an organic whole on the level on which it functions. Each is a complete universe in and of itself and is reflected in the patterns of the cosmos. Yet, humanity and the solar system are a part of one whole. There is no clear separation.[4]

Just as it is perceived in modern psychology that there are stages through which an individual must pass in the process of growth and development, so, in astrology, twelve major stages of development are recognized. The goal of both psychology and astrology is to integrate all of these stages into one smoothly functioning whole. But, astrology does not limit us to one lifetime to get ourselves together.

Ever since Ptolemy compiled all of the known knowledge regarding astrology (2nd century A.C.E.), students have been adding to the information through research and study. The old axiom used in physiology, "ontogeny recapitulates phylogeny" (the individual replays the history of the race), has been found to be true in astrology as well.

The zodiac, it has been discovered, is a map of the evolution of both the race and the individual. The patterns of one can be traced in the other. This is true even though the evolutionary paths are found to move in opposite directions (Figure 1). While the evolution of the individual is traced from left to right, or from West to East, the evolution of the race must be traced from right to left, or from East to West, because the precession of the sun through the astrological ages is in reverse order.

By allotting each of the signs of the zodiac a place in the life cycle of the individual, it becomes easier to

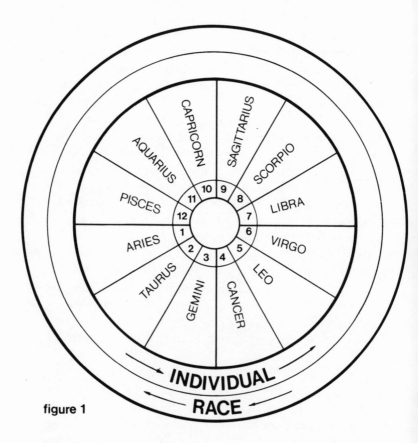

figure 1

understand the significance of the different signs. If, for instance, we say that Aries represents the new born infant and Pisces the old person, and all of the other signs are given their respective places between them as a part of the cycle of life, the evolutionary process should become more understandable.

While the evolution of the individual moves from infancy to old age, from left to right around the horoscope, the evolution of the race proceeds in reverse order with the precession of the ages. This reversed order of the precession of the ages has a strange effect upon the evolutionary process of the race. At one point there appears to be a sudden and rapid acceleration from a primitive society to a highly developed one, such as has been experienced in the past two thousand years. Actually, the greatest gains have been made in the last quarter of the Piscean age, or the past five or six hundred years.

It has been found that the vibrations of the ages overlap one another. So, the vibrations of the new age begin to be felt between five and six hundred years before it becomes fully operative. At the other end, the vibrations of the old age continue to be felt at a declining rate for a similar length of time. Thus it is that there is only about a thousand years or so in which the vibrations of any given age are clearly felt with little distortion from others.

Once the zenith point is reached, as will occur during the thousand year period between 2,500 and 3,500 A.C.E., a decline begins once more. And, for the next 20,000 to 22,000 years, the race will be on a gradual decline until it will once again reach its nadir in another age of Aries. But, the beliefs, mental attitudes and characteristics of an age are never completely obliterated. They are maintained intact throughout the solar year (26,000 earth years) by a few people from age to age until their time for full expression comes around again.

The Greek legend of the creation of mankind found in *Bulfinche's Mythology*[5] describes the first age as the

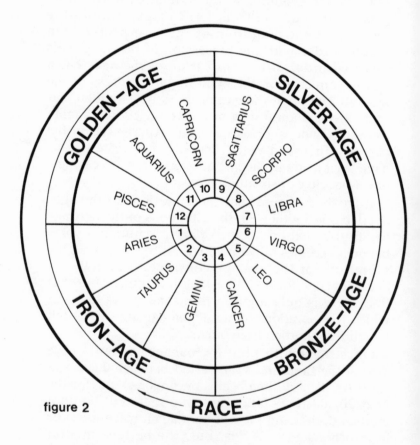

figure 2

Golden Age in which mankind was enlightened and lived in peace. They lived in a paradise in which the earth produced all the necessary food without the need for labor. The second was the **Silver Age**. Although inferior to the Golden Age, mankind was able to provide for all its needs by tilling the soil. In these two periods there was no private property, no need for artificial rules and regulations, and certainly no need for law enforcement.

The next was the **Bronze Age** in which mankind became more savage and inclined to fight at the slightest provocation. But it was not totally wicked. The worst was the **Iron Age** in which crime ran rampant, and truth and honor were no longer to be found. In their place was violence, fraud, cunning and greed.

A similar description is found in Plato's "Critias"[6] where he indicates that the Atlantean civilization began at a very high level. The people obeyed Universal Laws and revered the divine within themselves. But, when the divine element became diluted by mixing with mortals, their human characteristics began to dominate and degeneration set in.

This theme can be illustrated by dividing the zodiac into four quadrants (Figure 2). **The Golden Age** would be represented by the ages of Pisces, Aquarius and Capricorn, the **Silver Age** by Sagittarius, Scorpio and Libra, the **Bronze Age** by Virgo, Leo and Cancer, and the **Iron Age** by Gemini, Taurus and Aries. Each of these four ages could also be compared with the four seasons in nature but, for our purpose, a better comparison is with that of the ages of mankind (Figure 3): childhood, adulthood, middle age, old age. These in turn may be subdivided into three steps each, corresponding with the signs of the zodiac (Figure 4).

Childhood includes infancy, childhood, and the pre-teen years. Adulthood begins in the teens and includes young adulthood and the mature years. Middle age is the period which includes parents with teen-aged

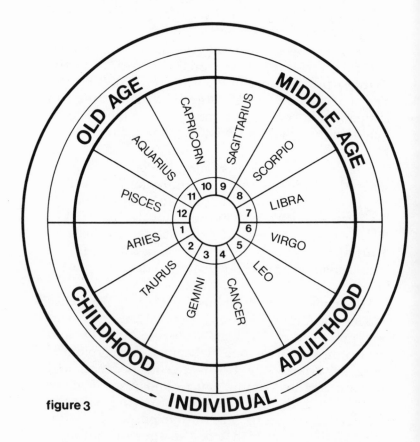

figure 3

children, parents with adult children, and the elderly or parents with grand-children. Finally, old age is the time in which one's responsibilities to the family have been met and one has time to give in service to others, in public service and in philanthropy. The last of these is the transition period between this life and the next in which one's thoughts are turned to summing up one's life and finalizing one's religious and philosophical beliefs (or understanding the meaning of life).

Another way in which to view the zodiac as it applies to mankind is to divide the circle into two halves with an upper and lower half (Figure 5). The lower half, as has been shown, represents the individual and the race in the early stages of development. The concerns of the young are strongly oriented toward the physical, personal and material side of life. The upper half, on the other hand represents the mature adult in the second half of life with an orientation toward the social, mental and spiritual aspects.

A further division into quarters provides another focus (Figure 6). The overall emphasis of each half remains the same, but the first quarter is seen to have a stronger emphasis upon the physical, while the second quarter has a stronger emphasis upon the social.

On the lower half, this reflects the characteristic of the pre-teen-aged child who is concerned about himself alone, while the teen and young adult has a greater concern for the self in the context of relating to others within a social setting. On the upper half, which is oriented toward the social, mental and spiritual, the quarter divisions are divided first with an emphasis on the personal and secondly on the social side. In the first, or personal quarter, relationships focus on one's spouse, children and grand-children. The last quarter, which is more socially oriented, is expressed through involvement in community service and, finally, in summing up.

In addition to these divisions, there are two ages in

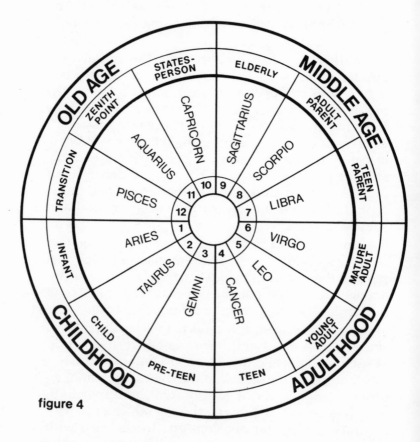

figure 4

the upper half of the horoscope which astrologers frequently describe as "The Age of Mankind" (Figure 7). The first is the age of Scorpio. This sign, it will be recalled, falls during the period which represents middle age. The sign Scorpio is represented by three symbols signifying the three aspects of our nature. The scorpion represents the lower, physical nature; the serpent represents the intellect or concrete mind, and the eagle is the symbol of the soaring spiritual mind.

It is at this period of life, when the children would normally be out on their own, that one has the opportunity to assess one's goals and purpose in life and to make adjustments. This is accomplished in the struggle to integrate the three aspects of the self: the body, soul and spirit.

The second sign designated as the "Age of Mankind" is Aquarius. It is presumably at this point in its evolution that mankind finds self-fulfillment in service to others. Hence the increased interest in the welfare of others and of the creatures of the earth. From the individual perspective, one has completed one's responsibilities as a householder and ceased active participation in the mechanics of society and is now free to choose the way in which to be of service to the community as a whole.

It is the time in which one is free to give of one's time without concern for getting something in return. Aquarius is the sign of Brother and Sisterhood and/or of philanthropy. Since the race is now entering into this age, these are the qualities that can be expected to become more evident as time passes.

If the idea of evolution through the ages is a valid concept, one would expect to find that in the Golden and Silver ages of the past mankind's philosophy and/or science would include the knowledge of the construct of the universe and the powers of nature. This information would be commonly known and each person would be capable of conducting his or her life in a responsible and peaceful manner. This, as has been shown, is the way legend describes those ages.

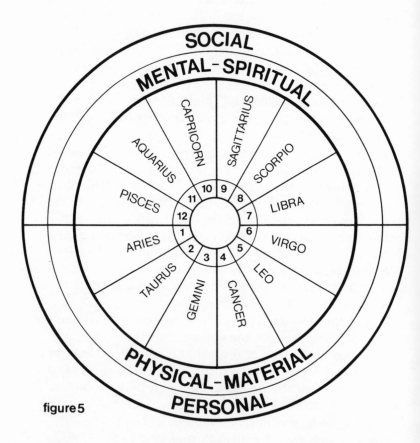

figure 5

Since everyone governed his or her personal life according to Universal Law, there was no need for separate laws or rules and regulations during these two ages. The only regulations needed were those which were necessary to allow an easy flow of commerce between people. Since there was no need for law and law enforcement, there was also no need for a priesthood.

When, in the Judeo/Christian Bible, the gods said, "Let us create Man in our image," they were not thinking of the physical form. This seems apparent since the word "man" means "thinker" and therefore does not relate to gender. It is the ability to think that sets mankind apart from the other animals. However, it has a meaning beyond the ordinary sense of the word.

Anyone who has spent much time around animals knows that they have the ability to think. What really separates mankind from the other animals is the ability to do "creative thinking." This includes not only the ability to harness the forces of nature and to build machines and sky-scrapers, but to build a harmonious society as well. These abilities are the qualities of the gods that we were given.

We were not created full-fledged gods. We are only potential gods. Just as children must learn and grow to become adults, adults must learn and grow to become gods. It is within the context of the astrological ages that we are provided the opportunities for certain experiences which help us to learn and grow, or evolve. Although in every age a variety of experiences are afforded us, each age has its own special emphasis.

The Ancient Wisdom says, as does modern science, that the universe was formed out of duality, or from positive and negative forces (from male and female principles). From these were born the male and female aspects of the natural/phenomenal world. It is,

47

therefore, in duality that the human race experiences life on both the physical and spiritual planes.

At its height, during the ages which lie above the

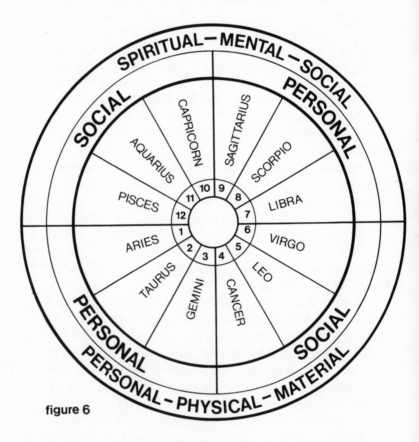

figure 6

horizon of the zodiac, mankind comes to recognize the duality of the universe. But by the beginning of the last quarter of the zodiac (the ages of Gemini, Taurus and

The Astrological Ages

Aries), degeneration has become so complete that the knowledge of the true nature of the universe is lost in the superstitious beliefs that develop.

As indicated, the lower half of the zodiac pertains to the stages of childhood and youth. It is during this period that, due to a lack of experience and, therefore, a poor understanding of the universe and our place in it, the race requires heroes and idols to emulate. During the astrological ages which correspond with this period, the need for a structured world with heroes and idols is satisfied by organized religion with its gods and priests. Powerful gods are invented to compensate for the growing lack of understanding and the consequent feeling of inadequacy to control the circumstances of life. The gods eventually becoming arbitrary and capricious, as was Jehovah, treating mankind as pawns in a giant game of chess.

Thus, it is found that religion is an invention of less mature minds and a phenomenon of the ages which are located on the lower hemisphere of the zodiac. This being the case, it is obvious that, as Jeremiah predicted, we are about to outgrow the need for religion as we come to understand the true meaning of life.

When religion is viewed by following the devolutionary (declining) path of the ages from Virgo to Aries, the emphasis seems to alternate from age to age between the Mother-goddess and Father-god religions (Figure 8). At first, the Mother/Father gods are regarded as benevolent benefactors who are seen as symbols of the life force. But, as the ages progress in reverse order, the gods assume more and more control over the lives of the people until the age of Aries in which they are no longer able to fend for themselves (psychologically/spiritually) and become fearful of the

49

dangers which threaten their physical lives. At this point they give up responsibility for themselves in favor of total dependence upon the Father-god.

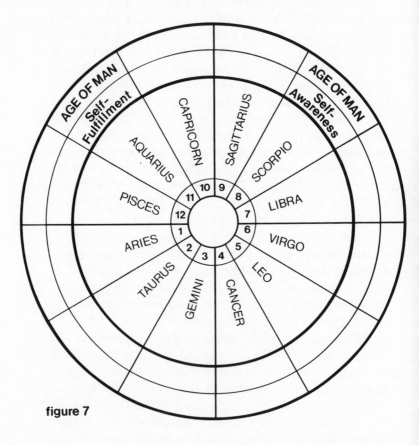

figure 7

Thus it can be seen that below the horizon, when viewed from the perspective of the evolution of the race, mankind gradually loses its autonomy. At first, in the age of Virgo, we begin to feel our dependency upon Mother Nature for our sustenance and create symbolic rituals by which to show reverence to her.

Under Leo, we become aware of our dependence upon the Sun and its life-giving energy, without which Mother Nature would not be able to provide her sustenance. This leads to the focus being placed upon the masculine Sun-god in his various forms.

With Cancer, the teen-age years of the individual, the emotions come into play. Now, the race is enamored by the Moon and her effects upon the emotional nature. It is the emotions that stir us to indulge our physical appetites which, in turn, cause us to have a sense of being alive.

During the ages of the last quarter of the zodiac, as consciousness regresses toward its lowest point, duality begins to be viewed, not in terms of cooperation between opposites, but in terms of competition. Prior to the changes in attitude from cooperation to competition, perhaps around the beginning of the age of Gemini, religion was more spontaneous and, therefore, less structured. But with the change came a highly structured and controlling institution which has been the character of all the major religions since then.

However, as we move closer to the age of Aquarius, enlightened people recognize that cooperation brings about greater freedom as well as more satisfactory relationships. Therefore, competitiveness is beginning to be seen as a negative factor in our lives and will eventually fade away.

It is likely that the idea of viewing the universal duality in terms of competition began with the Zoroastrian religion in Persia. Astrologically speaking, this event probably occurred during the age of Gemini between 6,500 and 8,500 years ago. This conclusion is not without support since some Parsees (the last

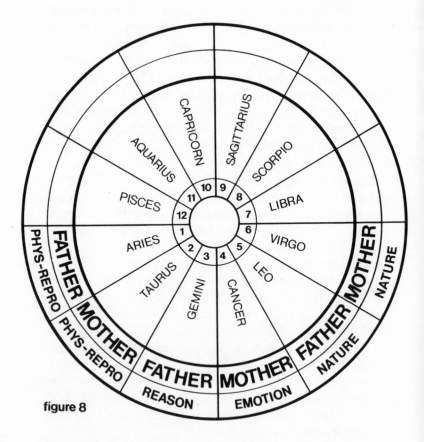

figure 8

remnants of the Zoroastrian religion) claim to be able to trace the source of their religion back into prehistory at least 8,000 years.

The Astrological Ages

The vibrations of Gemini generally bring out the rational side of our nature, but without the intuition. As a dual sign, there is much consideration given to opposites. But, in this age, the opposites with which they were concerned were not of the masculine and feminine principles but the qualities of "good and evil."

It was the Zoroastrians who created the myth regarding the creation of the universe which gave personifications to the various forces of the phenomenal and spiritual worlds found in Judaism and Christianity today. These were in the form of gods, angels, cherubim, etc. But, the creative forces were almost all masculine in principle. The feminine was given very little recognition. This has led to the Judeo/Christian belief in a creation devoid of the feminine principle.

Later, in the age of Taurus, when the goddess religions sprang up as a reaction to this slight to the feminine principle under the Zoroastrian and other God-dominated religions, duality was once again regarded as a male/female polarity. But, in this case, the symbology was taken literally and sex itself became the focus. Now, the female became the controlling agent. So, at the beginning of written history, or during the Taurean age, societies are found to have been matriarchal.

As previously indicated, the age of Taurus corresponds with the toddler age of the individual. The records available from that period show that the mental attitudes of the people at that time had a strong similarity to what is known of a child in that period of his or her life.

He or she is beginning to become aware of the self and the family within the larger community. Many children, at this time, discover and become obsessed with the genitals. But the interest is more one of a sense of discovery than of an obsession with sensation when the child is allowed to explore without interference from older people. This is also the time in which the imagination begins to develop and in which the child creates its own fantasy world. Included in these creations are often "boogie man" kinds of creatures, both animal and human.

It was during the age of Taurus that the Mother-goddess came into prominence and the male principle took the back seat. Consequently, men came to be treated as second class citizens. During this period, sex became a part of religious ritual and was considered to be a gift of the goddess to mankind.[8]

This state of affairs led to a severe reaction in the next age, the Age of Aries (2500 B.C.E to the present era). It was now the males' turn to dominate the females, and this was done with a vengeance. The repercussions from the fallout that followed this reversal of positions is still felt today. It will be discussed more fully in the chapter on the Politics of Sex.

By the time of the Age of Aries, which was dominated by the Hebrew religion, the level of awareness had regressed to that of an infant or pre-toddler. The religion was, therefore, designed to meet the needs of persons with the general awareness of very small children. It was only natural, therefore, that the Age of Aries would produce a Father-god who was responsible for the well-being of his helpless, non-responsible children.

So, we find that the "Laws of Moses" were given as commands without explanation because the "Children of Israel" were not able to comprehend the reasons behind them. Moses simply told them the laws were to be followed in order to insure them long lives. Does this not sound like an explanation a parent might give to a small child? Moses and the later priests had their hands full just trying to get the Children of Israel to accept basic social responsibilities. They were not ready for the truths of the Ancient Wisdom. An examination of some of the rules which Moses laid down demonstrates this point.

In one instance, Moses told them not to eat pork, which he said was an "abomination," or, disgusting. Today we know that improperly cooked pork can lead to infection with a worm called "trichina" which causes a debilitating disease, "trichinosis." Certainly, camping in the desert, they had no facilities to properly cook this meat. He also warned them not to eat food on the third day after preparation. It too was said to be an abomination. But today we call it botulism and ptomaine poisoning.

By the same token, some prohibitions were against certain sex practices which were also said to be an abomination. The reasons for putting them into place, it can now be seen, were twofold. First, there were hygienic reasons – to avoid the spread of venereal diseases, a problem then as now. The prohibition against homosexuality was, most likely, because Moses knew that many sexually transmitted diseases are transferred from the mouth and anus to the genitals. He also appears to have known that these diseases could be transmitted to the unborn children "to the third and fourth generations," he said. Today we know that they cause blindness, deafness, mental retardation, and perhaps other defects.

Secondly, a careful study of the scriptures reveals

Moses

that he restricted sexual intercourse to the period in which the woman was most likely to become pregnant. This, too, is based upon very valid reasons which will be discussed later.

While much of the Ancient Wisdom was preserved in the literature of the Hebrews, it was of little importance to the Children of Israel. For many years the books of Moses were stored away and forgotten. It was not until after their return from the Babylonian Captivity in the 6th century B.C.E. that these books were rediscovered and the people began to study them. It is clear that they contained the Wisdom which Moses had learned from the Egyptians in his youth.

During the ages of Gemini, Taurus and Aries, the Ancient Wisdom had faded from the memory of the race except in certain centers around the world where it was preserved. About the 6th century B.C.E., when it is believed by astrologers that the vibrations of the Piscean age began to be felt, the Ancient Wisdom began to be revived in various places around the world. Buddha in India, Lao Tse in China, and Pythagoras in Greece were the main leaders of this revival.

But, while Buddha and Lao Tse confined their efforts to the re-awakening of knowledge of the subjective/spiritual side of our nature, Pythagoras was concerned with both the subjective/spiritual and the objective/physical. He seemed to understand that each served as a symbol for the other.

Today, Pythagoras is regarded by many in the field to be the true Father of Modern Science. But his contributions to the spiritual awakening of Western minds had been lost, or rather hidden, from all but a few until recent years. It has now begun to resurface in many different forms, part of the changes which are taking place as we move into the new age of Aquarius.

It should also be noted that the Hebrew prophets of the 6th century B.C.E. (Jeremiah, Isaiah and Ezekiel) were, apparently, also influenced by the changes which were occurring between the ages of Aries and Pisces. Each of their teachings reflects this in their appeal to the individual to take responsibility for him or herself. Jeremiah and Isaiah both declared that the superstitious belief in blood sacrifice was not an acceptable substitute for self-realization. Nevertheless, even today, the belief continues to be the major part of the Christian religion which holds tenaciously to the belief in a crucified savior.

It was at this time that Jeremiah prophesied that there would come a time when there would be no more need for teachers (rabbis, priests, ministers, or gurus) because each individual would possess the truth for him or herself. The teachings of Jesus reveal that he attempted to fulfill this prophecy by teaching individual salvation through cooperation with Universal Law. But, as will be shown, his efforts were aborted as his teachings were driven underground by the religion which had greater appeal for the masses apparently not yet ready to take responsibility for themselves.

When Jesus appeared at the beginning of the Piscean age, he told the descendants of the followers of Moses that they no longer needed to be guided by the rules of small children. They were mature enough, he declared, to figure out a few things for themselves. Therefore, he said, if they were respectful toward the source of their being, their God, and toward one another, the rest would come about naturally.

But the age of Pisces represents the age of mankind

at the end of life, or in its "second childhood." It is commonly understood that those persons at this stage of life who become senile and revert to the mental attitude of children often become reluctant to assume responsibility for their own well-being. Having given up on life in this world, they tend to focus their interest upon what lies ahead in "life after death."

During the major part of the past two thousand years, because the majority of people were unwilling to assume responsibility for themselves, the vacuum was filled by a caretaker in the form of the Christian Church and Islam, both of which have used the concern for "life after death" as a hook to keep the masses tied to them.

The Christian religion is based upon a mythological savior god, the only son of the Creator God of the Zoroastrian religion. He was born of a Virgin, died, and was resurrected. After partaking of a "Last Supper" with his "Twelve Disciples," he ascended to Heaven where he shall remain until he returns to earth to carry those who remain his faithful followers back to heaven. They will be judged and separated from the infidels on the final judgment day.

If this sounds familiar, it is because the Christian Church adopted it, along with all of the rest of the ritual and dogma, from the Mithraic religion. One who is familiar with those religions will find a great deal of the same ritual and/or dogma in Judaism and Islam as well.

The story just sketched was a myth created to explain certain spiritual truths about the nature of the universe and mankind's purpose on earth. It was based upon astrology which was an integral part of the Mithraic religion. But, the people then, as now, were so unaware that they were unable to recognize the reality behind the symbols and came to regard the symbols as the reality.

Theoretically, by the time the race has reached the upper half of the zodiac in its evolution, it no longer should have a need for heroes and idols as guides to follow. There should instead be a universal understanding of the Laws of the Universe and of our place in it. Therefore, there should be no need for organized religion with its priests who are nothing more than blind leaders of the blind. It should be replaced by a philosophy which is based upon the objective/experimental outlook of science and the subjective/experiential introspection of the mystic.

✦

IV

History And The Astrological Ages

The Ancient Wisdom, which the Sumerian tablets say was imparted to mankind after the Flood, has been preserved in different times by various centers of learning. The original center was Sumeria. While much of the Wisdom was preserved by the Magi up to the beginning of the present age, it had largely become degenerate in its popular form by the time written history began in the age of Taurus (4500 B.C.E).

Since references made to the prehistoric past found in the ancient records are lacking in details regarding specific time periods, there is no way to determine with certainty where particular events fit chronologically. But, by showing that the historical ages follow the pattern of the ages, as described in Chapter III, it may be inferred that the prehistoric ages followed the pattern as well.

Egypt was the home of several centers of the Ancient Wisdom which persisted in a sea of growing superstitions for centuries. Early in the age of Taurus

the Great Pyramid was built, presumably by Cheops.[1]
It was here in the temple at Denderah where the starry
heavens were duplicated as a monumental form of the
Ancient Wisdom. It was also the Temple of Denderah
that served as the model for the temple Moses built in
the desert. Furthermore, the city of Jerusalem and the
Temple of Solomon were modeled after the same
temple. Thus it can be seen that the relationship
between heaven and earth (astrology) was a part of the
religion of Moses.

The age of Taurus, as indicated, corresponds with
the age of the child between the ages of two and four.
It is a time in which fantasy has a strong influence.
Lacking knowledge of the true nature of one's
environment, the child creates a fantasy world to
compensate for a lack of understanding and to
alleviate his or her fears of the unknown. This seems to
fit the picture of the general level of consciousness
during the age of Taurus.

It is significant to note that the cow and bull became
the symbols of this age. The cow was the symbol of
Mother Nature who nurtures mankind by giving
sustenance from her own body. The bull was the
symbol of the sun and was the fecundator of the
Mother-goddess. For a time they appear to have been
regarded as equally important.

However, possibly around the middle half of the
age, the goddess religion began to dominate the scene.
Each year in Sumeria the Goddess Inanna, or Ishtar,
took a new consort. At the end of the year he was
sacrificed in a ritual depicting the death of the sun,
and a new consort was taken to replace him. He
represented the new born, or newly risen sun.

As mentioned in the last chapter, the new Father-god religions which developed in the last quarter of the Taurean age (2500-2000 B.C.E) were formed in reaction to the excesses of the goddess religion which had been controlled by female priests. Men were not allowed into the priesthood until the end of the age. Even then they were not admitted until they had been castrated, which must have seemed to them to be an insult added to the injury of being sacrificed as part of the annual ritual.

In these religious rites, the blood of the male, like the rays of the sun, was believed to nurture new life on the earth just as the menstrual blood of the female nurtured the fetus. Later, under the new male-dominated religions, the bull was castrated before it was killed, making it female. Its blood was then regarded as the menstrual blood of the female, capable of nurturing life.

But, in a final act of revolt, the male-dominated religions inaugurated the sacrifice of women and children. Recorded history indicates that this was a wide-spread practice toward the end of the Taurean and the beginning of the Arien ages. It was one of the practices of the Druids of Europe as well as of various religions of the Americas.

While the goddess religion dominated the age of Taurus, due to the overlapping of the ages, god and goddess religions were practiced side by side for some time. The goddess religions were not fully replaced among the people of the Hebrew religion until the vibrations of the Piscean age began to be felt.

Although they had been ordered by their God Jehovah, through Moses, to give up the old religious practices, the Children of Israel continued to return to them. Up to the time of the Captivity (586-538 B.C.E.), the kings of Israel built pagan altars and sacrificed their children. And in Jerusalem, the Hebrew women were still practicing the goddess religion when Ezekiel returned there from Babylon toward the end of the Captivity. He found them at the north gate of the Temple of Solomon weeping for the death of Tammuz, the Sun God of the old goddess religion.[2]

True to the pattern of the evolution of the ages, the vibrations of the age of Aries brought about changes in the mental attitudes and behavior of the people. During the last quarter of the Taurean age this was experienced in the political arena. Prior to this time, the people had lived in tribes and city-states. But, around 2,600 B.C.E., this began to change when Sargon, a Semitic leader living in Akkad (Northern Mesopotamia), formed an effective army and began to wage war on neighboring states. He finally conquered the entire region of the Persion Gulf.[3] Speaking from an astrological point of view, when it is observed that the planet Mars, the ruler of the sign of Aries, is also the god of war, it seems only natural that the age should be one in which men began to develop the game of war into a "science."

History reveals that, not only were the Semites the harbingers of the new age of Aries, but their influence was to dominate the entire age. It is quite evident that the Hebrews were "chosen" to lead the rest of the race on the evolutionary path during this age. But much misfortune has arisen during the past two thousand years (the age of Pisces) because of the failure of both Christians and Jews to understand that this status was intended to be a temporary one.

Sargon's triumph was the beginning of wars which were to eventually mold the tribes and city-states into the nations which formed from them. The close contact between many diverse peoples which resulted from the larger social/political groupings which were formed served to further mankind's evolution by stimulating its intellectual processes. Although interrupted by a long hiatus during the middle ages of the Piscean age, this eventually led to the development of industry and technology in the last few hundred years. This, in turn, will no doubt lead to a global society in the age of Aquarius.

Although the nation which was formed under Sargon's leadership was divided for a time between its neighbors, it was reunited under Hammurabi, the sixth in line of the Amorite kings and the second great Semitic leader after Sargon.[4] Henceforth, empire building continued under the Semites until it passed into Roman hands about the 2nd century B.C.E.

It was Hammurabi who, after reuniting the Babylonian kingdom, introduced a code of social conduct which he claimed had been given to him directly by the god Shamash (Sun God). This code is found to be very similar to the Laws which Moses received from the God Jehovah, given to the Hebrew people during the Exodus from Egypt.

According to the Judeo/Christian Bible, Abraham, another Semite, was raised in the empire which Sargon and Hammurabi built and may have lived there during the time of Hammurabi's reign. However, a conflict in historical dating makes it impossible to determine for sure. We know that Abraham left Ur of the Chaldeas with his father and other family members to go to the land of Canaan. But on the way they stopped in Haran, a city in Syria where there may have been ancestral ties. After his father's death in

Haran, Abraham was instructed by the God Jehovah to continue on to the land of Canaan where it was promised that he would be the founder of a new nation.

As one of the harbingers of the age of Aries, it was Abraham who was to introduce the symbol of the new age. In the 22nd chapter of Genesis the story is told of how he was called upon by his god to sacrifice his son, Isaac, in the manner of the old religions. But, when he had shown his willingness to obey, his god relented and provided a substitute in the form of a Ram. It seems that this story was invented to indicate the transition from the old age of Taurus, in which the Bull was the symbol, to Aries which had the Ram as its symbol. Later, as the vibrations of the Piscean age began to be felt, the prophets preached against sacrifice altogether.

It now appears that it was the task of the Hebrews to preserve the Ancient Wisdom in the Western World during the decline of the Middle East. While Egypt had played the role of preserver during the age of Taurus and for a time in the age of Aries, she herself was on the decline and about to lose control of her own destiny and, along with it, the secrets of the Ancient Wisdom.

Moses, it seems, was instructed to rescue the Hebrews from the Egyptians and to form a nation as a means of preserving the Ancient Wisdom for a time when the race would once again be able to understand it. As Manly Hall says,[5] the picture of Moses surrounded by the twelve tribes of Israel recalls to mind the Astro-theology of the Chaldeans and Egyptians. It was this same truth which Moses preserved and imparted to the Children of Israel.

The View From Olympus

Apart from its historical significance, the Pentateuch (first five books of the Old Testament) seems to be a veiled account of hidden truths. Like the Greek Odysseus, it describes the wanderings of the human soul in search of the truth, or the promised land. Furthermore, the Tabernacle which Moses was instructed to build in the Wilderness was an exact duplicate of the Egyptian sanctuary at Denderah. The Tabernacle is said to be a microcosmic symbol of the universe or, perhaps more accurately, a miniature representation of the center of the universe, the home of the universal Sun and the dwelling place of the Most High.[6]

Clearly, the whole of the Hebrew ritual revolves around astrological symbols. The seven branched candlestick represents the seven planetary bodies as well as the seven days of creation, the seven races, and the seven spiritual centers in the human body.

The four faces of the cherubim on the Mercy Seat of the Ark represent the four fixed signs of the zodiac: Aquarius, Taurus, Leo and Scorpio. Together they are called the rulers of the four corners of the earth within whose bounds the mystery of creation occurs.

The priest's robes are hung with pomegranates and bells of gold representing the seventy-two stars (six in each zodiacal sign) and, on the earth plane, representing the seventy-two elders, six from each tribe.[7]

Within the Ark of the Covenant were three items symbolizing the three aspects of mankind: body, soul, and spirit. The manna represented the spirit; the staff of Aaron was the spinal column or "Kundalini," as it is called in the East. The blossoms represent the Chakras, or spiritual centers, which are to be awakened by spiritual awareness. The Tablets of the Law represent the physical body, which in turn signifies the mundane, man-made laws which were designed to help to steer the minds of the people in the direction of the higher levels of consciousness.

It is apparent that all the Hebrew symbology was intended to show the correspondence between the heavens and mankind and was presented to mankind as a means of assisting in the search for spiritual enlightenment.

While all of these astrological symbols were incorporated into the ritual of the Hebrew religion, their meaning was lost to the Children of Israel, whose level of consciousness was at such a low point that they were unable to comprehend it. One need only read the story of the Children of Israel[8] and the problems Moses and the later priests had in trying to change their mental attitudes to understand how degenerate the race had become during the ages of Taurus and Aries.

The Old Testament reveals that the tendency for abandonment to the physical appetites and the old superstitious beliefs was a difficult habit to change. Like intractable children, they persisted in following their lower instincts. Therefore, it appears there was good reason why the rules which Moses laid down were so harsh. The people were stubborn and could not be appealed to through reason. Beginning with Solomon and continuing until the Babylonian Captivity, the kings of the Hebrews habitually returned to the practice of the old religions. In the 9th century B.C.E., Ahab sacrificed two of his sons in commemoration of the rebuilding of Jericho.[9]

Just as the wars of conquest which Sargon began in

the 26th century B.C.E. sounded the first notes of the
trumpets of change between the ages of Taurus and
Aries, the Babylonian Captivity signalled the change
between the ages of Aries and Pisces. This celebrated
event was not, as many believe, a mass relocation of
the entire nation. It was only the leaders who were
likely to stir up trouble at home who were taken away.
They were, therefore, the intellectuals of their nation.

Because their minds were better trained than most,
they were also better equipped to profit from the
experience. History shows that it was while they were
in Babylon that the Jews came into contact with the
Zoroastrian religion and the belief in the supreme God.
Prior to that period they were taught that there were
many gods, but that theirs was superior to the others.
The idea that theirs was the one and only god came
from the teachings of the second Isaiah and was added
to their religion when Nehemiah and Ezra returned to
Jerusalem at the end of the Captivity.

It was Nehemiah and Ezra who were responsible for
restoring the Laws of Moses which had been lost and
forgotten for hundreds of years, but it was the liberal
attitude of the Persian conquerors that allowed them
to worship their own god without interference. And it
was this liberal attitude which also fostered the growth
and spread of Judaism and thus contributed to the
transformation of a local deity into a universal, cosmic
God.[10]

Regardless of all of its ideas of separateness and
superiority, when one gets down to the basic facts, the
Hebrew religion is just a composite of the religions of
all the past ages. There is nothing new in it which is
not found in those earlier religions.

After the Assyrian, Babylonian and Persian

conquests of Palestine, the Hebrews substituted Ishtar for the Canaanite Ashteroth. The Esther of the Old Testament is found to be a transliteration of the name Ishtar into the English language. The book of Esther, therefore, is a euphamistic way of telling the story of the old Spring New Year Fertility Rites. The qualities of the Egyptian Isis, whose name means "throne" are applied to the Kabbalistic Shekinah and to the "personified Wisdom of Proverbs."[11]

Like the older, Pagan religions, the Hebrew religion at one time conformed to the idea that the gods had consorts who were at once wives, daughters, and mothers. This was in recognition of the male and female principles in nature that play different roles at different times. In the 5th century B.C.E., Anat was described as the consort of Jehovah. But, this idea was discarded as the belief in the one, male god solidified.

These and other examples, along with the obvious connections to the Astro-theological beliefs and rituals of the Sumerian/Chaldeans and Egyptians show a direct reliance of the Hebrews upon the religions of the past.

There were two major events which occurred in Jewish history during the Persian period that influenced its future direction. From the Babylonian experience, the second Isaiah borrowed the Zoroastrian idea of the one god and declared that Jehovah, the Hebrew tribal god, was the one and only creator God. Therefore, it seemed logical that the worship of Jehovah should be the religion of the world. Secondly, the apocalyptic literature which was written at this time prophesied the future subjection of all nations to the Jews and their Laws. This firmed their belief in their mission to convert the world to the one "true religion." [12]

It was, no doubt, their strong sense of nationalism and belief in their chosen status which caused the Jews to fail to see the true meaning and purpose of their religion as the carrier of the Ancient Wisdom for the age of Aries only. In the 6th century B.C.E. they were unaware that they were living in a time of transition in which a new perception of life was being awakened by spiritual leaders all over the world. This included some of their own prophets.

But the appeal of Jeremiah and the second Isaiah for the people to assume their individuality and take responsibility for themselves fell on deaf ears. This message was the same as that which was being taught by their contemporaries in other parts of the world. It declared that the gods were no longer to be appeased by the ritual of blood sacrifice. The children of the emerging new age of Pisces were no longer children. Therefore salvation was, henceforth, to be the responsibility of the individual.

The 6th century B.C.E. is noted for the sudden awakening of the minds of mankind. This awakening was led by the Seven Wise Men of Greece (Thales, Pittacus, Bias, Solon, Clebulus, Periander, and Chilon), the Greek philosopher/scientist Pythagoras who later settled in Italy, Buddha in India, Lao Tse and Confucius in China. All seem to have acquired their knowledge from teachings which were ancient in their times.

The "Seven Wise Men of Greece" were a group of men renowned for their contributions to the Greek people. These contributions included knowledge of the arts and sciences as well as the accomplishment of bringing democracy to the governments of their respective city-states. Of the seven, Thales and Solon are the best known today. As previously mentioned, Thales was the first to substitute scientific for mythological interpretations of the nature of the physical universe. Solon was an ancestor of Plato, from whom he derived the story of Atlantis.

Confucius' teachings were based entirely upon a system of ethics which he expressed in the form of aphorisms. He did not believe in the use of coersion to get his point across. Education through the gentle persuasion of his pithy sayings was considered much more effective. He regarded human beings as essentially social beings, bound to one another by **jin**, or sympathy. Based upon this belief he proposed a system of morality, on both the individual and social levels, that would lead not only to peace and harmony but to a just and stable government as well.

Lao Tse (born 510 B.C.E.) based his philosophy on the rhythm of life. While he recognized Universal Law as a thing with which to be reckoned, he was most concerned with its application on the personal level and regarded simplicity to be a basic rule. The doctrine of "wu-wei," or inaction, which may be interpreted as **laissez-faire** or "live and let live," implies the element of free will or free choice. Therefore, the conduct of one's life is an individual responsibility.

Both Pythagoras and Buddha derived their teachings directly from the Ancient Wisdom. Buddha's background was in the Hindu religion, which is one of the repositories of the Ancient Wisdom in the Far East. Like all the others, Buddha was a reformer. His purpose was to overcome the superstitious beliefs which had developed in the Hindu religion and to remedy the abuses of the priesthood. The method by which he approached the task was to revive the part of the ancient teachings which related directly to the individual. His main purpose was to show the way to higher consciousness and attunement with the Cosmic Mind.

Pythagoras acquired his knowledge of the Ancient Wisdom from Egypt, Babylon and Arabia. Unlike the others, he was as much concerned with the nature of the universe as he was with the nature of mankind. Broadly speaking, he was interested in the interrelationship between people and the universe and in the means by which to work in harmony with the principles of nature. It was this understanding of the interconnectedness between the physical and spiritual aspects of the universe which led to his being influential in both the science and religion of the modern world.

However, the religion which he fostered had no connection to the superstitious beliefs of the other religions. It was based upon the same Universal Laws upon which his science was based. Many scholars believe the Essenes, of whom Jesus was almost certainly a member, were influenced by the teachings of Pythagoras.

The teachings of Jesus, the last great harbinger of the Piscean age, were also unquestionably based upon Universal Law. It was to this Law, and not the man-made laws of the Hebrew religion, that he referred when he said he had come to fulfill the Law. But, soon after his departure, these teachings were replaced by the ritual and dogma of the popular Pagan religion of the time. Thus, what has been known by his name for the past two thousand years has very little to do with him or his teachings. It is Christian in name only.

History And The Astrological Ages

But how, one may ask, if the teachings of Jesus regarding Universal Law and individual responsibility were meant for the Piscean age, has it happened that the so-called Christian religion with its vicarious salvation came to dominate the age? The answer to this question can only be found by reviewing the characteristics of the age.

In describing the astrological ages, it will be recalled, they were compared to the ages of the individual. It is said that the age of Pisces can be compared to a person at the end of life. At this point one often sees the future interms of death. Hope lies in "life after death." This, of course, has been the emphasis of the Christian religion throughout the Piscean age.

As indicated, this period of life has been called the "second childhood." At this stage people are often dependent upon others for their care and sometimes may be unable to make decisions for themselves. This seems to have been the case with people in general during the last 2,000 years, the age of Pisces. The Church, with its paternalistic, dictatorial attitude, has fulfilled the need for a caretaker.

Because the precession of the ages is in reverse order to that of the individual, the movement of the point at which Aries and Pisces meet has the effect of jumping from infancy to old age. So, it should not be difficult to see how some of the characteristics of the age of infancy would carry over into the age of the second childhood.

Not only does society as a whole show signs of the split between the child and the adult, this split is commonly encountered in individuals who find it difficult to take on adult responsibilities. While the adult in us sees the order and reason which characterizes the physical world, we often find it difficult to relate this to the subjective/spiritual side of life. For this reason, many continue to force themselves to accept the irrational teachings of organized religion whose major concern is to perpetuate its position of authority. The confusion this causes may be the reason for so much schizophrenic behavior in our society today.

You will recall that the vibrations of the new age begin to be felt five or six hundred years before the transition actually occurs. During the 14th and 15th centuries A.C.E., or five to six hundred years before the beginning of the Aquarian age, there was a new awakening of the cognitive faculties of Western people. These faculties had been repressed by the Church for over a thousand years.

By then, colleges and universities, which had begun to be established in the 12th and 13th centuries, were proliferating. Most, however, had been founded by the Church to train its priests and were, therefore, controlled by it so that its dogma would not be violated. Nevertheless, some students began to be carried beyond the bounds of propriety and made discoveries which were to challenge the doctrines of the Church. These discoveries were, in turn, to lay the foundation for more discoveries.

There were two major developments which took place in the 15th century that began to free the minds of Western people from the tyranny of the Church. The first was the explorations made by maritime explorers which resulted, not only in geographic discoveries, but in disproving the dogma of the Church which insisted that the earth was flat. This cast doubt upon the infallibility of the Church and opened it up to more scrutiny.

The second, equally important event was the invention of the printing press with moveable type. Between 1445 and 1500, more than 1,000 printing offices produced nearly 35,000 books with approximately 10,000,000 copies all told. This had a major impact because it increased the availability of information to a greater number of people and encouraged them to think for themselves.

The 16th century is noted as the beginning of the proliferation of scientific discoveries. This has led to the age of technology of today. Modern science was born in 1512 when Copernicus published his "Commentariolus" in which he challenged another of the Church's dogmas by declaring that the earth was not the center of the universe, but that it and the other planets revolved around the sun.

In the same century, Paracelsus established the foundation of modern medicine and taught his theories in various colleges in Europe. During that century, Tycho Brahe built a nineteen foot quadrant and a celestial globe five feet in diameter, Mercator published his "Cosmographia" with a map of the world, Galileo invented the thermometer and built a telescope, and Kepler published his "Harmonics Mundi" in which he states the "Third Law of Planetary Motion."

In addition to the proliferation of scientific discoveries, many other events played a role in preparing mankind for life in the new age which is emerging. The Protestant Revolution, the colonization of the "New World," the expansion of colonization around the world (in spite of the negative effects), the

The View From Olympus

Industrial Revolution of the 18th and 19th centuries, and, finally, the Technological Revolution of the 20th century have all had a part in our evolution, preparing us for the new age.

◆

V

The Influence Of Christianity In The Piscean Age

When Jesus appeared on the world scene, his message was no longer new. It was, however, directed more specifically to the individual than ever before. He was no elitist. His message was to ordinary people with whom he walked and talked. Whether they were men, women, or children, rich or poor, everyone had access to his time and attention.

His message was basic, simple and honest. It identified mankind as one with, not separate from, the creator. From this basic fact he taught the godhood of mankind and brought to others awareness of the god within and the creative power which is the natural heritage of all human beings. Finally, he offered instructions on how to use this power constructively. The parable of the Prodigal Son was his way of explaining human relationship to the godhead, the need to become aware of our true heritage and return to our true home, the source of all being.

After he had passed from the scene, his disciples

continued to teach and to suffer persecution at the hands of the established order. This order, of course, was the Hebrew religion as well as the Roman Empire and its' State religion. Eventually, however, one of their persecutors became dramatically converted. Soon after his conversion he changed his name from Saul to Paul and began to preach a message of his own. Although he taught in the name of Jesus Christ, the Christ of whom he taught was a transformed Sun God whom he patterned after the god of the popular religion of his time.

At first the disciples were very unhappy with his teachings, which were at odds with the teachings they had received from Jesus. But according to Paul, seeing that they could not change him, they finally withdrew their opposition with the stipulation that he confine his teachings to the Gentiles. They themselves would continue to teach the Jews.

But the disciples and the rest of the Jerusalem contingent failed to survive. There is no word concerning them after 70 A.C.E. when Jerusalem was destroyed by the Romans. From that time forward, although there were small pockets of people who followed the teaching of the disciples, the Christian religion was a Gentile religion with its authority vested in Paul. Scholars now credit him with the actual founding of the Christian religion that has dominated the past two thousand years.

For more than sixteen hundred years the Catholic Church has propagated the myth that the leadership of the Christian religion was passed from Peter to the first Bishop of Rome, now called the first Pope. But the evidence does not support this position.

The scriptures which are used to support the claim

that Peter received a mandate directly from Jesus are: Matthew 16: 13-20 and John 21: 15-25. The 16th chapter of Matthew describes an exchange between Jesus and his disciples in which he attempts to explain the purpose of his life and to prepare them for the future. As a test of their understanding he asks them who the ordinary people say that he is. Several of them reply that some say he is John the Baptist and others say Elijah, Jeremiah or one of the other prophets, reincarnated.

When Jesus asks who they think he is, Peter, the most vocal of the group, offers the correct answer. "You are the Christ, the Son of the living God." Jesus then replied that it was spiritual under-standing which allowed Peter to discern this truth and called him "a rock," or one who understands the truth. He next stated that it is "upon this rock I will build my church."

Ever since the Church began to seek to justify its position of power, it has claimed that it was Jesus' intention, based upon this scripture, to found his church on the person of Peter. But it is only five verses later that Jesus reprimands Peter for his failure to understand his mission. He says to him, "Get behind me Satan! You are a hindrance to me; for you are not on the side of God, but of men." This hardly sounds like an exchange that might have taken place between a Master and the one he has chosen to carry on his work.

It is possible to explain more clearly the intentions of Jesus by referring to another passage. In Matthew 7: 24, he says, "Everyone then who hears these words of mine and does them will be like a wise man who builds his house upon the rock." Clearly, the rock of

The rock which he speaks is a symbol of the truth he teaches. By the same token, the rock mentioned in the sixteenth chapter is the truth regarding his relationship to the "living God" which he claims elsewhere to be the same relationship held by all of mankind.

In John 21: 15-25 we find that, rather than indicating that Jesus had chosen him to assume leadership, Peter functions on the ego level and makes a nuisance of himself because of his jealous behavior toward "the disciple whom Jesus loved." In this instance, Jesus says to him in so many words, "The choices I make are none of your business. Tend to your own business."

Contrary to the Church's propaganda, the evidence indicates there were other disciples who had a greater understanding of the teachings of Jesus than did Peter. Therefore, had Jesus been inclined to choose a successor, it would most likely have been one of them. In fact, there is more evidence in both the New Testament and in the Nag Hammadi Library (the Gnostic gospels found in the Egyptian desert in 1945) to indicate that James, the brother of Jesus, assumed leadership .

Thus, it can be seen that the entire idea that Peter received the mantle of leadership from Jesus and was, therefore, in a position to pass it on to the next Bishop (or Pope) is a fabrication concocted to fool the people into accepting the Church of Rome as the center of the "Authentic (Orthodox)" Christian religion. There is no historical evidence to indicate that Peter ever set foot in Rome. Therefore, the "ancient tradition" that Peter and Paul died in Rome on the same day is also a story, fabricated to satisfy the need of the people to be a part of the "authentic, or orthodox" church.

Paul returned to Jerusalem from his third

The Influence Of Christianity

Missionary journey some time between the years 57 and 59. Soon thereafter he became embroiled in an argument with the orthodox Jews who accused him of teaching against the Hebrew religion and of defiling the temple by bringing Greeks into that holy place. Finally, in the year 60, he was sent to Rome to be tried by Caesar (Nero). But there is no record of a trial taking place at that time. Instead, he appears to have been free to teach openly and without hindrance for several years. From the time he arrived in Rome, in 60 A.C.E. until his death seven years later, he made his headquarters in Rome.

According to the Christian Church, Linus was the first Pope after Peter. The date of his rule is said to have been between 67 and 76 A.C.E. But, as II Timothy 4: 21 indicates, Linus was a co-worker of Paul and not Peter. This would indicate that he had received his position as a successor of Paul. This appears more than likely, since it would be expected that, had he indeed been the first Pope of Rome, a man with an ego like that of Peter would have chosen one of his own followers to succeed him rather than a follower of his rival.

The second Pope of Rome was Cletus (or Anacletus) of whom nothing is known. But we find that the third Pope was also a co-worker of Paul's. Clement I (88-97) is mentioned in Philippians 4: 3. In the light of these facts, it is difficult to accept the belief that Peter was either the founder of the Church at Rome or the founder of the Christian religion, thus providing a direct and unbroken link between Jesus Christ and all of the succeeding Roman Popes. Instead, a study of the subject shows that the Christian religion of today is much closer to the teachings of Paul than to the teachings of Jesus. In fact, Christianity has ignored the teachings of Jesus in favor of the teachings of Paul for the major part of the past 2,000 years.

A comparison between the teachings of Jesus and those of Paul soon makes it clear why the disciples were not pleased with Paul. It is evident that the teachings of Jesus are in keeping with the Ancient Wisdom and its grounding in Universal Law, placing the responsibility for salvation on the individual.[1] On the other hand, Paul's teachings are basically a mixture of Hebraic Law and the Mithraic religion (a branch of the Persian, Zoroastrian religion) with, perhaps, the addition of a little Stoicism. Drawing from these two religions, the very core of his religion is dependent upon vicarious salvation through blood sacrifice which the latter prophets, as well as Jesus Christ, had repudiated.

When Jesus sent his disciples out to preach, he gave them instructions to "shake the dust that is on thy feet"[2] when they left a community whose people refused to hear their message. But Paul says that the people who do not listen to his message "deserve to die."[3] He was also a tyrant when dealing with his followers. In his second letter to the Corinthians, he threatens those who disobey his rules with dire consequences. He says, "If I come again I will not spare them."[4]

In every letter he writes he reveals the strong anti-female position which he carried over from the Hebrew and Roman State religion which form the basis of his religion. While he suspends the Hebrew Law regarding circumcision, he is unwilling to make concessions to women whom he says should "keep quiet and be subordinate as the Law says."[5] The Law to which he refers is the Hebrew Law, not the Universal Law which Jesus taught. In his first letter to Timothy, he reiterates his strong feelings against women when he denies them any part in the service, demanding that they be silent and submissive to the men. "I permit no woman to teach or to have authority over men,"[6] he says. This position is justified by a reference to the story of Eve's sin, which we now know from the Chaldean Account of Genesis, was altered from the original in order to make it conform to the male-dominated religion of the Arien Age.

By contrast, Jesus visited in the home of Mary and Martha and accepted them as equals.[7] According to the Gospel of Mary,[8] all of the close associates of Jesus had met together after the crucifixion. Peter turned to Mary Magdelene, whom he said Jesus loved above all of them, and asked her to share some of the things Jesus had shared with her when they were apart from the others.

But, when she had finished sharing some very profound truths, Peter's male ego got the better of him and he questioned her veracity. "Did he really speak privately to a woman and not openly to us?" he asked. Mary, who was wounded at being called a liar, wept. Then, Levi came to her defense and called Peter a hot-head who contended against the woman as though she were an enemy. After which he countered Peter's argument by saying, "... if the Savior made her worthy, who are we ... to reject her? Surely, the Savior knows her very well. That is why he loved her more than us."

Paul was very concerned with the importance of coverings on women's heads, which was a symbol of their subordination. He seemed proud of the fact that the Corinthians had adhered to the Jewish tradition regarding the relative position of importance between men and women as they related to Christ. But Jesus, when confronted by the Pharisees with similar trivia, rebuked them roundly with a quotation from Isaiah. "This people honor me with their lips, but their heart is far from me, in vain do they worship me, teaching as doctrine the precepts of men."[10]

It is also clear that Paul has no understanding of Jesus' position regarding the Law. This is shown in his statement that the written law, "which held us captive," was replaced by a "new life of the spirit" not governed by law.[11] Women, of course, were the exception. But Jesus teaches the opposite. He states that he has not come to abolish the Law of the prophets but to fulfill it. "Not an iota, not a dot, will pass away until it is accomplished,"[12] he says. Since he has already taken a stand against man-made laws, it is clear that the law of which he speaks is Universal Law.

In keeping with the **Law of Karma**, or cause and effect, he says, "Judge not that you be not judged. For with the judgment you pronounce, you will be judged."[13] He warns against the effects of the **Law of Compensation** when he says, "... whatever you wish that men should do to you, do so to them; for this is the law and the prophets."[14]

The function of the **Law of Reincarnation** is beautifully described in the allegory of the Prodigal Son. It is the story of the Soul which leaves its spiritual home and spends many lifetimes enjoying the pleasures of the flesh until it finally remembers who it is. It then enters the path "back to the Father's house,"[15] or the place of spiritual enlightenment.

He also asserts the effectiveness of the **Law of Manifestation** which affirms the creative power of the mind when he says, "Ask, and it will be given you; seek, and you will find; knock and it will be opened to you. For every one who asks receives, and he who seeks finds, and to him who knocks it will be opened."[16]

Paul teaches that Christians should "present your bodies as a living sacrifice."[17] But Jesus, quoting a passage from the Old Testament, clearly shows that God "desires mercy and not sacrifice."[18] Where Paul makes Christ a mediary between God and mankind[19] (according to Mithraic tradition), Jesus admonishes his followers to "pray to the Father"[20] directly.

Paul sees justice in the God of Moses who has a whimsical attitude toward mankind. "For he says to Moses, ' I will have mercy on whom I have mercy, and I will have compassion on whom I have compassion.' So, it depends not upon man's will or exertion, but upon God's mercy."[21] But Jesus presented a heavenly Father who regards all of mankind as his children, who is always compassionate and can be counted upon to be consistent. As indicated in the discussion of the "Law of Manifestation," he says, everyone who asks receives,[22] not just those whom the god decides to favor on a whim.

While Jesus is peaceful, accepting, loving and compassionate, Paul is militant, unfeeling and tyrannical in his relations with his followers. He is even more of a tyrant in his attitude toward unbelievers.

Thus, it is clear to see that those scholars who give credit to Paul as the founder of the Christian religion are accurate in their assessment. For it is apparent that far more of his teachings have become a working part of the Christian religion than have the teachings of

Jesus. In fact, many of the teachings of Jesus are regarded as "heretical" by orthodox/fundamentalist Christians.

While it is true that Paul includes some of the Gnostic teachings of Jesus in his religion, their high sounding tone is lost in his dogma requiring unquestioning loyalty to himself and the Church. However, it is these high sounding teachings, in combination with the Mithraic mythology of a savior god, which make his religion so appealing to the idealism of the masses who are not inclined to think for themselves.

The Mithraic teaching of the death, resurrection and ascension of the god became the very core of Paul's religion. Without it, he says, he would not have a religion. By teaching that Christ was the ultimate sacrifice for the salvation of mankind, he fails to understand that he legitimizes all sacrifice, which is not only contrary to the teachings of Jesus Christ himself, but also of Jeremiah and Isaiah, the later prophets who had condemned it six hundred years before.

While Paul embraced the Mithraic dogma of the crucified and risen Christ, the later Church Fathers went the distance and adopted all of the Mithraic rituals, including baptism and the eucharist. The Sunday Sabbath and December 25th as the birthday of the god, as well as all of the Saints' days, were also borrowed from Mithraism and other Pagan religions. The idea of the Virgin Birth and of Mary as the "Mother of God" were inserted into the Christian religion by the Bishops of North Africa who were familiar with the Egyptian religion in which Isis was called by the very same name hundreds of years before the birth of Christ.

While it has managed to convince the masses of its divinely inspired uniqueness, the truth is that the Christian religion shares the major part of its doctrines and rituals with the Pagans whom it supplanted. As one searches into its background, it becomes evident that there is nothing original about it.

It can be seen that the story of the virgin birth of Jesus Christ is obviously a contrivance of the Church Fathers when one discovers that someone slipped up while tracing the ancestry of Jesus back to David. Although, according to the virgin birth scenario, he had no earthly father, his lineage is nevertheless traced through Joseph's line rather than that of Mary.[23]

It is also obvious that the three Persian Wise Men, whose astrological calculations led them to the Messiah, were not looking for a Jewish Messiah, and they did not go near Palestine. The star which they followed was toward the East, not West to Palestine. They looked, instead, for their own savior god, Mithra, who was born in a cave of a virgin mother and had all of the characteristics which were later ascribed to Jesus perhaps six hundred years later.

We are indeed fortunate that, when the Church Fathers set about to edit the scriptures to make them conform to their dogma, they did a sloppy job and missed some pertinent information. Consequently, we not only have evidence from the recently unearthed, deleted scriptures with which to impeach them but from their own scriptures as well.

Although it was responsible for most of the deaths of heretics during the Inquisition, the Roman Catholic Church was not responsible for all of them. After the Protestant Revolution, when they had the power to do so, the Protestants were just as inclined to violence as the Mother Church. In 1553, for instance, Miguel Servetus was burned alive at Champel, near Geneva, for declaring that the Council of Nicea had made a serious mistake in regard to the Trinity. This event was engineered by the Protestant leader, John Calvin. Martin Luther was also guilty of harsh treatment toward dissenters in his Church.

Servetus' crime was that he espoused the Arian Heresy which had been disavowed by the Council.[24] While the leaders of the orthodox Christians held the Pagan belief that Jesus Christ, as a Son of God, was of the same substance (consubstantial), the Arians (followers of Arius, a Libyan theologian based in Alexandria) taught that he was divinely created but was neither God nor man. He was a demi-god. What really put Servetus outside the pale of Church tolerance was that he dared to question the competence and authority of the early Church leaders, who by that time were regarded as infallible.

Perhaps it would be well to briefly examine the nature of the men who founded the Christian religion and created, or more correctly edited, the literature that is regarded by Catholics as canonical and, therefore, sacred, and by Protestants as the "inspired word of God." Just who were these men and what did they believe?

Although the Roman Church claims to have acquired its Papal authority from Peter, as indicated, it is clear that Paul, whose teachings were contrary to those which were understood by Peter, was the true founder of the Christian religion. Wherever the Church has followed the teachings of the early Christians, it is more consistent with those of Paul than of Jesus. It has definitely assumed Paul's military stance and dictatorial attitude regarding the authority of the Church leadership over its followers.

After Paul, these attitudes are first apparent with Clement I, Bishop of Rome from 88-97 A.C.E. in a letter written to the Corinthians reproving them for quarrelling among themselves. He tells them that, "God delegates his 'authority to reign' to 'rulers and leaders on earth.' " These designated rulers are the Bishops, Priests, and Deacons of the church, he goes on to tell them. Those who refuse to submit to this authority are guilty of rebellion against God himself and receive, "the death penalty."[25]

Ignatius, Bishop of Antioch (d. 110 A.C.E.), Paul's home Church, was another prominent early Church leader who placed his stamp on the dogma of the Church. It was he who first used the word "Catholic" to describe the Christian Church. In his writings he warns the laity to revere, honor and obey the Bishop "as if he were god."[26]

Thus, it is clear to see that the tone of the Piscean age was quickly changed from that of the teachings of Jesus of individual responsibility to that of the custodial responsibility of the hierarchy of the Church over the minds of the people who were once again to be treated as children. By the middle of the first century, soon after the departure of Jesus, the tide was turned away from the belief in personal contact between a person and the deity back to the Old Father-God of the Hebrews with an added ingredient: the intrusion of a mediary or middle man, as found in Mithraism.

Had the majority of the people of the first few centuries been willing to take responsibility for themselves, the Church could not have imposed its dictatorial powers over them. The history of the past two thousand years would then have been different. But, as a study of the astrological ages indicates, it was a necessary part of our evolution for it to happen as it did.

Only a few held on to the belief in individual responsibility and a personal experience of enlightenment. The general term used to describe these people was the Greek word "Gnostic," which signifies belief in a personal experience. This was a positive, intuitive knowledge of spiritual matters which did not require the interference of a third party or priest.

This belief was "anathema" to Paul as well as to the Church leaders who followed him.[27] It was an affront to his and their power and authority which could not be tolerated. As we shall see, henceforth, the power and authority of the Church hierarchy takes precedence over spiritual enlightenment or moral and ethical integrity.

Irenaeus (125-202 A.C.E.), Bishop of Lyons in Gaul (France), is regarded as the expositor of Orthodox Christianity. It was he who set forth the main tenets of belief in the "Incarnation" (Jesus as God), the Resurrection, and the importance of the Eucharist. All of these, it should be recalled, are derived from Mithraism, a branch of the Persian, Zoroastrian religion. Since Irenaeus was born in Asia Minor, from whence Mithraism had spread, it is likely that he was raised in that religion, as were many of the early Fathers. Like Paul, who seems to have been strongly influenced by it, he too found it natural to incorporate Mithraism into the religion of Jesus Christ.

The Influence Of Christianity

Irenaeus is also considered to be the real founder of the Canon. He chose the present four gospels from among many because, as he said, "there are four quarters of the earth, four universal winds, and animals have four legs."[28] Incidently, he also claimed that Jesus' ministry had lasted twenty years and that he was fifty years old when he was crucified. The number of years of his ministry and his age at death seem to have been altered at a later date in order to conform to a number system of the Pagans.

Tertullian (150-230 A.C.E.) was the son of a Centurion and was a Pagan in his youth. We can assume his religion was also Mithraism, since it was the religion of soldiers and had been adopted by the Roman soldiers as a result of their conquest of the Middle East. He was well educated, especially in Roman Law, and, no doubt, contributed to the trend of the Church to structure itself after Roman government. It was also he who is noted for twisting the meaning of Paul's statement, "the foolishness of God is wiser than men," into the statement "it is certain because it is impossible."[29]

It seems a paradox that an educated man such as Tertullian should be responsible for justifying the nonrational approach to religion that was adopted by the Church. But, the nonrational approach has been the basis upon which the Church has justified its arbitrary rulings and has allowed the clergy to exert unlimited power over the people under its control for most of its history.

Until 325 A.C.E., the Christian religion had very little influence. As previously indicated, the predominant religion of the Roman Empire was Mithraism. It was the religion of kings and soldiers and, therefore, excluded women. This, and the fact that Mithra was a mythological savior, were two of its weaknesses.

Since Christianity, under Paul and the later Fathers, had incorporated into its dogma the major part of the Mithraic religion, by the 4th century there was little difference between the two. But it was those things which made up that little difference which gave the Christian religion an advantage. First, it admitted women (although in a subordinate role in the manner of the Hebrew religion) and, secondly, its god was an historical figure, which gave him greater importance in the minds of the people of that day.

When the Emperor Constantine I (274-337 A.C.E.) came to power at the death of his father, the realm was in disarray. While his co-rulers and advisaries had persecuted the Christians during his father's reign, after he had defeated them he reversed the policy and issued an edict of tolerance in the hope of bringing about peace and stability. But quarrelling over dogma continued between the Christians and the Mithraites. Eventually he concluded that the only way to have peace was to have one State religion. Although the Christians were in the minority, he was inclined to favor them because of their strong organization. But he could not openly choose them over the Mithraites without risk of having a Pagan reaction.[30]

While Christianity differed very little from Mithraism, there were differences of opinion within its own ranks. This presented a further need for compromise. Constantine called a Council of the Christian Bishops to meet at Nicea. It was at this Council, over which he presided, that the compromises were worked out, creating the climate for the Catholic Church to be given official approval. One of the concessions which Constantine made to the Christians was to declare that the cross, an ancient symbol of the Sun-god's "Cross of Light," would henceforth be the Cross of Christ.[31]

Not only had the Church structured its organization on the basis of Roman Law, it had divided its territory according to the divisions of the Dioces of the Empire. Now, with the Council of Nicea, Constantine was to make it the "alter ego" of the State. In so doing, he gave it concrete unity on the order of a political entity. He wanted "a universal Church that could stand beside the universal Empire and worthily support its labours."[32]

From this time forward, the Church, which had already placed power and authority before the spiritual virtues, turned its efforts to the consolidation and expansion of its control over the minds of the Western World. One of the means by which this was accomplished was to destroy all of the Mithraic literature in its reach. It was to become more and more politicized until, in a few years, it would assert its authority over the secular empire as well.

During the first Council of Nicea (325 A.C.E.), there were four major things accomplished. 1. The sabbath was changed from Saturday to Sunday. 2. The time of Easter was changed from that of the Jewish Passover to a time which coincided with the Pagan Spring rituals. 3. The question of the divine nature of Christ was settled upon and his precise relationship to the universal Creator God determined, as explained previously.

As stated, there were two opposing factions regarding this last question. There were the so-called orthodox and the Arian factions. The dispute over the substance and nature of Christ was settled when Constantine chose what is today the orthodox position, which conforms to the Mithraic belief. He stripped Arius of his position in the Presbytery and sent him into exile. 4. In addition, the Council settled on twenty "Canon" as guides in the conduct of Church business. Among the rules, the clergy was forbidden to keep female consorts in their houses.[33]

The most serious outcome of the Nicean Council was that it set the tone which was to characterize the Church from that time to the present. It was at this juncture that dogmatics was permanently separated from rational thinking and the anti-rational came to be equated with the sacred.[34]

What were Constantine's qualifications for making the rules for a spiritual institution? About the same as those of Henry VIII of England. He was "willful, voluptuous, and self-conceited."[35] He was also rapacious and prodigal. These qualities eventually cost him the loss of the esteem of his subjects, but had no effect upon the Church Fathers. Even today, modern Christianity (both Protestant and Catholic) eulogizes him in terms reserved for saints. He could not allow anyone to assume a position of equality with himself. When his son Crispus, who had fought his father's wars since he was seventeen years old, was shown esteem and admiration by the army, the court and the people at large, Constantine had him murdered. The same fate was meted out to his sister and nephew as well as his own wife, Fausta.

The next great landmark in the history of the Church centers around Ambrose (339-397 A.C.E.), Bishop of Milan. He was educated in Rome in the

The Influence Of Christianity

Classics and Law and became Governor of Liguria and Aemilia. He was made Bishop by popular demand, although he had not been formally trained for the clergy.

This man was a strong, dominant figure who insisted upon the superiority of Church authority, even over the Emperor. He once forced the Emperor, Theodosius I, to do penance on pain of excommunication. Theodosius capitulated and was baptized into the Christian Church in 380 A.C.E. Immediately afterwards, he issued an edict making Christianity the official religion of the empire, commanding that all of his subjects adhere to the faith outlined at the Council of Nicea.[36]

It seems that Theodosius was as weak as Ambrose was strong. In addition to the above, he allowed the Church to establish its own courts. By the time of his death (395 A.C.E.), the Christian Church was totally independent of the State, and the basis of the power of the Medieval Church had been established.[37]

Both Constantine and Theodosius had hoped that their affiliation with the Church would save the empire. But they had put their faith in the very institution that would destroy it. As the power of the empire slipped from secular hands, it was grasped by the Church. This power remained intact until Henry VIII defied Pope Clement VII in 1532 and declared himself the head of the clergy of England.

There are two men who have dominated the philosophy of the Christian Church from the 4th century to the present. They are Augustine (354-430 A.C.E.), a contemporary of Ambrose, and Thomas Aquinas (1225-1274 A.C.E.).

Augustine was born in Tagaste, a small town in

Augustine

North Africa where his father was a minor official and a Pagan. His mother was a Christian. For a time in his youth he belonged to the Manichaean Sect (later the Albigensians or Cathars). His conversion to Christianity was brought about by the influence of Ambrose. It seems that his attitude toward "heretics," which was soon made evident, was greatly influenced by his reaction against the Manichaean beliefs.

The nonrational, unphilosophical and unhistorical approach to thinking which had been firmly established by the Nicean Council allowed Augustine to support almost any tenent with the aid of references from the Bible. He despised the sciences, which by then were in a largely dormant state. For him superstition supported by the Bible was not superstition; it was the incomprehensibility of God.[38] All that mattered to him was blind obedience to God which he equated with obedience to the Church. Knowledge was based upon faith, and faith was founded upon the dogma of the Church.[39]

The early Christian view of the Church as a congregation of saints had been abandoned by the 4th century. It was only upheld by the Montanists, Novatianists, Donatists and Priscillians. They, along with other Gnostics, were among those whom the Church condemned as heretics. Salvation was now regarded as right belief and membership in the organized Church.[40] This belief is still held by many Protestants and most Catholics.

The first heretic to be put to death, around 385 A.C.E., was Priscillian. He was the Bishop of Avila and was suspected of Manichaean and Gnostic tendencies because he stressed puristic ideals, favored asceticism as a means of perfection, and dabbled in astrology.

The Influence Of Christianity

While Ambrose expressed shock at the death and censored the Ecclesiastics who were responsible, nevertheless, he had no objections to the suppression of heretical meetings.[41]

In his early writings, Augustine discouraged coercion of nonbelievers, but this gave way later to the demand for their compulsory inclusion in the Church. This change of attitude came about in 404 A.C.E. When the Bishops of North Africa appealed to the State for intervention in regard to the Donatists, fines were levied on the laity, and the clergy were banished by the Emperor. The result was a wholesale return of the Donatist lay persons to the Church due to the fear of physical harm from the military. These results led Augustine to see the efficacy of coercive action.

In his apology for coercion, he likened the persecutor to "a kind father who disciplines a wayward son." This was followed by the comparison of the heretic to a diseased part of the body which must be surgically removed for the good of the whole body.[42] This, coupled with Paul's statement that heretics did not deserve to live, laid the foundation for the Inquisition of the Middle Ages.

There was little left for the Middle Ages to add to the theory of persecution which had not been elaborated upon by Augustine. He had already stated that heresy, which destroys the soul, is worse than murder. While he stopped short of giving approval to the death penalty, he was not unwilling to inflict the punishment of banishment, even though it was often the same as a death sentence.

Thomas Aquinas added the argument that "the counterfeiting of the divine truth is worse than forging money," which was then punishable by death.

The View From Olympus

Innocent III (1160-1217) and Frederick II (1272-1337) both declared that "heresy is worse than treason" because, they said, it was an offense against God while the other only offended a temporal ruler.[43] With these declarations, the rational for the Inquisition was complete.

The Church which Paul founded was democratic in form in that the ministers, deacons and other elders were elected by the congregation and could, therefore, be fired as well. But this was quickly changed as the Church came to be structured after the temporal government. By the 4th century the power no longer filtered up; it filtered down instead. But, by the time it reached the laity, there was no power left. The individual was even stripped of the power to control his or her own life.

Very soon, corruption began to creep in, and the means by which clerical positions were secured were so degenerate that preference was given to the unscrupulous rather than to the deserving.[44] The wealthy abbeys and powerful bishoprics came to be the means by which to provide financially for the younger sons of the noble class or to improve positions of power for the leading families.

There was no distinction observable between the plundering of the Feudal Lords and the servants of Christ in the minds of the ravaged peasants. The records of those terrible times bear witness to a clergy that was not only rapacious but flagrantly criminal in every conceivable way.[45]

Early in the twelfth century the Archbishop of Tours called in a favor from the king. He demanded that he be rewarded by having the vacant See of Orleans given to a youth "whom he loved not wisely, but too well."

The Influence Of Christianity

His sexual profligacy was so flagrant that in town he was mockingly called by the name of a well-known local prostitute.[46]

By denying the masses the right to be educated, the Church was able to keep them enslaved. Because their ignorance left them defenseless, the clergy were provided a powerful advantage. But, while the people may have been ignorant and superstitious, they were not stupid. For centuries the bitterness seethed in the breasts of the victimized people. And there was no sorer point than the issue surrounding the subject of sex.

The priesthood which, by the vows of celibacy, was deprived of the opportunity for sexual gratification in marriage, managed to avoid the restrictions by devious means. The least offensive was to acquire a mistress. The worst was to capitalize upon the position of power to take advantage of the women (wives and unmarried young women) and children of the parish. This assault upon the integrity of the family by the lust of the priesthood added to the antagonism of the people toward the Church.[47]

Corruption within the Church was rampant. The priests were free to do anything they pleased so long as they did not marry or threaten the authority of those above them. All too often the abbeys were centers of this corruption. The monasteries functioned like feudal castles in which the monks lived lives of debauchery. They plundered their neighbors and accumulated large holdings of property in this manner. Nor were the nuns exempt from the corruption. The convents became nothing more or less than houses of prostitution.[48]

The sale of indulgences (pardon for sins) was begun

with the first Crusade, which was organized by Urban II at the end of the eleventh century. It became the means by which all of the "holy wars" were financed thereafter. During the period of the Crusades, it was commonly understood and frequently expressed by the troubadours that if a man escaped the perils of the Crusades themselves, he was bound to return home a "lawless bandit."[49]

There is no question that Lord Acton (1834-1902), the famous British historian, had the Church in mind when he said, in a letter to Bishop Mandell Creighton, "Power tends to corrupt and absolute power corrupts absolutely."

The history of the Councils, which were called periodically throughout the centuries in order to canonize scripture and determine Church rules, is full of accounts of the most disgraceful kinds of conduct. There always seems to have been at least two rival factions in attendance, each determined that its position would prevail at any cost.

The third general Council, held at Ephesus in 431, is an example of such a meeting. It can only be described as a melee. Cyril was the leader of one faction, while Nestorius and John of Antioch led the other. The latter two arrived with armed escorts, followed by mobs of ignorant rabble prepared to protect themselves against the forces of Cyril. The two factions fought a bloody battle in the streets until the contending bishops were arrested and the mob disbursed by the emperor's soldiers.[50]

The canonization of the Roman scriptures was not completed until after the Protestant Reformation which began in 1517 when Luther posted his 95 Thesis protesting the sale of indulgences on the Castle Church door. Thenceforth, the Bishops were forced to work together in order to have a source of written authority by which to refute the arguments of the Protestants.

But, it was not until the Westminster assembly in 1647 that the Protestants adopted the present list of books which form the Protestant Bible. With the exception of the Old Testament apocrypha, it was the same as the Catholic list. It was, however, printed in the back of the Bible in an appendix until 1827 when the British and Foreign Bible Societies, followed by the American Bible society, decided to delete it altogether.[51]

This has been a brief sketch of some of the high points of the two thousand year history of the Christian religion and its influence during the age of Pisces. It is shown that the dogma and ritual of the Church has never been based upon the teachings of the man Jesus Christ. Nor are the scriptures which are used as texts the sacred and "inspired word of God." They are, instead, a collection of writings from past ages which were assembled by ignorant, violent men and edited to support the dogma which they propounded.

In spite of its history of distorting the truth and its practice of repressing the people through threats and the use of violence, the Christian religion still maintains a strong hold on the minds of the Western World.

Although it is overwhelmingly evident that the Christian religion, as well as all other organized religions, has failed to fulfill the promise to bring peace on earth, the priesthood persists in spreading the propaganda that it holds the key to the answers regarding the meaning of life. The sad and unfortunate fact is that there are still many people who, rather than take responsibility for themselves, are willing to allow priests and other would-be leaders to do their thinking for them.

◆

VI

Ancient Wisdom In Modern Religion

There was time in the far reaches of prehistory when religion and science formed one body of knowledge. But, as previously indicated, in the process of devolution through the ages of mankind's childhood and infancy, this knowledge gradually degenerated into superstitious beliefs. The objective, rational part of this knowledge became obscured as a priesthood arose which preyed upon the emotions of the people and fostered ignorance as a means by which to control their minds.

One of the attitudes which organized religion has fostered is that of a sense of alienation from the source of our being. This sense of alienation or separation is the product of ignorance. We have no understanding of ourselves or the nature of the universe and, therefore, lack the necessary tools for successful living. Without understanding, everything beyond our physical bodies seems to pose a threat to our well-being. Consequently, we see ourselves in terms of "us" and "them" and feel compelled to compete with "them" for our survival. But competition is the name of a game in which everyone is a loser. As long as we fight each other we have no chance to dispel the ignorance that causes our sense of alienation. We remain trapped by the fears that keep us enslaved.

In the Middle Ages when, after a thousand years of religious tyranny, science had once more freed itself, it replaced the irrational mental attitudes of the Church regarding the physical/objective universe with reason. The result was a greater understanding of the workings of the physical world which has freed mankind from fear of the unknown forces of nature.

But religion, which has assumed responsibility for revealing the nature of the psycho/spiritual world, has failed to bring reason to bear on the subject. Instead, it issues decrees designed to keep people trapped in ignorance of the subjective side of life. When this fails to bring the desired results, it resorts to coercion to gain by force the obedience that is not freely given.

The Protestant Revolution came into being as a result of the corruption within the Mother Church. Since then, the Protestant Movement has been splintered into multiple factions. Each new branch is formed with the idea of making improvements over the previous one. Yet none has succeeded in providing humanity with an understanding of the psycho/spiritual side of life. Instead, each clings to the old belief in mankind as a helpless pawn of the forces of nature and/or a capricious god.

Although it is apparent that organized religions have failed to live up to their promise to bring peace and tranquility to the human race, the truth which holds the key to the fulfillment of this promise still lies hidden and, therefore, untapped within the literature of these religions. It remains for us to extract these truths and the truths found in other places and make them a part of a new reality.

The teachings of both Moses and Jesus were derived from the Ancient Wisdom. But, in their times, people were not ready to accept them. Therefore, they were hidden away where they remained until recently. Now, in this age of information, the minds of many have matured to a point where they are willing and able to comprehend the material contained in this ancient body of knowledge.

Since it emerged out of the Dark Ages, science has assumed the role of exploring and explaining the physical universe, its construct, and the laws which govern it. But religion, which has claimed the role of interpreter of the spiritual laws, has failed in its responsibility. Instead of teaching Universal Law, as science has done, it has concocted laws of its own which are contrary to the laws of nature.

The result of this lack of agreement with Universal Law has been social disharmony. But instead of recognizing the cause of the disharmony, religion has responded with more of the same kind of coercion that created the chaos in the first place. Today, when people turn to drugs and an excess of sex to fill the void religion has failed to fill, religion does as it has always done: it goads government into perpetrating violence upon the people it professes to cherish.

Jesus[1] said that he had come not to abolish the Law and the prophets, but to fulfill them. But Christian priests and ministers have distorted his meaning regarding the Law and teach that it is related to their Pagan belief in the death and resurrection of their sacrificial god. They further presume that Jesus Christ is that sacrificial god. Yet, both Jesus and the prophets of whom he spoke were clearly concerned with the righteousness which stems from obeying Universal Law, not man-made law. This righteousness recognizes the unity of all things and follows the laws which allow all the parts to function as one harmonious whole. It is also the Law upon which the Ancient Wisdom was founded.

Moses derived his knowledge of the Ancient Wisdom from the Egyptians.[2] Since Jesus was called "Rabbi" and was allowed to preach in the Synagogues, it must be assumed that he was well versed in the Books of Moses. Also, many scholars have concluded that he was affiliated with the ascetic Essenes. This group has been shown to have direct connection with the Ancient Wisdom.

Other scholars have suggested that Jesus travelled to centers of learning in Egypt and India and had direct contact with and training in the ancient knowledge from those who had charge of its preservation. Thus, it seems his teachings, although grounded in Judaism, are very much in agreement with the teachings of several branches of Yoga, the principles of which were derived from the Vedas, the ancient scriptures of the Hindu religion.

The Vedas, which means "wisdom" or "science," is the oldest literature in the world.[3] Scholars who have studied the age of these scriptures agree that they date back to at least 5000 B.C.E.[4] But the system of Yoga was obscured within the philosophy of Vedanta until Patanjali extracted and restated it for the benefit of people in the fifth or sixth century B.C.E.

Yoga is called the supreme science of all sciences

because it deals with the ultimate truths pertaining to mankind, its nature and purpose of life. It is also characterized as a "scientific and spiritual" way of knowing and entering the kingdom of heaven in the here and now.[5] It can safely be called a science since it has been shown that wherever, whenever, and by whomever the methods are followed, the results are the same. One eventually becomes enlightened.

Although it is obscured in the teachings of Judaism, Christianity and Islam, the path to enlightenment is basically the same in each of them as in Hinduism, Buddhaism and Taoism. The ultimate goal of them all is the union of the individual with the eternal, the source of all being. The Hindu philosophy has no problem with the fact that all religions are similar in their basic tenets since it teaches that truth, although it may be expressed in many different forms, is universally the same.[6]

The Sanskrit word "Yoga" has the same meaning as the "yoke." A Yogi might explain its meaning as a system which yokes the Lower Mind with the Higher Mind in order to make one's life function in harmony. Jesus, speaking from his Higher Mind (the Christ Mind), admonished his followers to "take my yoke upon you ... for the yoke is easy and the burden light."[7]

As one departs from the Pagan interpretation of the life of Jesus and casts the light of the Ancient Wisdom upon it, it becomes clear that he intended, through his teachings, to lead his followers out of the Pagan superstitious beliefs and into a more mature spiritual understanding. However, the people of his time were surrounded by and steeped in the Pagan beliefs and were, therefore, unable to understand. Because the Pagan beliefs prevailed over the teachings of Jesus, this lack of understanding has been perpetuated in the Christian religion to the present. This becomes evident when the teachings of Jesus are compared to the teachings of modern Christianity.

A discussion between Jesus and some Pharisees regarding the Kingdom of God is an example. When asked by the Pharisees about the time in which the Kingdom would come on earth, Jesus replied that the coming of the Kingdom is not an event that can be observed on the physical plane. It is, instead, a condition or state of being. The Kingdom is not a geographic place for "behold the Kingdom of God is within you."[8] Nevertheless, modern Christians are still looking for the Kingdom of God as though it were an event which is to take place in the future.

The death and resurrection of which he spoke are clearly events which occur within the self and take place in the context of multiple life times, or reincarnations (a Vedic concept). In a discussion which took place between Jesus and a number of Sadducees, Jesus corrects their misconceptions about the resurrection by explaining that it occurs on the mental plane.[9] Nevertheless, many Christians still look forward to the day in which their resurrected physical bodies will be carried up to heaven in the "rapture" where they will live for the rest of eternity.

On the subject of reincarnation, Jesus states that those who "are accounted worthy," or who attain the world of higher consciousness, "cannot die anymore"[10] Chatterji explains that, in the older texts, the idea of reincarnation was expressed in terms of "redeath" instead of "rebirth."[11] Thus, the perfected man or woman need not die anymore since he or she need not be reborn.

Clearly, the aim of the teachings of Jesus was the perfection of mankind. The miracles he performed were not unique to him. They are the abilities of a perfected person. For he says that those who live according to his teachings will not only be able to do those things but "greater works than these will he do."[12] But he warns the aspirant that, in order to have access to the benefits of the Law of Manifestation (upon which these works are based), one must seek first the Kingdom of God. All else will follow as a natural consequence.[13] The Kingdom of God is, of course, the higher levels of consciousness.

This too is in keeping with the philosophy of Vedanta, which states that only those who can develop self-control can achieve a balance between the conscious and the unconscious minds.[14] Without this balance one cannot achieve enlightenment or, as Jesus put it, one cannot "be born again."

All religions are expressed on two levels. The exoteric, or outer expression, which is based upon the worship of dieties who are concerned with mankind and its mundane affairs. Based upon the masculine, or Yang, principle, these religions participate in the visible, overt side of life. The esoteric religions place an emphasis upon the feminine, or Yin, principle and are concerned with the hidden (occult) or spiritual side of life. The ultimate goal of the esoteric religion is to aid in raising consciousness so that one can transcend the lower, mundane part of one's self.

In those ages in which the people are unwilling or unable to take responsibility for themselves, the exoteric religions appeal to the masses. Only a few follow the esoteric way which requires that each person take responsibility for his or her own salvation.

The View From Olympus

Throughout its history it has been the esoteric "heresies" which the Christian Church has feared the most.

While the Christian, Hebrew and Islamic religions are exoteric in their "orthodox" form, their literature contains some of the original esoteric teachings of the Ancient Wisdom. Within their ranks there have always been those who have discovered the ancient truths on their own. But these people have not been appreciated by the hierarchy of their respective religions, especially when their awareness leads them to criticize that religion or they attempt to teach others to take responsibility for themselves.

In the East, the "Mantram" is recognized as an aid in the process of consciousness raising. There seems to be a definite connection between vibrations of sound and the opening of the chakras.[15] Mantras, when accompanied by the release of control by the Lower in deference to the Higher Mind (or, when one has what the Judeo/Christian Bible describes as a "humble and contrite" attitude), produce a sense of lightness and an altered, objective perspective on the mundane affairs of life.

The word "mantra" is defined by dividing it in two: "man" and "tra." The root meaning of the word, "man," means "to think" in both Latin and Greek, while "tra" is used to form words which mean "tools" or "instrumentality." Thus it can be seen that the mantram is a tool which aids the thought process. It is through the mental pictures which the mantram elicits during meditation that one is able to raise his or her consciousness by becoming aware of the thought processes as they occur.

In *The Mantram Handbook*, Eknath Easwaran says,

"The mantram enables us to direct our attention at will from negative to positive channels."[16] Lama Anagarika Govinda describes words as "the audible that clings to the inaudible; the forms and potentialities of thoughts which grow from that which is beyond thought."[17]

Contrary to popular belief, the mantram is not unique to Eastern religions. It is used by the devout of all major religions, whether Hindu, Buddhist, Taoist, Hebrew, Christian, or Muslim. It is the utterance used by all as a focus in their devotions and as a means of calming the tense and troubled mind.

A mantram may be either a name regarded as holy or a formula which symbolizes the ultimate reality for a particular religious group. In most modern religions, however, the Pagan dogma to which believers adhere has the effect of dampening true spiritual fervor. For all but a few diligent aspirants, the raising of the consciousness through the use of the mantram is a temporary condition which seldom lasts beyond the Temple, Church, or Mosque door. Only a few persist in raising the consciousness to a point at which it becomes a continuous state, lasting throughout the daily routines of life.

The mantram "Aum," used in the practice of Yoga, is said to contain the vibrations of all the vowels of the alphabet. The Hindus call it the "perfect symbol of the godhead." So it seems it is the vowel sounds that set up the vibrations which act as keys to open the chakras. Some have found the "U" sounds to be effective on the lower chakras, the "O" sounds on the next higher, followed by "A," "I" and "E" at the highest chakras. Some scholars suggest that the Hawaiian language is the remnant of a once "sacred language" which was used in ancient times for the purpose of raising the consciousness.[18] This seems possible since the language makes a generous use of the vowel sounds.

The theory behind the use of the mantram, as explained in the ancient Hindu scriptures, is in agreement with the discoveries of modern science which state that the vitality of the universe is vibration just as matter is concentrated energy.[19] Many Westerners believe that the use of sound vibrations for the purpose of consciousness raising is unique to the East. They forget that their own formulas are of the same nature and have the same purpose as the mantras of the East. Furthermore, few recognize that the West also has its own special kind of mantram which may be just as effective.

In the book of Acts in the New Testament,[20] there is a report of an event regarding the disciples of Jesus which took place after his death. They were in an "Upper Room" praying for the "Comforter," which Jesus had promised would come. Soon tongues of fire appeared and sat on the heads of each of them accompanied by the sounds of rushing winds. These are similar terms to those used to describe the rising of the Kundalini fire from the base of the spine. With this, they began to speak in other tongues, or to utter sounds that were unintelligible to them. The experience caused such a sense of euphoria that the onlookers, who had not experienced this "baptism," thought they were drunk from too much wine.

The aftermath of this experience was that those who had been a part of it were filled with a sense of love for all mankind. The "haves" pooled their resources and shared them with the "have nots." Not only were they compassionate toward others, they seemed to have acquired a wisdom or intuitive understanding they had not had before.

Peter became so overjoyed with the experience that he began to preach to the onlookers. As an explanation of what was happening, he quoted the prophet Joel, who had prophesied that, after mankind had endured many trials and tribulations and had repented of its evil ways, God would pour out his spirit upon all of mankind, and the young people would prophesy (or develop their intuitive awareness), and the old men would dream dreams.

The experience of the disciples on that day of Penticost was manifested by many people soon after the event, but it seems to have lost impetus and faded out of the picture with the passing of the disciples, or by the end of the first century when the Church began to be organized as a political entity. However, the phenomenon continued to occur from time to time as small brush fires.

It did not recur in strength however until soon after the turn of the twentieth century. The result then was what has been called the "Pentecostal Movement." It gave birth to many new denominations of the Protestant faith based upon the experience of what began to be called "the baptism of the Holy Spirit." At first, this baptism had a profound effect upon its recipients. What occurred was what one might describe today as a "raising of consciousness." The lower, selfish emotions seemed to give way to the higher emotions of Brother and Sisterhood and compassion for one's fellow human beings.

But, as time passed, the fervor wore off, and people began to seek the experience of speaking in tongues as a status symbol. Those who had "received the baptism" took pride in the fact that they had "it." It became an accepted belief that those who conformed to the Penticostal Churches' standards of morality and who learned to make unintelligible sounds (without embarrassment) were the "Chosen People of God." All others were "lost." Of a certainty, those who failed to embrace this form of religion were going to hell, much to the satisfaction of the "in crowd."

At the beginning, most of the people who became involved in this movement were poorly educated. While this is not as true today, emotions still supercede reason. They are not inclined to think for themselves but, instead, continue to adhere to the Pagan belief in a vicarious salvation, bought and secured by the crucifixion of a physical man whom they have elevated to the status of a god.

Since their salvation comes from outside themselves, they fail to see the need to examine their own lower emotions. There is no understanding of the chakras and the kundalini fire, nor of the existence of the divisions between the lower and higher minds (the soul and the spirit).

Because no mandate is given for the individual to take responsibility for him or herself, no matter how uplifting an experience may be at the time, it soon degenerates into a means by which to gratify the lower emotions of competition, greed, jealousy and lust for power. And, instead of examining their own short-comings, they often engage in an attempt to force others to their way of thinking or, as Jesus described it, to engage in trying to remove the dust from the eye of someone else when they have a log in their own.

If, however, one separates the "charismatic experience" itself from the religions that have been built around it, one discovers that it has a validity very much akin to the experience of a Yogi.[21] Thus it can be seen that, when one ceases to view all other beliefs on the basis of differences and sees them, instead, as similar in form and identical in their goals, one can easily find something of value in all religions. From this vantage point, it becomes possible to recognize the Brother and Sisterhood of all mankind as a fact and not just an ideal.

But, because of the long history in which organized religions have been steeped in their individual dogmas and because of the power structures which have grown up around them, it seems unlikely that any major changes will occur within these institutions themselves.

Jesus described the problem when he used the examples of the new cloth on an old garment and of new wine in old wine skins.[22] The old garments and old wine skins represent old paradigms which are unable to accommodate new ideas. In order for the new ideas to work we must start from scratch with a new basic premise.

Although the Ancient Wisdom has been a part of the literature of organized religions from their inception, it has been ignored and/or denied for too long for them to embrace it now. Therefore, it is evident that New Age philosophy will continue to evolve outside of these organizations. In spite of them, not because of them.

✦

VII

The Gnostic Heretics

Modern scholars have concluded that the Jewish Essene and Christian Gnostic theology flowed from the same stream. It seems quite certain that Jesus was a member of the Essene community since it was the source of the scrolls (which are in keeping with his teachings) found near the Dead Sea in 1947.

Some, noting the similarity between the Essene/Gnostic teachings and those of Pythagoras and Buddha, suppose that there was some direct connection between them.[1] The presumption is that both Pythagoreans and the Essenes had been directly influenced by Buddhism. But Pythagoras and Buddha were contemporaries teaching in separate parts of the world at the same time. Furthermore, it was not until three centuries later that Asoka (264-227 B.C.E.), Emperor of India, sent Buddhist missionaries to Ceylon, Kashmire, Tibet, Persia, Antioch, Egypt and Greece. Therefore, it is most likely that their philosophies evolved separately.

The Gnostic Heretics

This is confirmed by the facts known about each of them. Buddha had access to Hindu literature which, in turn, shows signs of having a common source with the Parsees in old Persia. On the other hand, Pythagoras acquired his knowledge directly from Greece, Egypt, Arabia and Persia.[2] The one common connection between the two of them is that of Persia, the seat of a prehistoric society now believed to be the source of modern civilization.

So, on one hand, we can trace Buddha's connection through Hinduism to Persia, and, on the other, we have Pythagoras with a direct connection to Persia. It would seem, therefore, more logical to assume a connection from Pythagoras to the Essenes rather than from Buddha. However, the idea that the Essenes may have had some contact with Buddhist missionaries cannot be ruled out.

Whatever the case may have been, it is clear that the teachings of Jesus were not new in themselves. It was the time, place and circumstances under which they were presented that made them seem revolutionary. He appeared at a **time** in which superstition among the general population was the norm. The **place** at which the teachings were given was that of a conquered nation under the control of the Roman Empire. The **circumstances** under which they were given were those of political unrest. Finally, the people to whom he preached were unhappy with their position of subjugation. Many were engaged in plots to free themselves from the control of the Empire by force. There is no doubt but that some of Jesus' followers were members of at least one of these militant groups. The new Testament states that Peter was a "Zealot," actively engaged in plots against the

Empire.

The political unrest in Palestine, which had begun two hundred years earlier, continued for another thirty-five years or so after the crucifixion. But in 70 A.C.E., the Romans became determined to put a stop to it once and for all. After a siege of five months, the city of Jerusalem was sacked and the structure of both the Jewish religion and state was dissolved. The Jewish Christians in Jerusalem were apparently annihilated since there is no record of their activities after that date.

The fall of Jerusalem is of critical importance to the history of Christianity because, with it, Jewish Christianity faded from the scene and, henceforth, Christianity became a Gentile movement.[3] While there were many separate groups of Christians planted around the eastern end of the Mediterranean Sea, the strongest were the followers of Paul, who had died a short time prior to the fall of Jerusalem.

In recent years it has become more and more evident that there is a great deal of difference between the teachings of Paul and those of the disciples of Jesus. Although there has been an attempt to minimize it, Paul's letters show that there was indeed a conflict between himself and the disciples in Jerusalem who were led by the original apostles of Jesus. His unorthodox views regarding the nature of Jesus along with other points in his dogma were clearly rejected by the Jerusalem Christians.

Nevertheless, he continued to teach and to gain converts. As has been suggested, his success may be attributed to the fact that his religion did not contain the need for individual responsibility which marked the teachings of Jesus. History shows that, soon after the fall of Jerusalem, Paul's teachings became the accepted "Christian teachings" while the teachings of Jesus became regarded as "heretical." This condition remains today.

When Jesus chose peaceful over violent solutions to problems, it placed his followers in a precarious position with the Empire. Their defiance in refusing to serve in the Roman military was viewed as a threat to the stability of the Empire. Also, it was never understood that the Kingdom of which Jesus taught was not an earthly kingdom. Therefore, to the Romans, those who were not for them were against them.

While Paul also made the distinction between heavenly and earthly kingdoms, he was militant by nature and, therefore, had no scruples about engaging in war and violence for the cause of his religion. This was in keeping with the attitude of the Mithraic religion, a religion of kings and soldiers. It also supported the belief in the divine right of kings, which Paul and the Church Fathers who followed him transferred to the Church hierarchy.

The idea of "Christian soldiers" came from Paul who, in his second Epistle to Timothy, used this metaphor to describe the followers of Christ.[4] Elsewhere he speaks of the "armor of God," the "helmet of salvation," and the "sword of the spirit."[5]

As soon as the so-called "Orthodox Church" was given preferred status over other religions, it began a concerted effort to silence all dissenters. This included the true followers of Jesus as well as other groups who believed in individual responsibility for salvation and to whom the Church referred, collectively, as "Gnostics."

During the first four centuries of the Christian era,

apart from the "Orthodox Church," there were many different sects which regarded themselves as followers of the teachings of Jesus Christ. Much like the denominations of the Protestant Christian religion today, they had minor differences of opinion. While there may have been as many of these as there were followers of the Pauline doctrine, their diversity of allegiance made them vulnerable and unable to sustain themselves against the overwhelming power which the organized Pauline Church eventually acquired.

As Gnostic literature reveals, the original disciples regarded Jesus as an ordinary human whose purpose was twofold: 1. as a political leader, to free the Jews from the bondage of Rome, and 2. as a spiritual leader, to bring individual freedom to those who became self-aware through the knowledge and understanding of Universal Law. After his death, they dropped the belief in his political purpose and became wholly involved in seeking to understand his spiritual teachings.

But Paul, who was steeped in the beliefs of the Hebrew religion as well as the Mithraic and other Pagan religions, seized upon the personality of Jesus and inserted him into the myth of the Savior-god of the Pagan religion. Based upon his belief in "original sin," which could only be erased by the death and resurrection of a god, he turned an ordinary spiritual teacher into a sacrificial god.

By circulating the fiction of Jesus' physical resurrection, he was able to bring that myth into reality. In replacing a mythical god with an historical god, he made the beliefs of the Mithraic religion more credible and made it possible to create a new religion with greater appeal to the masses. However, by making a god of Jesus, he distorted Jesus' purpose to bring enlightenment through an understanding of Universal Law and made him a tool of the priesthood by which the Church has been able to keep Western people in a benighted state for another two thousand years.

Many of the followers of Pauline Christianity were converts from Mithraism. Once Christianity had been declared the official religion of the Empire in the 4th century, they really had no choice. However, it was no problem for them to accept the new religion since the ritual and dogma were almost identical.

Several of the early Church Fathers of the second and third centuries were not only converts from Mithraism but were also trained in Roman law. Since they had been trained in the law, it was only natural for them to structure the Church organization after that of the Roman Empire. As has been shown, it was the organization of the Church which tipped the scales in its favor and prompted Constantine to choose Christianity over Mithraism. In spite of, or perhaps because of, their legal training, it was these same Fathers who advocated a doctrine based upon blind faith and the emotions rather than reason and spiritual awareness. This, of course, would insure greater control over the masses.

In recent years, it has become evident to scholars that the New Testament reflects very little of the views of Jesus' followers. The material, it seems, was instead selected to support the views of the followers of Paul. Besides containing the dogma and ritual of Paul's teachings, the books of the New Testament, which, incidentally, were written during the one hundred years after the fall of Jerusalem (70 A.C.E.), had three major concerns. One, to preserve the traditions of the

Hebrew religion (including the belief in the coming Messiah). Two, to preserve the illusion of being derived from the teachings of Jesus. Three, to overcome Roman hostility toward them by distancing themselves from the nationalism of the Jews who had been defeated.[6]

Facts which have come to light within the last half century reveal that the scriptures were altered to fit the beliefs of the faction in power. Furthermore, the Christian religion which has survived into the present as the "Orthodox" (whether Catholic or Protestant) is in fact the true "heretical faction."

It has been only since some of the material from the Nag Hammadi Library (Gnostic literature discovered in Egypt in 1945) and the Dead Sea Scrolls (found in Palestine in 1947) has been published that we have had any direct contact with the "Gnostic heretics." The only information previously available was to be found in the works of the Church Fathers which were written to discredit Gnostic beliefs. Therefore, they were not a true representation of these beliefs. Now that it is possible to compare the Gnostic literature with the Christian Bible, it is clear to many that the Gnostics were in closer agreement with the teachings of Jesus than the religion that has held center stage for the past two thousand years.

One of the major points of difference between the Gnostics and the Church was the Gnostic contention that the true Christ is without bodily form. They, therefore, denied that Jesus rose from the dead in the physical state. In the Nag Hammadi Library books, the visitations of Jesus after the crucifixion are described by the disciples as visions.

Their idea of redemption was both individual and

cosmic. It dealt with the liberation of the spiritual from the material and with the freedom of the soul from enslavement to the appetites of the physical body as well as from attachment to the material world in general. As Jesus taught, they believed that they should be "in the world but not of it."

A clear connection can be made between the Christian and Gnostic literature which provides evidence of editing on the part of the Christians. There are at least four apocryphal Old Testament books which are a part of the Gnostic literature but do not appear in the Christian literature. They are: *The Book of Jubilees*, *The Book of Enoch*, *The Testament of the Twelve Patriarchs*, and *The Assumption of Moses*.

In the New Testament *Epistle of Jude*, Verse 9 makes reference to an incident found only in the *Assumption of Moses*. Verse 14 is a direct quotation from *The Book of Enoch*. In addition, there are passages quoted in the New Testament as though from the Old Testament which are not found there but are found in the Dead Sea Scrolls.[7]

The prevailing view among scholars is that the Dead Sea Scrolls belonged to the Essenes, whom Philo and Josephus placed in that area.[8] A study of the scrolls leads one to the conclusion that the Christian religion was not a phenomenon which burst onto the stage suddenly but, instead, was gradually developed over a period of years by a segment of dissenters within the Hebrew religion.[9]

Among other things, the Essenes were influenced by wide-spread belief in the Cycle of the Ages, which is rooted in the Ancient Wisdom. It was believed at the time that a cycle was about to end and that the transition to the new age would be spearheaded by a

Messianic leader. They hoped that they could have some influence upon the closing days of the old and the birth of the new age.[10]

The belief in the myth of a child whose birth would herald the beginning of a new age is an ancient, worldwide idea to which the Hebrews also subscribed. From ancient times, in many parts of the world, it was the custom to stage pageants which depicted the combat between the old symbols and the new, in which the new was always triumphant.

In ancient Babylon, it was the victory of Marduk (the god) over Tiamat (the goddess). This was, it seems, a celebration of the transition from the age of Taurus to that of Aries, when the goddess religions were replaced by the god or male dominated religions. Vestiges of this myth are found in the Old Testament in which Jehovah (Marduk) is said to have triumphed over the sea monster, or dragon, Leviathan (Tiamat). However, in the Hebrew religion, which denies the female principle in the universe, the female dragon has been replaced by a male.

In the New Testament the war between Gog and Magog may also depict the transition between the ages of Aries and Pisces. There seems to be no question but that some of the tales regarding dragon slayers in the Middle Ages were based upon this theme.

The Church has established its authority in the teachings and pronouncements of Paul, who admonished his followers to "obey your leaders and submit to them for they are keeping watch over your souls."[11] They declare that there is no authority except from God and that those earthly rulers who exist "have been installed by God. Those who resist, resist God and, therefore, shall be punished ... for he does not bear the sword in vain."[12]

The Catholic Church has taken this and other declarations by Paul regarding the divine right of tyranny to extend to the Church as well. Throughout its history it has favored dictatorship over democracy. However, it has been adamantly against Modern Communism since it was founded as a reaction to the excesses of the Church as much as the Tzarist regime and, consequently, has been an enemy of the Church.

After the 4th century, when the Pauline (Catholic) Church assumed predominance over the other religions in the realm, the hierarchy used every means possible to silence the true followers of Jesus and his disciples. This included assistance from the military forces of the Empire.

For the next one thousand years the institution which is called by the name of the man it designates "The Prince of Peace" increased its membership at the point of a sword or a musket and kept the people enslaved by the constant threat of extreme punishment or death. Eventually, however, when the people could no longer tolerate the violence and corruption of the Church, they began to convert to the Gnostic sects which had survived the earlier purgings underground.

But the new exodus was soon noted with alarm by the Church, and it was not long before it took steps to stem the flow. The result was the mass murder of thousands of peace loving people in what history calls "The Inquisition" and the Church calls its "Holy Wars." Those who dared to challenge the authority of the Church were tortured and burned alive at the stake. Their property was confiscated and added to the holdings of the Church.

Even today, Protestants and Catholics alike justify

this slaughter on the grounds that those who died were heretics and, therefore, deserved to die. After all, did not Paul sanction the death penalty for unbelievers?

The sale of "Indulgences" began with the slaughter of the Gnostic Albigenseans, or Cathars, as they were also called. They were peace loving, prosperous people living in Southern France from the 12th to the 15th centuries. The faithful members of the Church who assisted in the slaughter were guaranteed direct access to heaven immediately following their own demise. Thus, they would be spared the inconvenience of spending time in purgatory. None of the heretics was spared. They included men, women, children and unborn fetuses (for which the Church professes so much concern today). The lucky ones were those who were killed before their mutilated bodies were thrown upon the pyre.

Attitude toward authority is one of the major differences between the teachings of Paul and Jesus. It is quite evident that Jesus had no intention of setting up a church ruled by a hierarchy with dictatorial powers since he said, "Call no man father on earth, for you have one Father, who is in heaven."[13] Nevertheless, a common connection between the Pauline Church and the Mithraic religion are the terms "Father" and "Pope" as designations for persons in authority. The bishop's "mitre" was also borrowed from Mithraism.

To Jesus, the word "faith," as indicated in the three Synoptic Gospels, was a belief in the Universal Laws and the creative power within each of us. It was this kind of faith which could move mountains.[14] Paul's faith, on the other hand, was grounded in a belief in the Mithraic myth of a dead and resurrected god. As he explained, his faith was "in the redemption in Christ Jesus whom God put forward as an expiation by his blood, to be received by faith."[15] Contrary to Paul's teachings, it is clear that Jesus did not think of himself as the medium through which redemption was to be acquired. He accepted the designation of teacher, but rejected the title of "Master."

The word "salvation" is not mentioned in the Gospels. Jesus' concern is shown to be that of spiritual enlightenment and the freedom which it brings.[16] But Paul, putting Jesus in the position of a sacrificial god, teaches the vicarious salvation of Mithraism saying, "God has not destined us to wroth but to obtain salvation through our Lord Jesus Christ,[17] without whose blood, he also says, there is no salvation.

It is difficult to understand how the need for a blood sacrifice can still be acceptable in a modern world in which science has revealed the basic facts of "Natural Law." Under nature's law, death and resurrection are a part of the cyclic side of its nature. There is no need to appease the forces of nature through such rituals. There is, however, a great deal of evidence of a need for self-understanding and of cooperation with Universal Law.

Why should a modern, intelligent person continue to be intimidated by Paul's pronouncement that "He who doubts is condemned," and "Whatsoever does not proceed from faith is sin"?[18] His faith is in the myth of a resurrected Sun god, not in the power to control one's own destiny as Jesus taught.

One of the major points of conflict between Paul and Jesus revolves around the nature of Jesus. Is he God or Man? Repeatedly, throughout the gospels, Jesus speaks of himself as the "Son of Man." And, in the Gnostic

Gospel of Thomas, he disclaims any position of superiority over others when he says, "I am not your Master."[19] Furthermore, he explains that they have gained their experience of enlightenment through their own efforts.

Yet, in every Epistle, Paul persists in describing Jesus as the "Son of God." His description of the nature of Jesus is identical to that of Mithra as given in the Zoroastrian/Mithraic stories in which Mithra is the creator of the world and its inhabitants and acts as mediator between mankind and his father, the Supreme God. Paul says, "He is the image of God, the first born of creation ... all things are created through him and for him. He is before all things and in him all things exist."[20]

The question here is, who knows the nature of Jesus best: Jesus himself or Paul?

Jesus says the Kingdom of Heaven is within us. This statement is not only found in the New Testament, but is also found several times in Gnostic literature[21] But, to Paul, the Kingdom is shrouded in a mystical cloud in which God operates outside Universal Law to transfer mankind "to the kingdom of his beloved son."[22] This belief must, of course, be accepted by faith since it is impossible for it to be proved.

Regarding the subject of the "death and resurrection," Jesus indicates that it has spiritual, not physical, implications. In the Gospel of Philip he says, "While we are in the world it is fitting for us to acquire the resurrection for ourselves, so that when we strip off the flesh we may be found in rest."[23] In the New Testament, in his confrontation with the Sadducees, he also indicates that death and resurrection are spiritual events.[24]

But Paul is unmoved by this. He persists in his belief in the Pagan myth. Not only does he hold that Jesus was raised from the dead and ascended to heaven, but, also like Mithra, he will return in the clouds to raise his followers in their physical bodies and carry them off to heaven with him to live in eternal blissful idleness throughout eternity.[25]

"Rebirth" is another prominent teaching of both Jesus and Paul. But there is little agreement between them on what it means. In his exchange with Nicodemus, Jesus says that one must "be born again" in order to "see the kingdom of God." When Nicodemus wonders how one can return to his mother's womb, Jesus explains that rebirth is a spiritual and not a physical matter.[26]

To the contrary, Paul presents Jesus as a mediator who saves mankind from enslavement to "elemental spirits," from which bondage "God sent forth his son" (the reluctant Jesus) to redeem those who are under the Law so that we might "receive adoptions as sons."[27]

This last statement reveals Paul's position on the nature of mankind, which is not only separate but different from the nature of God. This is contrary to both the teachings of the Hebrew religion and Jesus, who reaffirmed that we are "gods" in our own right as offspring of the creator. Thus, there is no need for "adoption."

Throughout the literature which contains the teachings of Jesus and Paul, it is obvious that, while Jesus bases his upon Natural or Universal Law, Paul's are based upon Pagan myth which relies upon the belief in a supernatural force in the universe. This force, or God, operates outside the laws of his own creation as he behaves in a capricious manner. Because of the unpredictable nature of his God, there is no way to prove the validity of his teachings. They must, therefore, be taken on faith. There is an added threat of dire consequences for those who fail to conform.

In regard to the physical body, we again find Paul on a collision course with the teachings of Jesus. Not only do his teachings conflict with the teachings of Jesus, they appear to be in conflict with each other. On one hand he speaks of the body as "sinful" and "vile," and on the other he calls it "a temple of the Holy Spirit within you which you have from God."[28] Paul also finds sex to be a dangerous impediment to the spiritual life. He is concerned with the "redemption of the body"[29] and warns that the "body is not for fornication" because those who indulge "sin against their own bodies."[30]

While, in the new Testament, Jesus has nothing to say about sex per se, in the Gospel of Philip he makes a specific statement about our attitude toward the body which, once again, is in disagreement with Paul. In his usual way, he takes the middle of the way approach and says, "Fear not the flesh nor love it. If you fear it, it will gain mastery over you. If you love it, it will swallow and paralyze you."[31]

In the last chapter we showed that the religion which is called by the name of Christ is not the Christian religion. It is the religion of Paul, who infiltrated the religion of Jesus Christ and converted it into a completely different set of beliefs. There is only a surface resemblance between the religion of Paul and the philosophy of Jesus Christ.

We have also shown that the "Gnostic heretics" who followed the teachings of Jesus and other great

The Gnostic Heretics

teachers whose philosophy is rooted in the Ancient Wisdom, have been persecuted by the Pauline Church for two thousand years. It is they who have been tortured and murdered for daring to believe that they are responsible for their own destiny.

But, now that science and reason have been restored in certain circles of learning, it is becoming clear that the philosophy of the Gnostics was and is based upon the ancient symbols or metaphor which explain the truths of the Ancient Wisdom.

✦

VIII

Ancient and Modern Science/Philosophy As Metaphor

From time immemorial mankind has been on a quest for knowledge and understanding. The search has been two-pronged. One points downward and outward to the objective/phenomenal world while the other points upward and inward to the subjective/spiritual. Throughout the ages the language which has been used to explain these two worlds has been symbology.

The workings of the objective are discovered through the use of mathematical symbols and explained with pictures, graphs and sketches. These may later be translated into mechanical and technological devices and used in human commerce. On the other hand, the subjective world is revealed through pictures that are conjured by the mind and explained by symbols which are drawn from the objective world of nature and the mechanical/technical world.

While the objective describes the phenomenal world, the subjective explains its nature and how it is to be used. Thus it is that the two are interdependent. Each is incomplete without the other. The truth of each is only half-truth until it has been merged with the truth of the other. For half-truth often has the practical results of untruth.

The Ancient Wisdom, it now appears, was a sophisticated system of knowledge that could only be understood by a technologically advanced society. Only now, as science has come close to the source of creation, have the truths contained in the ancient lore become comprehensible and the interdependence of the objective and subjective become recognizable once again.

In recent years both science and the lay public have begun to become aware of the limitations inherent in scientific knowledge.[1] In the process of research within their special fields, a number of scientists have made discoveries which have forced them to make some re-evaluations. For they have come close to a reality that cannot be explained in terms of modern mechanistic science.

Men like Fritjof Capra, David Bohm, Rupert Sheldrake, and others have, through their studies in physics, biology and other sciences, discovered a reality that leads them "to a view of the world which is very similar to the views held by mystics of all ages and traditions."[2] This view is what modern mystics refer to as the Ancient Wisdom. It is an all encompassing body of knowledge which embraces all of the sciences as well as religion and philosophy.

But, while modern science approaches knowledge from an objective/quantitative view point, the Ancient Wisdom perceives the universe in a subjective/qualitative way. It might be said that the objective world of experience is internalized by the experiential/subjective world.

With the advent of the basics of twentieth century physics, the quantum and relativity theories, many scientists have been forced to recognize the reality of the mystical or metaphysical part of life. They have found that "the methods of physical science leads ... to a shadow world of symbols which they cannot penetrate."[3] Some have conceded that they are "forced to see the world very much in the way a Hindu, Buddhist or Taoist sees it."[4] These religions, as has been explained, have their roots in the Ancient Wisdom.

Therefore, the new science which is evolving out of this new understanding has a belief in common with the Ancient Wisdom of the prehistoric past. This common belief is in "the undivided wholeness of the universe."[5] The underlying cause and purpose behind it all is a conscious agent which transcends it. Some would call this agent "God" while others call it "Mind." While it is complete within itself, all created things partake of its nature. Or, put another way, we might say that God and creation are one. Organisms of all levels of complexity are reflections of the transcendent whole from which they were derived.[6] The Ancient Hermeticists phrased it in the axiom "as above, so below."

Put simply, the universe is a "hologram" in which the created world is a mirror image of the whole universe which is composed of many universes. Because of the enfolding or intertwining nature of the universe the observer cannot be separated from that which he or she observes.

Alfred North Whitehead is credited with having traced European philosophical tradition back to Plato.

Ancient and Modern Science/Philosophy

But we now know that he stopped too soon. The evidence reveals that Plato's source of knowledge goes back many generations to Pythagoras, to whom he was deeply indebted. Plato was a pupil of Archytos and, as such, was ninth in line from Pythagoras.[8]

Pythagoras is not only the fountain from which modern philosophy flows but also the source of modern science and religion. The basis of modern mathematics, upon which science is dependent, is the geometry of Euclide, who drew inspiration for the first segment of his system from the Pythagoreans.

Although the religious/philosophical and scientific factions later parted company, the early Pythagoreans saw no difference between their science and their religious philosophy. For Pythagoras, number was not only a universal principle, it was divine as well. The two were inseparable.[9]

Modern Western civilization has its roots in Greek civilization which, in turn, is indebted for its knowledge to the Babylonian, Egyptian, and perhaps, Indian cultures, all of which had their roots in prehistory.

Thales (636-546 B.C.E.), who is generally regarded as the Father of Western civilization, was the first to substitute scientific for mythological interpretations of the Ancient Wisdom. One of his first pronouncements regarded the belief that water is the source of all created things.

Anaximander (611-547 B.C.E.) was a pupil of Thales. He postulated the "boundless as the primary source of all things" concept and speculated on the "law of compensation." He also anticipated the theory of evolution. It was his belief that mankind achieved its physical state by adaptation to the environment; that, not only had life evolved from moisture, but that human beings had developed from fish.

Pythagoras (582-507 B.C.E.) was a student of both Thales and Anaximander before he set off on his own to gain first-hand knowledge of the Ancient Wisdom in Egypt, Babylon, Arabia and Persia. While it is known that Anaximander was knowledgeable in astronomy and also cast horoscopes, it is understood that Pythagoras developed his skill and understanding of numerology and astrology from the Chaldeans and Babylonians.[10]

Throughout history mankind has had two major approaches to comprehending its relationship to the ultimate reality or creative source. These are science and religious philosophy which, when the shadows of prehistory are pierced, are shown to have been one single integrated system of sophisticated knowledge. However, during the ages that lie below the horizon of the zodiac, religion based upon superstition and bred of ignorance almost completely replaced science and philosophy as the ancient knowledge became distorted. The people, having lost knowledge of the nature of things, were afraid of the natural forces of both heaven and earth. From this fear came many fanciful tales of gods and demons and the ways in which they controlled helpless people.

However, in a few remote segregated areas of the world there remained some who retained memories of the ancient knowledge. Although they too had lost most of the knowledge of the nature of the objective/physical universe, they still retained a little knowledge of the subjective/spiritual powers of which their ancient ancestors had been aware. This second group, called "Shamans" by the Russians, have not only survived into the present time but are growing in their numbers and influence.

Both religion and Shamanism have had the tendency in the past to interpret the symbols of earlier ages in a literal way, thereby distorting their meaning. But, in religion, the priests created power bases by reserving education to themselves and, in so doing, kept the people dependent. From this power base, they were able to create a theological system which they alone could understand. This allowed them to be not only the messengers of the gods but their agents as well. Thus they were endowed with the final word on earth regarding the conduct and destiny of the individual.

On the other hand, while the Shamans lost most of the over-all understanding of the true nature of the universe, they did retain the practical knowledge of how to work with nature and to utilize the elements of nature for their personal benefit. Although the Shaman priests sometimes yielded to the temptation to use their knowledge to control others, the basic tenets of Shamanism were geared to the individual and allowed each person to make his or her own spiritual discoveries. Scholars have found that Shamanism in both ancient and modern times has been characterized by the personalization of the spiritual or mystical experience.[11]

The term "Shaman" is most often thought of as pertaining to the priesthood of a particular belief system. But in recent times it has been broadened to embrace all systems of belief which not only explain the relationship between mankind and the universe but also serve to develop latent creative powers so that one can literally become a "co-creator with God."

In the past, the word "Shaman" was often viewed as

synonymous with "magician" because both were endowed with similar characteristics. The signature of both was the ability to understand and work with the forces of nature and, in some cases, to communicate with wild animals. The true magician or Shaman established his or her credentials by performing "miracles."

Pythagoras was said to have had the abilities described above and, therefore, may rightfully be called a Shaman. By the same standards, Jesus Christ might also be classed among the Shamans since he too was reported to have performed the miracles ascribed to a magician. Furthermore, his teachings provide for the personalization of the spiritual or mystical experience. The ultimate goal of this experience, as he explained, was to develop the creative powers which he exhibited and some which he had not yet performed.

It has been reported that Pythagoras was able to enter into a trance state in which he could leave the body (astral travel). Scholars say that the philosophers of Pythagoras' time regarded the cultivation of psychic powers an essential element of their profession. To travel by means of a "magic arrow" was a metaphor for this phenomenon.[12] In Plato's "Phoedo," Socrates, speaking of the soul in search of the truth, says that thought is the best when it is withdrawn and untroubled by the things of the mundane world, "when she takes leave of the body."[13]

The belief in reincarnation is inherent in the science of astrology, a subject to which Pythagoras gave much consideration and study. It fitted naturally into his study of the cycles of nature, of birth, death and rebirth on both the universal and individual levels. Like

Like Norm Shealy

Apollonius of Tayana, a first century philosopher who believed he was the reincarnation of Pythagoras, Pythagoras was said to have recalled his previous lives.

Pythagoras travelled widely throughout the known world to "assimilate the wisdom of the ancients wherever it might be found."[14] We are told that he spent twenty-two years in study and research before he began to teach. He became a many-faceted man, a philospher, physical scientist, religious thinker, and political theorist. In addition, he found music and art to be of basic importance and made a knowledge of them a prerequisite for entry into his school.

The Pythagoreans regarded number differently from the quantitative way in which it is understood today. For them number is the living, qualitative basis of reality and can only be comprehended through the experiential method. Their science was not concerned with the investigations of "things" but rather of "principles." One of the principles to which they adhered was that of the unity of all things which contained within it the principles of both Limit and Unlimitedness.

Plato's later dialogues contain many mathematical allegories. Among them are: Timaeaus, Statesman, The Republic, Critias, and Laws. In Philebus he gives credit to the ancients who, he says, lived closer to the gods and were, therefore, superior. He states that they should be believed when they say that everything that exists "consists of the One and the Many which contain in themselves the ... principles of Limit and Unlimitedness."[15] Both Pythagorean and Platonic Cosmologies weave Limit and Unlimitedness, along with Form and Matter, into a numerical harmony. Plato shows how the creator of the universe distributes the basic units of creation "according to numerical proportions of the musical scales."[16]

Every relic and tradition of ancient times shows that there was only one numerical code upon which mathematics, music, astronomy, chronology, metrology, and the arts and crafts were based.[17] This is the same code which was brought to light by Pythagoras and passed down through Plato as a legacy for the present age.

From the maxim of Pythagoras, which states that everything revolves around number, a new perspective on the meaning of life is revealed to the modern world. But, although it is new to us today, in all the known civilizations of the ancient world this "cannon of number" was revered as the very source of life and a guide to human conduct.[18] This cannon of number contained the code of the dimensions of the universe, the ratios of music and geometry, and the sacred measurements of the ancient religion as well. To the ancients, the universe was a living, sacredly created thing based upon divine Law. And mathematics was the key to its understanding.[19]

It now seems apparent that both physics and metaphysics resolve into one point of focus: the creative force which lies behind the phenomenal universe. It is none other than consciousness or Universal Mind. But, as the focus comes close to the source, the picture becomes blurred. It cannot be defined in the old way. In order to clarify it, it becomes necessary for both physics and metaphysics to resort to a different language. This is the language of metaphor. The ultimate reality, it is found, can only be explained by reducing it to symbols.

As Roger Jones explains,[20] physics is the metaphor by

which the ultimate source is revealed in the objective/quantitative mode. But he goes beyond this to see metaphor "in the larger context in which all things are related" and points out that the theory of relativity reveals that "space and time are the same as matter and energy, while geometry is gravity."[21] Thus, when the objective and subjective aspects are joined together they become reduced to concepts of the Mind and must be perceived in the subjective mode.

As we struggle to understand ourselves through symbolism, we can bring vitality to the metaphor by renouncing mechanistic scientism and embracing rational mysticism and by "accepting responsibility for our own creative part in the universe."[22]

The Ancient Wisdom pictured human nature as having dual qualities derived from the physical/phenomenal and mental/noumenal worlds. This ancient system was founded upon Universal Laws which are based upon a rational system of number. Because it is rational, it requires no "act of faith" to be understood.[23] The Ancient Religious Philosophy is to the world of Mind or Consciousness what physics has become to the physical world: a means by which to bridge the gap between abstract and concrete reality. Together, they point the way to ultimate reality.

The astrological zodiac is a symbolic map of relationships in the universe.[24] Based upon natural principles, it represents the relationships between all created forms. It is also concerned with the cycles of seasons and of the ages, is the symbol of the many and the one, and represents the fall of the spiritual self into the material world. Finally, it points the way to "salvation," freedom from the force of the attraction of matter.

Clearly, the mysteries of the Ancient Wisdom were explained long ago by the use of metaphor. The various principles of nature were often personified and used as allegory as a means to illuminate the dark corners of the mind.

The serpent[25] is probably the most universal and the most frequently found symbol because it lends itself to many interpretations and, therefore, can describe many different aspects of nature. It is used to describe both the male and female principles as well as the idea of self-creation. It is used as a symbol of death and destruction and also as the periodic renewal of life. Thus, it can only be understood when interpreted within the proper context.

When coiled by itself, the serpent suggests the cycles of manifestation such as the seasons and the reincarnation of the human soul, of latent power, and the potential for good and evil. Coiled around the egg, it represents the process of fertilization. Coiled around the tree or pole it is the awakening of the dynamics of growth. Coiled around a woman, who is the lunar Mother, it becomes the Sun, and together they represent the male and female relationship. Cosmologically, it is the symbol of the ocean of life. These are only a few of the many representations of the serpent found around the world.

In the Christian religion, the serpent has lost its place in the creation myth except as the representation of evil. There it becomes Satan, the god of evil and the tempter of mankind, and the cause of its fall into sin. Thus, it is the enemy of God. And, while the Christians look to the death of a god on the cross as the way to salvation, the Ancient Wisdom pictures the serpent raised on the cross as a prototype of the spiritual energy which lies at the base of the spine (the tree in the garden of Eden) when it is raised to the level of Christ Consciousness (the 6th Chakra) "for the healing and salvation of the world."[26]

Long before the Christians adopted the ritual and dogma of the Mithraic religion, it too was familiar with the symbology of the serpent. In a relief of that religion, Mithra is shown encircled by the snake and surrounded by the signs of the zodiac,[27] revealing astrological connections to the religion.

The Cosmic Egg, which is also symbolized by a sphere, represents the life principle, the germ of creation. It is also the womb and the matriarchal aspect of the first cause.[28] The idea of the Easter Egg was originally developed from this understanding and was used as a symbol of the cosmos and its creative aspects.

The tree[29] is another important ancient universal symbol. As the representation of the feminine principle, it depicts the nourishing, protecting, sheltering and supportive aspects of the Mother. It also represents the whole of creation and, as demonstrated in the Scandinavian Yggdrasil, or Cosmic Tree, it "grows from the nether world through the world of men and into the realm of the gods, uniting all three."[30] It is also the tree upon which the god Odin sacrificed himself.

The Tree of Light, or Heavenly Tree, is the tree of rebirth, and each light on the tree represents an individual soul. The lights on the Christian Christmas Tree originally represented the Cosmic Tree, and the lights were symbols of the sun, moon, planets and stars.

The Evergreen Tree represents everlasting life, while the deciduous tree represents the cycle of death and regeneration. The many branches of both, rising from the single root, are the symbol of the Many included in the One.

The Tree of Life, which grows in Paradise, is a symbol of the cycle of the ages. It suggests that, when the larger cycle (the Manvantura of the Hindus) has been completed, the created universe will return to a state of oneness. This idea might be expressed by an astronomer who understands the concept with the statement that, at the end of the great cycle, the universe will collapse upon itself to form something like a "black hole."

On the human level, the Tree of Life is the spine which contains the nerve centers or plexus (or chakras) from which the life force is distributed throughout the body. When the energy is consciously raised to the sixth chakra (the Christ or Buddha level), one is enlightened and becomes aware on all levels of one's being.

The Tree of Knowledge signifies mankind's responsibility to use its free will. The Tree of Knowledge of "good and evil" implies the ability to make choices. When one makes choices which are in harmony with Universal Law, he or she partakes of the fruits of the Tree of Life, or immortality.

The Inverted Tree, with its roots in the heavens, represents mankind's roots in the Cosmic Mind, thus showing that knowledge flows from above or from the higher to the lower levels of consciousness.

The stone represents durability. Together with the tree it signifies the everlasting nature of the creative power and changing nature of creation.

These are but a few of the many symbols used by mankind throughout its existence to explain the nature and meaning of life. In the context of the cycles of the ages, during those periods of time in which mankind has an understanding of the true nature of the universe, the symbols are understood as they are intended: as the symbols behind the principles which govern the universe. But, during the ages in which the consciousness is on the decline, understanding of the symbols becomes lost, and the race begins to see the symbols as the things themselves and to interpret allegorical representations literally.

The distortion of the meaning of the symbols leaves a void which causes childish fears to arise among the people along with a sense of need for someone or something wiser and stronger to look after them. Instead of behaving as co-creators and integral parts of Universal Mind, mankind in a degenerate state sees itself as a helpless pawn.

It is from this helplessness that the race creates its religions and from the distorted understanding of the symbols that superstitious beliefs and practices arise. The idea of a sacrificial god is one example of how a symbol becomes the focus of a superstitious belief. During the age of Taurus this kind of distortion led to the literal sacrifice of both animals and humans. This idea has continued to the present time in the Christian religion which is based upon a belief in salvation purchased by a sacrificial god.

In the myths and traditions of many cultures the world was said to have been created from parts of a sacrificial god. In the Babylonian creation myth, the dismembered body of Tiamat, the Goddess of Chaos, formed the substance of the created universe. The allegory of the sacrifice of the goddess eventually became a reality. For, from a lack of understanding of the true meaning of the creation story, came the system of blood sacrifice.

Another example of the distortion of the meaning of a metaphor into a superstitious belief and practice is that of the Sacred Cow of India, which Christians regard as ridiculous. The cow is another ancient symbol of the Great Universal Mother which represents the nourishing, productive aspects of the earth. It signifies both procreation and the maternal instincts. But, it became distorted when the cow became the thing instead of a symbol.

The idea of blood sacrifice to propitiate the gods is one of the oldest beliefs known to mankind. At the beginning of written history it was believed that the masculine principle, personified by the Sun which stimulated the growth of vegetation, became transferred to the person of the king. As the growth and vitality of vegetation began to wane, it was thought that the king had also lost his fertility and that he should die as the Sun was thought to die at the Winter Solstice. It was believed that his blood, when sacrificed to the Earth Mother Goddess, would provide virility to the new king. The sacrifice, which was literally carried out for a long time, took place during the Winter Solstice, the twelve days of chaos between the death and rebirth of the Sun. This myth is the source of the twelve days of Christmas of the Christians. Later, a scapegoat was substituted in place of the human king.[31]

In the age of Taurus, the sacrificial animal was the Bull, while, in the age of Aries, it became the Ram. It seems the ritual sacrifice was done in recognition of the creation of the universe as well as of the cycles of life and death. In animal sacrifice, the head represented the dawn, the eye was the sun, the breath represented the wind, the back the sky, the belly the air, and the underbelly the earth.

In the ritual of the blood sacrifice, the sacrificer and the sacrificed are thought to be fused into one in which the microcosm and macrocosm meet to form a unity.[32] In the Christian religion, the bread and wine represent the body and the blood of the crucified god or Jesus Christ (formerly, Mithra).

Now that we have entered a new technological age in which there is a scientific understanding of the phenomenal world, we no longer need to believe that the soul's salvation can be bought by a crucified god. The consciousness of the race has evolved far enough that we should be able to understand the metaphor of science and philosophy which makes us gods in our own right and, therefore, as creators, we are not dependent upon the caprices of an imagined god.

✦

IX

Universal Law and Reason: Tools of Enlightenment

The New Gnosticism does not seek to duplicate the beliefs of the Gnostics of the early Christian era. Since the old Gnosticism did not have the advantage of modern scientific knowledge, it was at a disadvantage. Because it did not have a firm understanding of the Laws which govern the physical universe, it lacked a basis for understanding the Laws of the noumenal or spiritual universe. In its desire to be eclectic, it embraced not only the science of Pythagoras but the angelology of Zoroastrianism as well as the allegory of ancient myths. Consequently, it had difficulty in making a distinction between the real and the unreal. Today, with the assistance of scientific knowledge, we have a new and more solid ground upon which to understand the universe and our place in it.

The first law to which the New Gnosticism adheres is that which requires the individual to take responsibility for him or herself as the Gnostic Jesus taught two thousand years ago.

Universall Law and Reason

It seems an unfortunate fact that, after two millennia of the violence and dis-ease caused by the ignorance of organized Semitic religions (Hebrew, Islamic, and Pauline Christianity), there are still very few who have the courage to try it the way it was taught by Jesus Christ. The same is true of the so-called New Age Movement. Even though they disassociate themselves from the fundamentalist religions, New Agers are equally reluctant to take responsibility for themselves. They would rather let every self-styled guru who comes along with a gimmick do their thinking for them.

But the New Gnosticism takes the position that the only valid truth is one which the individual has discovered for him or herself. The final test of its validity, however, is the test of its practical application. It must harm no one, but add peace and harmony to human relationships. The ancient Greeks, who nurtured the Ancient Wisdom in their own flawed way, summed it up very succinctly in the axiom "Know Thyself and Know God." For it is from an intimate relationship between the soul (Conscious Mind) and the Higher Mind that one is able to make one's life flow smoothly and in harmony with the world.

The remainder of this book is dedicated to providing some basic principles by which the individual can, without the need for a priest or guru, come into harmony with his or her inner self and with the world without.

Modern psychology has attempted to fill the void which organized religion has left in the area of self-understanding. But it has made the same mistake the ancient mythological goddess made when she

The View From Olympus

color

attempted to create beings from her emotional level of consciousness without the aid of the god, her higher Spiritual Mind.

From the beginning, psychology, like modern science, has denied the existence of the Higher Mind. Consequently, it has been unable to correct the distortions or deformities in us that religion has created from its warped view of life. While it has used mythology as a metaphor in an attempt to bring about self-understanding, it has failed because it has based its conclusions upon false interpretations.

Before we can understand the ancient myths, it should first be understood that the mythology of the ancients was a part of their religion/philosophy. All of the ancient religions from which these myths were borrowed, including that of the Greeks, had a belief in the three aspects of mankind: body, soul and spirit. The myth of Psyche and Eros is no exception. While the myth was told in several different ways over time, the fundamental structure of the story contains three, not two, gods. They are Eros, Psyche and Anteros.

Contrary to the interpretation which psychology has put upon the myth, Eros was not the god of passion (the libido). He was, instead, the god of love, or agape (altruistic love). His brother, Anteros, who opposed him, was the god of the Unconscious (reactive) Mind (as will be shown in the next chapter) and, as such, was the god of passions.

Psyche is the soul (Conscious Mind) in search of her mate. But, for much of her life, Eros is unknown to her because she has been seduced by Anteros, the Lower Mind, and has fallen into a sub-conscious state. But eventually she comes to realize that Anteros is not her true mate and goes in search of Eros, her Higher

Consciousness, and is finally united with him for eternity.

In the Gospel of Philip, we find that the Old Gnostics believed the purpose of Christ's coming was to reunite Adam and Eve, the male and female principles in each of us. They knew there had been a time when mankind had been androgynous, both physically and mentally/spiritually. But when the sexes became separate, mankind was faced with a new set of circumstances with which to deal. This was the need to overcome the pull of attraction of the physical appetites which keep us trapped on the lower levels of consciousness. They quote Jesus as saying, "He who comes out of the world is above desire and fear. He is master over nature."[1]

It is an unfortunate fact of history that we have been controlled by our emotions for thousands of years. Even in these modern times in which science and technology have freed us from the need to fear the forces of nature, we still tend to put more faith in our feelings than in the higher levels of consciousness. One wonders why we persist in doing things the old way when the results are so unsatisfactory.

When it comes to the subjective side of our lives, the part which pertains to our personal and social relationships, it is not only the under-educated who rely upon their emotions. The elevated position of the emotions has been a part of our culture for so long that even the best educated fail to recognize when their reasoning faculties have been switched off.

While seven levels of consciousness can be identified, as will be shown in the next chapter, they come under the control of three major divisions which the religions of the world list as the body, soul and *spirit*

151

spirit. The body is controlled by the emotions or Lower Mind, the soul by the sub-conscious and the will or Conscious Mind, and the spirit by the Higher Consciousness or intuition.

It should be understood that today, when we speak of the Higher Consciousness or Spiritual Enlightenment, what is at issue is a question of emotional/mental maturity. This entails the integration of all levels of consciousness which, in turn, requires that we take responsibility for ourselves by making a conscious choice to get in touch with and be guided by our super-aware-self. But before this commitment can be made successfully, we must first become aware of and take control of our reasoning faculties, our conscious/intellectual awareness, which has been subordinated to the emotions for thousands of years.

Our best defense against the unruly Lower Mind is our cognitive faculties in cooperation with the higher levels of consciousness. Therefore, it would seem that the first step toward an integrated, enlightened life is to control the Conscious Mind by learning to think straight.[2] To do this, we must become aware of the way in which we think as well as the way in which we communicate with others.

Logic is the study of the rules of reason and is, therefore, a means by which to discipline our conscious minds. It is only a disciplined mind that is capable of making the kinds of choices which lead to higher awareness. The study of logic has a threefold effect. First, it helps us to learn to communicate more successfully with one another, thus avoiding misunderstandings which tend to destroy relationships. Secondly, it helps us to think more clearly, thereby making it possible to arrive at more satisfactory conclusions. Finally, it provides us with a weapon against the unscrupulous who would manipulate and control us by appealing to our lower natures: our emotions. It is the lack of logic that has allowed us to be kept enslaved by our emotions for these many thousands of years.

Therefore, the first step toward becoming enlightened is to become aware of the fallacies in our thinking processes and replace them with valid reasoning. At first this will require a great deal of concentration since, as logicians report, there are many ways in which our minds can go astray. Perhaps, by becoming aware of some of the most common fallacies of reasoning, we can learn to avoid falling prey to them. By disciplining our reasoning faculties we may also become more discriminating in what we accept as truth from both our own Lower Minds and from others, especially those who wish to be our leaders and/or want to do our thinking for us.

Here are a few of the more common fallacies which we are likely to encounter in ourselves and others as we begin the quest for truth. It would be well to take the time to examine each of them very carefully in the context of your own personal relationships.

The first is **Accent,** or **Lifting Out of Context**. It is the tool of propaganda and is used to obscure the truth in order to persuade others to a point of view they might not accept if they knew the whole truth. It occurs when an argument is presented with only favorable facts. The negative or unfavorable material is omitted. It is a common fallacy employed by ministers (priests, rabbis and gurus), politicians and, sometimes, even scientists.

The View From Olympus

Authors of books and magazine articles, reporters and advertising agents often emphasize a point so that it gets more consideration than other points of equal or greater importance by such means as italics, full capitals, or special positioning on the printed page. It is usually used as an appeal to the emotions.

The **Leading Question** implies that a point of reference has been previously agreed upon as an established fact when, in fact, it has not. To ask, "Why do dogs make better pets than cats?" implies that two or more people involved in the discussion have agreed that dogs make better pets. If this conclusion has not been previously agreed upon, it is a "leading question."

The **Complex Question** is a leading question which may involve more than one question and imply more than one answer. It has no basis in fact and is usually used to best one's opponent. "Why do people set up abortion clinics? Is it because they do not believe in God, because they have no respect for human life, or is it for the money they make from it?" This complex question implies that all of the possibilities have been stated and also implies that the motives of the clinic operators have been established to be negative. It does not allow for the possibility that they may have given a great deal of honest thought to the subject of abortion and that their motives may be purely for the good of society, making them just as valid as the motives of those who hold the opposite position.

Extension is the introduction of irrelevant extremes into a discussion in a bid to appeal to the emotions of the hearer. A Fundamentalist Christian author states that New Age people think they are a Super Race. Furthermore, these people say that the rest of us will not be around during the New Age. This, she says, means that they plan to slaughter all Christians, Jews, Moslems, and anyone else who does not agree with them. This statement introduces irrelevant extremes and is, therefore, a fallacy of reasoning. Furthermore, it is an irresponsible attitude calculated to incite violence.

The **Appeal to Ignorance,** or **Argument Ad Ignorantium**, makes a case based upon the absence of any evidence as proof to the contrary. The Fundamentalist Christians say, "Since science cannot prove the theory of evolution, the Biblical version as interpreted by the Theologians, must be true." On the other hand, scientists say, since the Biblical account of Creation as interpreted by the Theologians is ridiculous, evolution must be a fact.

The Theologians say, "We know the human soul is immortal, because no one has proved it does not survive after death." On the contrary, scientists say, "Man is an accident of Nature. When he dies, he is dead. We know this is true because no one has proved to our satisfaction that we survive after death." In these instances, both are engaging in the use of fallacious reasoning which should be disregarded by a thinking person.

An **Argument Ad Hominem** employs the tactic of depreciating the value of the person in order to devalue his or her ideas or abilities. "Do not listen to that person; he or she is a Secular Humanist, Fundamentalist or Catholic Christian, believes in reincarnation, or holds some other unpopular belief."

The **Tu Quoque Argument** states that, if you do something wrong why should I not do so as well. Or, two wrongs make a right. Politicians often justify their misconduct by pointing to the wrong doing of their predecessors. But we should know that good government requires leaders who follow the rules regardless of what others do. This is in the best interest of the people whom they represent as a whole.

Where the problem of child sexual molestation by priests is concerned, the Catholic Church argues that it is not a problem because the priests are no worse than the general population. The conclusion the general population should draw from this argument is, if the clergy is not any better than the general population, why do we need a clergy?

Pettifogging, or **Nit Picking,** is a devise used, either consciously or unconsciously, to divert attention from the main line of discussion which may cause one of the conversants to feel uncomfortable. It may be used as a means to embarrass the other person by making him or her appear ridiculous. One of the more common means used is to correct the other person's pronunciation of words. Another diversionary tactic is to pounce upon double meanings of words and expound upon them as though they were of great importance. Still another is to ask complex questions or to postulate a fallacious argument unrelated to the subject at hand in order to keep the "opponent" off balance.

In short, the pettifogger, or nit picker, is not really interested in communicating. He or she engages in conversation as a deadly sport. The aim is to score points against an "opponent" by befogging the issues of the discussion until the opponent drops out of the game. In this manner, the pettifogger survives as the victor. By clever manipulation of the conversation, he or she has succeeded in making him or herself "right" by making the other person "wrong."

Universall Law and Reason

The winner of this kind of contest may go away feeling smug, vindicated, righteous, and self-satisfied. But it is quite likely that he or she will also be lonely. For no one enjoys being made "wrong." Therefore, in order to avoid a repeat performance, the victim will avoid the villain who engages in such sport.

In the fallacy of **Accident** or **General Rule**, the discussion is moved from a generally accepted rule or principle to an individual case which may lack some of the basic characteristics of the general rule. What is good for the majority is perceived to be good for the individual. Or, what is good for one society is good for another. This was the fallacy under which the Christian Missionaries operated. Since people in Christian Europe wore clothes, they felt the natives of Africa, Asia, and the South Pacific must also wear European clothes as part of the requirement of becoming "saved."

While democracy may be a good system of government for those who are prepared to function under it, in some cases it may not work. For instance, few of the African nations which have gained independence from European overlords have been able to function as democracies. The same may be said of many of the Latin American countries. They tend toward dictatorships, perhaps because the people, who have been subjugated by the Church for so long, are not prepared to take responsibility for living under a democracy which requires self-determination.

The hasty **Generalization** moves from the specific instance to state a general rule. This is done when a characteristic of one individual person or thing is ascribed to all persons or things within a given category. We often refer to this kind of reasoning as "jumping to conclusions."

During the years of expansion in the United States, the white man regarded all Indians as dirty and untrustworthy. The Indians regarded the white man in a similar manner. When women first began to drive automobiles, some, who had had no experience with mechanical equipment before, were not very adept in handling a vehicle. Many men generalized that all women were poor drivers. The opinion is still occasionally voiced even though statistics indicate that women drivers are involved in fewer accidents than men. Some other common generalizations are: blacks are born with a natural aptitude for rhythm; all politicians are dishonest, and all Jews are shrewd bargainers.

The **Post Hoc Ergo Propter Hoc** fallacy reasons that, because an event occurs after another, it was caused by the preceding event or "after this, therefore, because of this." If this were always valid, it would follow that lightning is the cause of thunder. But science has shown that thunder precedes lightning. We see the lightning before we hear the thunder because light travels faster than sound.

Some Westerners, aware of this fallacy of reasoning, have gone to the extreme of classifying a belief in the connection between one's attitudes and desires and their fulfillment as a **Post Hoc** fallacy. However, psychology has confirmed Jesus' teaching that we attract that upon which we focus our minds. It is demonstrably true that we are drawn to the things we fear or resist as well as to the things which we desire or love.

Many of us are prone to solve problems by **Oversimplification**. Management is apt to blame the higher cost of their products on the high wages demanded by unions. Unions, on the other hand, blame poor management. Politicians have a habit of blaming the opposing party for the things that go wrong and taking credit for everything that goes right. But the problems continue under both party's administration. Finally, many people, including the Fundamentalist Christians, believe that they can correct the problems of the world by getting laws passed designed to force others to live by their standards and beliefs. All of these are examples of the oversimplification of complex problems which require complex solutions.

A person who sees the world in **Black and White** is unable to see "shades of gray." They cannot allow for modifying factors or extenuating circumstances. This is sometimes referred to as "false dilemma." The person is stuck with two alternatives, neither of which assesses the situation accurately. "He that is not for us is against us" is a statement made from the black and white point of view. The correct statement may lie somewhere in the middle.

Begging the Question is the term used to describe "arguing in a circle." It is usually expressed as statements rather than questions. Two friends were reminiscing about their high school days. One made repeated derogatory remarks about some of their old classmates. The second asked, "Why do you say such things about them?" To which the first answered, "I would not have said anything negative about them if you had not brought up the subject of the past."

The person who claims to believe the Bible is the word of God because the Bible says it is, is engaging in circular reasoning. Just as one word needs others to define it, so a book can be judged only by verification from outside itself. A rose is a rose is a rose may be poetic; it is not a definition.

These are just a few of the ways in which we make it difficult to discover the truth about ourselves and the meaning of life. We keep going in circles or end up going down blind alleys because we do not know how to think straight. And, because we do not know how to think straight, we fall easy prey to the fast talker who appeals to our emotions through the use of fallacious reasoning.

We keep walking into their traps and when we discover our error, instead of taking responsibility for our own blunder, we put the blame on the other person. It matters not what kind of so and so the other person may be, we are still responsible for the mistakes we make, which includes falling into traps other people set for us. Furthermore, we cannot correct our mistakes until we are willing to admit that mistakes have been made and take responsibility for making the necessary changes. A disease cannot be cured until it has first been diagnosed.

Reason is an orderly process of the Mind. Just as there are laws which govern the harmony of the physical universe, there are also laws which govern the harmony of the mental world. These Universal Laws are the true "Laws of God." As previously stated, the teachings of Jesus are based upon these Universal Laws, the Laws which he said he had come to fulfill.

Now that we have learned to distinguish between valid and invalid reasoning, we should be able to profit from discovering some rules by which to govern our lives. There are seven major laws which may be helpful tools in your search for self-understanding. Although some of them were mentioned in Chapter V, they bear being repeated.

The first Law is the **Law of Manifestation**. This is the law which governs the creation or bringing into being of both the macrocosmic and the microcosmic universes. The Ancient Wisdom teaches that mankind creates the world in which it lives by the way in which it thinks. This is true both in the life of the individual and of the community. The Judeo/Christian Bible states that God said, "Let there be light and there was light."[3] This seems to suggest the power of the Mind over Matter and to demonstrate that Mind is the force behind creation.

Since mankind is made in the image of God[4] and is endowed with a mind, it must follow that we are also creators. This is what Jesus postulated when he was taunted by the Jews because he made himself to be God. His reply was a quotation from their own scriptures which says, "I said, you are gods."[5] Clearly, it is Mind which gives us our god quality, the power to create. It would seem, therefore, that the first step a seeker after enlightenment should take is to become aware of what happens in his or her own mind.

Logic leads us to the conclusion that the fact we are endowed with minds is an indication that we are, ipso facto, creators as well. This is the position taken in the Ancient Wisdom which says that we are the creators of our own little worlds and the circumstances in which we live. It is not a God in some heavenly world remote from us who is responsible for what happens to us when things go wrong. It is the Lower Mind within ourselves attempting to play "god" without the aid of the Higher Mind.

The View From Olympus

One of the early creation myths found in the ancient Gnostic literature is of the Universal Female, Physical Principle (emotions) trying to create without the aid of the Male, Spiritual Principle (reason). The result was a population of deformed monsters who turned the world into a chaotic mess. The moral of the story is that there must be a balance between the masculine and feminine aspects of our natures on both the physical and spiritual levels, both in individuals and in society as a whole, in order for us to live in harmony with the rest of the universe.

The second Law is the **Law of Correspondence**. Simply stated, this Law indicates that what occurs on the macrocosmic (or universal) level also occurs on the microcosmic (individual) level as well. This is what modern physics has discovered in what it calls the "Holographic Universe." The Hermeticists expressed it in the axiom "As above, so below and, as below, so above." It was based upon this principle that the Greek Oracle could say, "Know Thyself and Know God."

The third Law, the **Law of Cycles,** or **Periodicity** has been discussed in connection with the subject of astrology and the cycles of the ages. As applies to mankind, it is evidenced as a repetition of certain types of circumstances until we learn to deal with them constructively. An example may be found in the life of persons who have had multiple marriages or liaisons, each of which is a repeat of the preceding one.

It is also the Law under which reincarnation operates. What we do not learn in one lifetime we must learn in another. This Law operates on the social level as well and is expressed in the saying "History repeats itself." Whether as individuals or as a race, we keep making the same mistakes until we learn to avoid them.

Reincarnation is governed by a combination of the **Law of Cycles** and the fourth Law, the **Law of Conservation,** which states that nothing is lost, it simply changes form. When something dies, the physical elements are returned to the earth to be recycled into different forms. Similarly, the soul returns to the world of formlessness where it functions until it returns to another body for further experience and growth. It is said that the soul must continue to incarnate until it has learned to deal positively with every aspect of life and the consciousness has been raised to the level of the Super-Consciousness (or Christ Consciousness). When one has arrived at this state it is no longer necessary to incarnate.

The fifth Law is that of **Devolution/Evolution**, which was discussed in connection with the cycles of the ages and needs no further explanation.

The sixth Law is the **Law of Attraction**. We often say "Likes attract likes," or "Birds of a feather flock together." This is one form of attraction, but there is another meaning as well. As psychologists have discovered, we become like the person or thing about which we have strong feelings - whether it be love or hate.

When Jesus said "Judge not that you be not judged," he must have had this Law in mind. For he certainly knew that those who are super critical of others take into themselves the very characteristics which they criticize. By the same token, we also take into our lives the qualities in others which we admire.

The seventh Law is the **Law of Compensation**, the Law of Cause and Effect, or Karma, as the Eastern religions call it. Paul, as Jesus before him, warned of it when he said, "Whatsoever a man sows, that shall he also reap."[6] But he interpreted it to mean that his anthropomorphic God would punish the wrong doer, while Jesus recognized it as a natural law that would bring about natural results. History makes it clear that war has never ended war, it has only sown the seeds of the next one, for violence begets violence.

Before we try to absolve ourselves of the responsibility for the wars our country wages by putting the onus on the politicians, we should think again. Whether or not we vote, the leadership of our government reflects the attitudes of the individuals who make up the given nation or state. So, if we are not pleased with our government as it is, we should first change our own personal attitudes to a more peaceful stance. This will radiate into the ether and eventually be tuned into by the leadership.

In the final analysis, the leadership does not dare to do other than the "will of the people" when the people are informed and express attitudes they want the leadership to act upon. Therefore, the reality is that the individual does have an influence upon the greater society, but that influence must begin at home with one's personal relationships.

✦

X

Evolution of Consciousness

For thousands of years we have been taught to rely upon our emotions and follow our leaders like mindless automatons. In spite of the great advances science and philosophy have made in the past two thousand years, the majority of people in the world are still ruled by the superstitious beliefs of religions that were founded when the consciousness of the race was at its lowest ebb.

It was a time when the application of reason was regarded as a sin against God. God was a mysterious tyrant who was all powerful, all knowing, and all seeing, whose laws must be followed blindly, without question. The priests were God's anointed leaders whose interpretation of his laws were to be regarded as infallible. It was the duty of the people to obey or suffer the consequences of the rath of God, usually administered by the priesthood.

We live in an insane world where the conduct of our lives is controlled by rules which are contrary to the facts of the real world. The rules and regulations of organized religion which were instituted in order to regulate a community of mental/emotional children are an insult to people of the modern world. The reactions to these insults, however, are as unreasoned as the rules which prompt them. The result is a world in chaos. Our only hope for the return of sanity to the world order, it seems, is to stop and make an assessment of who we are and what we want to accomplish here on earth. This requires that we utilize all of the knowledge and understanding that is available to us.

Science and philosophy are the two major branches of learning under which all other branches of learning fall. The word "science" is derived from the Latin "scientia," meaning "to know, to discern or distinguish." Modern scholars have broadened its meaning to include a field of study by which to categorize facts, principles and methods. Its basic concern is with the systemization of our knowledge of the physical universe.

The word "philosophy" was coined by the Greek scholar Pythagoras in the 6th century B.C.E. Its original meaning was concerned with love of and the search for wisdom and knowledge. But modern scholars define it more specifically as the theory of logical analysis of the principles underlying conduct, thought, knowledge and the nature of the universe. Included in philosophy are: ethics (orderly social conduct), aesthetics (the study of beauty and its effects upon the human psyche), logic (the science of correct reasoning), epistomology (the study of knowledge, its origins, nature, methods and limits), metaphysics (concerned with abstract thoughts based upon first principles – particularly ontology, the nature of being which is distinct from physical existence), etcetera.

The etcetera is, of course, religion which, during periods of mankind's lowest levels of consciousness, takes the place of rational philosophy. While rational philosophy is founded upon the principles of logic or correct reasoning, religion is based upon the emotions or nonrational conclusions. It is from a nonrational position that organized religion has taught us to believe that we are not subject to Natural Law. We have been made to believe that, in some unexplained way, we are apart from nature. The Gnostic Jesus, however, taught that, not only are we subject to Natural Law, but freedom and control over our personal lives can only be obtained by learning to understand and live in harmony with that Law. This is the same law with which science and philosophy are concerned.

One of the first laws of nature we have learned from modern science and philosophy is that our minds and bodies are inextricably bound together. We express our thoughts and attitudes through the body in the form of speech and in what is called "body language," or gestures. It is also found that our attitudes are imprinted upon the fibers of the body and reflected in either "good health" or "disease."

Furthermore, we are now learning that the imprints which are made in one lifetime are carried over into future lifetimes. For instance, it has been found that the scars of wounds which caused traumatic death in a previous incarnation often appear on the body in a subsequent incarnation. In recent years it has been discovered that these scars are imprinted on the psyche as well and can be healed by physical and psychological therapies. These will be discussed in

The View From Olympus

Chapter XII.

Apart from the traumas received during an untimely death, the major traumas of our lives occur in childhood and/or at times in which we are at the mercy of others or otherwise feel out of control. One may be out of control when ill or when forced to comply with the will of another under such conditions as kidnapping or rape as well as when controlled by the tyranny of church, state, and/or parental authority. All of these infringe upon the integrity of the psyche of the individual and leave scars which must be healed through a process of self-understanding.

The place to begin our quest for self-understanding is at the beginning. While nature provides us with physical bodies by which to experience and discover, that is as far as she can take us.[1] The rest is up to us. How we respond to our experiences will either make or break us. They can be used either as stepping stones to higher and better things or as the quagmire that sucks us under. Therefore, our first chore is to learn how to act from reason and the facts rather than react from our emotions. Before we embark upon the path to enlightenment we are nothing more than machines (or automatons) which act on cue to having our buttons pushed. Until we learn to act from inner awareness instead of reacting to outside stimulus, we are only flotsam and jetsam on the sea of life.

It seems that we all have a need to know the source of our being. Just as we have a need to discover our "roots" or biological ancestry in order to heal psychological wounds, it is equally important to become aware of our spiritual/mental heritage in order to come to terms with our spiritual/mental nature.

The story of the Prodigal Son[2] is the story of

mankind's spiritual journey through numerous incarnations on earth. His decision to arise and return to his father's house is the symbol of the decision that each spiritual aspirant must make. But in order to know the right direction to take, we must have something to guide us.

The Judeo/Christian Bible was intended to be such a guide, but, because it has been garbled in translation, Western people have lost their way. While the Bible appears to be accurate in its basic details, because of a lack of understanding the meaning has become distorted. For thousands of years mankind has believed the universe was created by a super-human being (male) who resides outside of his creation. It is also believed that this creation was accomplished in an arbitrary and capricious manner and continues to be run in the same way. This is the belief held by most religious people in the modern world, even though science has found a more satisfactory explanation.

Various people have attempted to correct the misunderstanding about creation and our place in it, but none has done it better than Arthur Young,[3] who has reinterpreted the story of creation by explaining it in terms of modern physics. Mr. Young's approach not only agrees with modern scientific understanding of the nature of the universe, it also fits into the picture described in the Ancient Wisdom as preserved in the Eastern religions.

Surprisingly, when a new assessment is made, the meaning of the symbolic language of the Judeo/Christian Bible is discovered to be in agreement as well. When God said "Let there be light," he began the process of creation. This is described in science as the "Big Bang" and by the Hindu religion as the

The View From Olympus

"Awakening of Brahma," the Father-God and Creator of the Christians. The sequence of events is much the same in all three accounts .

If the spoken word or God or Brahma was the driving force which created the universe, the question arises, what was the source of this command? By following the natural sequence of events back to the source one finds that action is preceeded by thought. But thought does not exist on its own; it is a product of Mind. Both science and religion agree with mysticism that Mind is the source of all being. Since God has all the attributes of Mind – omnipresent, omniscient and omnipotent – it must be concluded that Mind and God are one and the same.

Thus it must follow that mankind, being created in the "image of God," is also Mind. The Fall, therefore, is a symbolic term used to describe the gradual clothing of Mind with increasing layers of matter until it is fully clothed in the flesh of a physical body. The ascent or journey back to the Father's house, or the creative source, begins with the recognition of one's "godhood."

The Fall, Young says, does not deal with mankind alone. It is an integral part of the function of the universe which is composed of two major phases. These are the devolution (or fall into matter) and evolution (ascent away from the pull of matter) of the Mind. The primordial state of Mind is undefined. The Fall, therefore, begins with an undefined state and culminates in a defined state in matter. The ascent, or return to the source, begins with the awakening of the consciousness within the several kingdoms.

The number seven seems to have great significance in the structure of the universe in both the Judeo/Christian Bible and the Ancient Wisdom. While science has only recognized three kingdoms (mineral, plant, animal) in the physical world, Arthur Young[4] describes seven kingdoms which he believes are the warp and woof of creation and the evolution of both the universe and mankind.

Just as in the Judeo/Christian Bible, Young says, the first element is found to be light. It is also learned that, as the process moves from the simplest to the most complex forms, each succeeding step after the first contains all of the elements which precede it. Therefore, since it contains all the elements which precede it, the seventh is the most complete. Perhaps this is the reason the Ancient Wisdom teaches that mankind, found on the seventh level, is a miniature universe, since it contains within itself all the elements of the entire universe.

For graphic purposes, the process of evolution is described by Young with a symbol in the form of a letter "V." (Figure 9) The top left (1) represents the primordial state in which light was first made manifest. It also represents the beginning of the Fall into matter.

Step Two (2) is the development of nuclear particles. Step Three (3) is the formation of atoms from the first two. Step Four (4) combines all of the first three and adds an element to become the visible form of matter, molecules, which are the building blocks of all of the next three stages. Step Five (5) combines all of the above to bring the plant kingdom into being. Step Six (6) is the creation of the animal kingdom, and Step Seven (7) is the creation of mankind.

An interesting point is made by Young in showing that the first two kingdoms on the ascending side (plants and animals) are divided into species, genus, family, order, class and phylum, while mankind has only one species and no other subdivisions. This may be explained by the fact that, since we contain all of the

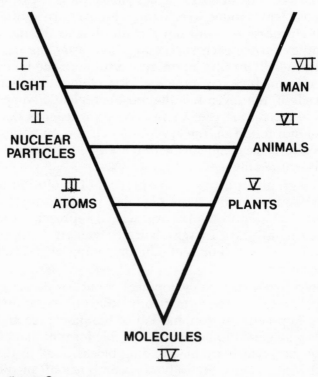

figure 9

elements of all the other stages of evolution, there is no need for further subdivisions.

A further explanation lies in the ancient

understanding that mankind is spiritual or mental in nature but experiences the material world through physical bodies. Therefore, in order to understand ourselves, we must not confine our search to the physical plane. What is learned from the Ancient Wisdom is that evolution occurs on two levels: the physical and mental or spiritual.

Exact science is concerned only with the kingdom on the left side of Young's "V," or the objective side. It is not equipped to explain life as it occurs on the right, or ascending side. Perhaps this is because there is an added element in the higher kingdoms which is not present in the lower ones. This element is described as that of "voluntary" action rather than "random" action as found in the first three stages.[5] Voluntary action is governed by the subjective/mental side.

While mankind has not been subdivided into different species, it has been divided into races and cultures. But these are environmental conditions and, therefore, incidental to our evolution. They fall under the category of learning experience. From the Ancient Wisdom we learn that the subdivisions of the human race are on the mental rather than the physical plane, since that is the level upon which the evolution of the human race occurs. But because we are gods and therefore free agents, the subdivisions are chosen by us and not arbitrarily set by nature.

Just as the universe is divided into seven kingdoms, mankind (being spiritual or mental in nature) is divided according to seven mental levels. Therefore our evolution is determined by the level of consciousness on which we function. The return journey of the prodigal back to the creator's home is up Jacob's ladder: the seven levels of consciousness which are located in what Eastern Yogis call "Chakras."

Although the terms used to describe the various levels of consciousness in this chapter are borrowed from psychology, they may not have the same meanings. They have been chosen because they have become familiar to a large segment of the population, even to those who may not have formal training in the field.

In lieu of a diagram of a physical body showing the locations of the seven levels of consciousness which correspond to the Chakras and nerve centers, we will use a vertical line with seven steps (circles or points) to designate the different levels (see Figure 11). One should understand that the division of consciousness into seven levels is an artificial separation designed to help us understand the way in which the mind works. There is no clear break between them because each level partakes, to some extent, of the characteristics of the next higher level. Each higher level includes all of the levels beneath it. Thus, the higher is aware of the lower, while the lower is only dimly aware of, but has no understanding of, the higher levels.

The majority of people in the modern world function on the first three levels most of the time. Few ever become aware enough of the higher levels to function on those levels at all. While they may tap into them momentarily from time to time, they lack the greater understanding that true higher awareness brings. According to the Ancient Wisdom, the purpose of life is to learn to function consciously on all seven levels at all times. To act consciously rather than to react unconsciously.

The first and lowest level in our chart is designated as the **Unconscious** (latent) and is related to the

Evolution of Consciousness

Chakra in the area of the coccygeal ganglia of the pelvic plexus. This level is not related to mankind's consciousness as such because, in a sense, it is a world unto itself. It pertains exclusively to the physical body and relates to the life of the cells and organs of the body. Scientific studies in recent years have confirmed what the Ancient Wisdom has always taught, that every cell in the body has a consciousness which allows it to find its place and do the job to which it is assigned. One of the marvels which biological science has discovered is the precision with which the body functions when it has no interference from other agents.

The physical body is only a vehicle through which the true self functions and experiences. Therefore, the consciousness of the body is only indirectly connected to the higher consciousness. Its functions are totally under the control of the brain, which performs like a computer through the autonomic nervous system. Nevertheless, it is now understood by various health practitioners that the condition of other levels of consciousness affect the functioning of the body's consciousness and may result in "psychosomatic illness."

The second level is the **Unconscious** (reactive), located in the area of the sacral ganglia of the pelvic plexus (the Sacral Chakra). Theosophists, who describe these various levels in terms of "bodies," call this body the etheric double (of the physical body), but, because it functions on a higher vibratory level, it is not visible to most people. It is believed that, in actuality, the connection between the body and the brain does not take place in the body itself but on this second level, which operates within the bounds of stimulus and response, or instinct. The message is then relayed from the **Unconscious** (reactive) to the **Unconscious** (latent). It is, therefore, on this level that the need for food, water, elimination, and sex are acted upon. It functions independent of the higher levels of consciousness unless the **Conscious Mind** makes the choice to bring it under the control of reason and/or intuition.

This, then, is the level of the body appetites and the passions. The Greek myths say it is ruled by Anteros (Ant=against and Eros=love). While he is the brother of Eros, he is opposed to him and, therefore, is the antipathy of love.

It is at this level that, when the new born child feels hunger pangs, it instinctively roots about until it finds something for its mouth to grasp and begins to suck. If it finds the mother's breast, its hunger is satisfied. But if it finds only a button on her blouse, its efforts will be frustrated. In this case the stimulus becomes painful and results in a response characteristic of this level of consciousness. At first, it will experience the **fear** of not being able to satisfy its hunger. Then it begins to **despair** of ever finding the source of nourishment. This is followed by a feeling of **hopelessness**, then **panic** and, finally, it gives vent to its emotions in a fit of **hysteria**, crying at the top of its lungs.

Its concerns are exclusively with its own survival. Since it is unable to see itself as part of a larger whole, it sees everything and everyone outside itself as a potential for either satisfying its personal needs or as a threat to its safety. Being ignorant of the whole and its place in it, it has no way of knowing how to cope constructively with these felt threats. Therefore, when it experiences pain it becomes afraid for its safety and survival and judges the perceived threat to be perpetrated by an enemy. The fear soon becomes **anger** or **rage** which triggers the instinct for self-preservation into a **violent reaction** as a means to eliminate the threat of danger. In older people it becomes translated into the feeling that it must "kill or be killed."

The **Sub-conscious** or psychic/emotional on the third level is our Animal Mind, which is instinctive in nature. On the positive side, the Sub-conscious mind is like an antenna which picks up signals from the ether which provides information on what is transpiring at a distance and/or out of sight. We call this E.S.P. It is also Psyche in her somnambulistic state.

Because it lacks full consciousness, it is unaware of the meaning of the signals it receives. It has two choices regarding the disposition of this information: 1. to seek advice from the Conscious Mind, or 2. to be governed by the Unconscious (reactive) Mind (or Anteros). If it takes the way of least resistance and allows Anteros to be in control, it may act out of fear and panic. Or, it may act from a need to control others and make inaccurate interpretations of what has been perceived. The results are likely to be chaotic. On the other hand, if it appeals to the Conscious Mind and gets a response, it may find that a course of action is taken that has positive and harmonious results.

This would be especially true if the Conscious Mind has, in turn, sought advice from the higher, Intuitive Mind.

When the Psyche functions without the light of reason from the Conscious Mind, it feels alienated from others and perceives them to be a threat to its existence. Since it is ignorant of the nature of the universe and its place in it, it is not aware of its interrelationship with others and, therefore, feels the need to compete with them for its survival. **Competition** leads to **greed** (or aquisition) which creates the need to be **right**, to have **more**, and to be **better than** others. When it is frustrated in these goals, it is **discontented**, **jealous**, and **envious**. These, in turn, breed **resentfulness**, which is expressed in **hostility** and **vengefulness**.

These three levels of consciousness are the levels upon which most people function in today's world. Most, however, have no conscious awareness of their psychic (ESP) level. This, unfortunately, includes many of those who regard themselves as spiritually enlightened. It also includes those who call themselves "Born Again." Since their salvation is purchased by a crucified god, they see no need to deal with their lower emotions. While there is lip service given to this need, it does not seem to be taken seriously, since many are critical of others who do engage in self-examination. They express the opinion that such people are "under the influence of the devil." However, many Fundamentalist Christians have a highly developed psychic awareness, but they attribute the information received from this level to be from "the Lord." It is therefore interpreted according to their religious beliefs.

Because there is so much confusion in most minds regarding the nature and role of the psychic level of consciousness, we will go into greater depths to explain it so that it can be utilized more constructively.

The term "ESP" (or extrasensory perception), presumes that this level of consciousness is related to a "sixth sense." However, it is not really a sixth sense since it operates on a different dimension from the five physical senses. It is rather a mental perception which is interpreted through the five senses. One whose psychic perceptions are developed may see, hear and feel things that are beyond the five senses. But, as part of our animal instinct, this awareness remains in the twilight zone of consciousness until the Concrete Mind accepts the message from the psychic level informing it of unseen events and conditions.

When the psychic level of consciousness senses that something is about to occur which has the potential to affect the individual, it may send a message to the Concrete Mind in the form of either pictures or a feeling of restlessness, which is a signal to listen. The message may be either on a positive note, heralding a pleasant change, or a negative note, foreboding an unpleasant event to come.

There is a great deal of confusion regarding the nature of ESP because most people, including so-called "psychics," do not realize that true, meaningful ESP is a combination of two levels of consciousness: the psychic (third level) and the intuitive (sixth level). Most tend to use the terms interchangeably as though there were no distinction between them. But, while the Animal Mind (instinctive nature) is able to detect certain imminent changes, the information is of no practical use unless there is some way to know what to do with it.

The information is of value only if, when a message from the psychic level is received, the Concrete Mind calls upon the higher, intuitive levels above it for an interpretation and instructions on what action to take, if any. In any case, it makes it possible for the individual to be forewarned and therefore able to take evasive actions when they are called for, or be prepared for the consequences of changes which cannot be altered. In this way, one can cope with change in a calm and controlled manner.

There are some who have awakened to the psychic level of consciousness without having awakened to the higher levels. They often claim to have the ability to give guidance to others through knowledge gained by this means. But, from the point of view of Universal Law, to follow such advice is dangerous for both "psychic" and the person who relies upon him or her for advice.

The psychic sense, when confined to the psychic level and acted upon by the Conscious Mind without input from the Higher Mind, becomes "Black Magic" and is used for personal, selfish gain. Its effects can be destructive to both the person using it in this manner and to those who rely upon information second hand from such people.

There are two reasons why this is so. First, the information gotten by the so-called psychic is likely to be tainted with his or her prejudices and, therefore, not valid. Secondly, the person who seeks the advice does so at the expense of his or her own autonomy. It robs one of the responsibility to take charge of their own life. It does not, however, relieve him or her of the consequences of attitudes and actions taken as a result of such advice.

On the other hand, when psychic awareness is used according to the guidance of the Intuitive Mind, it becomes "White Magic" and can be used in a constructive way as a guide for one's daily life. But this magic is for personal use only. It is never to be used to give others advice as to how to conduct their personal lives.

As indicated, the lower levels of consciousness

cannot comprehend the higher levels. The psychic level can only report what it perceives through the five senses. It does not have the capacity for judging the value of the information it receives. This is the function of the higher levels.

Those who function on the higher, intuitive levels are aware that they do not have the right to give advice to others. They know the consequences of interfering with the responsibility of another to make his or her own decisions. The adviser becomes responsible for the actions of the person to whom he or she gives advice. Therefore, the truly enlightened person is inclined to avoid such activity. Instead, he or she will attempt to assist the individual in learning to get guidance from his or her own higher levels of consciousness.

There are, however, certain people, such as Edgar Cayce, who have clairvoyant ability and can see mental and physical problems in others. Such people can conduct their healing in a purely altruistic frame of mind and, therefore, do not cause harm. Jesus Christ was one of these. When he healed someone, he always put the responsibility on the person who was healed by admonishing him or her to give up the habits which had caused the illness to occur. He said, "Go and sin no more. "

Seeking advice from another is not a short cut to higher understanding. Anyone who develops the intuitive level (the **Super-conscious**) will automatically develop the psychic level along with it. As Jesus put it, when one seeks the kingdom of heaven (or enlightenment) first, the rest comes along as a part of the package. It is also the reason why legitimate teachers of the technique of Yoga teach their students to concentrate upon the sixth Chakra, or the third eye, and to raise the Kundalini from this perspective.

Only when the intuitive level of consciousness is brought into the decision making process can one satisfactorily utilize the knowledge acquired through the psychic level. It is just so much static without input from above. When followed without the guidance from the higher mind, it leads to chaos.

The **Concrete Consciousness** or the fourth level is sometimes associated with the Greek god Mercury, who was the messenger of the gods. But one of the characteristics of Mercury was that he was frequently unreliable. Likewise, the Concrete Mind cannot be trusted to be totally accurate in its conclusions since things are not always as they seem. It can, therefore, only be trusted when it is guided by the higher levels of consciousness.

Situated mid-way between the higher and lower levels of consciousness, its purpose is to gather knowledge from experience on the physical level and relay it to the higher levels for interpretation. When it does the job for which it was designed, it acts as the helms-person to steer the course of the lower self toward higher awareness. Thus, it acts as the contact point between the Higher and Lower Self.

Sometimes, however, it forgets its purpose and becomes side-tracked and trapped in the quagmire of the lower appetites. And, like the Prodigal Son of the New Testament, it "wastes its substance in riotous living." But in time (after many lifetimes) it catches on to the truth that the "good times" which can be had on the physical plane are like the husks the swine herd feeds the pigs when compared to a life lived under the control and direction of the Higher Mind (or Eros, the

Evolution of Consciousness

Christ or Buddha consciousness).

The **Abstract Consciousness** on the fifth level is the repository of the memories of experience passed through by the entity in each incarnation and of the faculties which are developed from these experiences. Therefore, it contains the knowledge of the lessons learned and those yet to be learned (or karma) which the personality creates during its incarnation. The knowledge derived from the experience of many lifetimes is stored here and may be made available to the Concrete Mind when it is made receptive to receiving such information.

Because it combines knowledge accumulated by the Conscious Mind with the Wisdom of the Super-conscious Mind, this is also the level of consciousness which comprehends higher math, science, music, philosophy and the arts. It is the level from which a "genius" operates. Unfortunately, even the most intelligent of us only tap this level in infrequent, periodic intervals. According to the Ancient Wisdom, our goal should be to maintain this and higher levels of consciousness at all times.

The **Super-Conscious (Intuitive Mind)** on the sixth level is related to the Cavernous Plexus which contains the pituitary gland, often regarded as the seat of the "third eye." It is the mediary through which the Supra-conscious (or Cosmic Mind) transmits divine knowledge to the Ego or Soul. It conveys to the Conscious Mind through the Abstract Mind what action to take regarding information it has acquired from the lower levels of consciousness. As the agent of discrimination, it is the faculty for discerning "right and wrong," "good and evil," etc. In other words, it is our conscience.

The View From Olympus

When this level is sufficiently developed, one has an awareness of the oneness of all of creation. This translates into feelings of tenderness and sympathy for all living things. When reflected in the emotions, it is spiritual love or love without an object, without possessiveness.

This level of consciousness not only enables one to recognize higher truths, but it is also the source of reliable guidance in the ordinary conduct of one's daily life. The direct perception which it inspires is firmly rooted and therefore provides one with a sense of completeness and stability. When one remains centered in this consciousness, he or she is not easily shaken by the winds of uncertainty. And the old need to compete with others is replaced with the desire for cooperation.

The **Supra-Conscious** on the seventh level is related to the carotid plexus which contains the pineal gland. However, it is said by mystics to have its sphere of influence outside the confines of the physical body. It is, nevertheless, the link between heaven and earth, as it were, since it is the root which connects us to the Universal Consciousness.

Another way of visualizing the levels of consciousness is to lay them out in the form of the letter "V." (Figure 10) In this example, the Concrete Mind is seen to occupy a level by itself at the bottom, or pivotal point. You will recall that the Concrete Mind is said to be the go-between for the Higher and Lower Minds. The Lower Mind is shown on the left side with the different levels in descending order, revealing that the orientation of the Lower Mind is toward the Concrete Mind, or conscious awareness. The Higher Mind, on the other hand, is oriented upward from the

Concrete Mind.

Thus the Concrete Mind, located at the pivotal point, is connected to both sides and can therefore

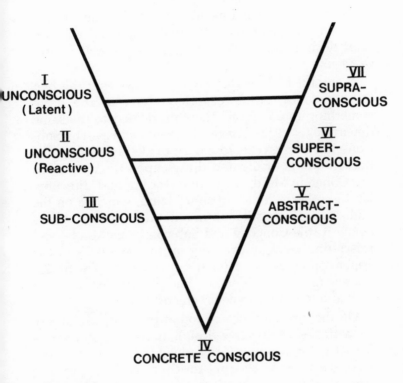

figure 10

move in either direction. It is in the command position and can direct its energy either way. From this description it becomes clear that we are indeed masters of our own destiny.

On the next step up we have the numeral III, Sub-Conscious Mind, on the left and the numeral V, Abstract Mind, on the right side. On the next step up we have the numerals II and VI with their respective designations of Unconscious-Reactive and Super-Conscious. At the top are the numerals I and VII with their designation of Unconscious-Latent and Supra-Conscious.

A careful look at this lay-out shows that the two levels of consciousness that share a line have something in common. They are related to the same departments of life but on different octaves. The Sub-Conscious, or Psyche, found on the left deals with the unseen affairs of life and draws upon the next level, the Concrete Mind, for understanding and direction. On the other side the Abstract Mind, which is on the higher octave, gets its information from the two levels below it (the Concrete and Sub-conscious Minds) and raises one level by drawing on the resources of the Super-conscious Mind (or Intuition). Armed with this knowledge, it is able to combine the unseen with the seen and to put it to a new, "creative" use.

On the next step up are found the numerals II and VI with their respective designations of Unconscious (Reactive) and Super-Conscious (or Intuitive). These two are related to one another in that they are concerned with the creative aspects of life.

It may be recalled that the second level is in the area of the sacral ganglia which is related to sex and procreation. The Super-Conscious, on the other hand, deals with creativity on the mental/spiritual level. We have also said that the second level is ruled by Anteros, the god of passion and the antipathy of Eros, the god of love, situated on the right side of the same line and representing the higher octave of creativity.

It has been found that, when the passions are aroused through the frustrations of unfulfilled desires on the Unconscious level, or the need to control others on the Sub-conscious level, they will generally result in actions taken on the physical level which are discordant if the emotions are not modified by higher levels of consciousness. The most common action, which has been the approved way of organized religion for several thousand years, is that of "Recreational Sex" for the purpose of releasing tensions of frustration and/or the need to control others. However it frequently results in the "creation" of undesired and/or unplanned for human beings. Furthermore, when the activity is engaged upon with multiple partners, it spreads diseases among the participants which cause deformities in the bodies and minds of future generations.

Nevertheless, the use of the procreative act in this manner has been declared by religion and echoed by all levels of modern society to be an imperative which must not be denied, especially to men. It is implied that denial of this imperative will cause permanent physical and psychological damage to anyone who does not avail him or herself of this means by which to release pent up tensions.

Much of modern medicine and psycho-therapy is based upon this premise. Because we have forgotten who and what we are, there is a great deal of confusion in the minds of many people. While Jesus said that we are "gods," or spiritual beings with the power to create and the ability to control our own destinies, organized religion has taught us that we are helpless pawns in a great chess game between a good god and a bad god. Now modern psychology has come along to add further confusion by telling us that we are "sexual beings" and, as such, were created as slaves to our physical appetites.

But it has already been shown that our true selves are Spirit/Mind. Sex, being one of the lowest levels of consciousness, is a primitive urge and as such must be modified by the higher levels of consciousness in order to activate one's god qualities. When one focuses one's Conscious Mind on the lower level of consciousness for the sake of the appetites without input from the Higher Mind, one becomes a miscreator because the results of one's actions become out of synchronization with the rest of life and, therefore, discordant.

When one is out of touch with the higher consciousness, one tends to emphasize the lower, physical side. Since sex is the lower octave of the creative aspect, if the higher creative expression is thwarted, the individual tends to express his or her frustrations through recreational sex. When the frustration is extreme, it is often expressed through sexual abuse of others or in various forms of self abuse such as the misuse of food and drugs or the infliction of injury directly to the body.

The problem is not that we are sexual beings whose expression is repressed by a lack of sufficient sexual intercourse. Nor has nature played a dirty trick on us by giving us more sex drive than we can handle. It is rather that the other creative avenues are blocked and the energy built up by frustration is concentrated on the lower levels. The cure is to unblock the higher creative centers by turning one's attention in that direction.

On the highest step of our "V" symbol are numerals

Evolution of Consciousness

I and VII with the designations of Unconscious (latent) and the Supra-conscious Mind. On one hand, the vibrations of the lowest level of consciousness, or the physical side, are too far below our ordinary consciousness to be tapped by most people. The vibrations of the Supra-conscious, on the other hand, are too high for most to tap. These levels require a supreme effort and can be reached only by the most highly developed adepts. In modern times, certain Yogis and Shamans have been found to reach these levels. They are able to see the workings of the body and to control the autonomic nervous system and the organs of the body at will from the seventh level or Cosmic Consciousness.

Those who operate from the lower levels of consciousness lack the benefit of the higher reasoning and, therefore, have no understanding of how to guide the Conscious Mind. Thus, they have no means by which to control their lives. Consequently, they are adrift on the sea of life without direction. This does not mean that, to be enlightened, one must give up all commerce with the mundane world. It simply means that one no longer has the need to react to the fluctuations of life as others do. In other words, one does not act on cue to having one's "buttons pushed." He or she "acts" from conscious awareness instead of "reacting" from unconsciousness. Reaction is a blind response to forces which are not understood. Action, on the other hand, is reasoned and comes from within. It is not, therefore, controlled by outside forces or circumstances. Thus, one who is able to act from a position of awareness is in control of his or her life.

It is upon this understanding of the levels of consciousness that the various systems of Yoga in the

The View From Olympus

Hindu religion were founded. The seven Chakras represent the seven levels. The raising of the Kundalini power is the same as the raising of the serpent of Moses and part of the process of becoming awakened to one's spiritual/mental nature.

Today we know that knowledge of the levels of consciousness, or of the Chakras, was a part of many world religions in the past. In addition to the Eastern religions, it was known to the Sumerians. The tale of Gilgamesh has been found to be a description of the awakening of the Chakras. The Mayans too are said to have been acquainted with the Kundalini and the Chakras. It now also seems quite likely that the meaning of the seven Churches and Seven Candlesticks in the book of **Revelation** in the New Testament is also related to the seven Chakras.

There is no doubt that we are dealing with allegory in this book since the author explains that he is describing something which came to him in the form of a vision. In the first chapter he introduces "one like the son of man" or, as we have learned from the study of symbology, the prototype of perfected mankind. He is seen standing in the midst of seven lampstands holding seven stars in his right hand. The meaning of his vision is also revealed here. And, when it is examined, it is found to be strikingly similar to the teachings of the seven levels found in the Ancient Wisdom. He is told that the seven stars are the angels of the seven churches and the seven lampstands are the seven churches.

Students of the Ancient Wisdom such as James M. Pryse[6] see the lampstands as representing the seven Chakras. The lampstands (or churches) are receptacles of energy (or light); they are not energy itself. The

Evolution of Consciousness

seven stars (or angels/messengers) represent the energy (or light) which is brought to the receptacle in order to bring it to life. Thus it can be seen that, if the churches represent the Chakras, the stars which are the energy in the form of spiritual fire are the kundalini energy which activates them and raises the consciousness to higher levels.

The Ancient Wisdom teaches that mankind is on a sojourn in the physical body and that its purpose is to rise above the pull of attraction to the physical plane and to raise its consciousness to the spiritual/mental plane. Therefore it is obvious that the allegory of the seven lampstands and the seven stars is a way of telling mankind what is required in order to arrive at the necessary state of perfection or the state which Jesus called "born again."

Once again we find the old Hermetic adage "As above, so below" applies as much to the Chakras as it does elsewhere. We find that these seven spiritual/mental centers correspond with the major nerve centers found along the spine and known in the medical field as "plexus."

The two lowest Chakras occur in the area of the coccygeal ganglia and the sacral ganglia, respectively. Together they form the **Pelvic Plexus**. The third Chakra is located in the area of the **Solar Plexus**, the fourth in the area of the **Cardiac Plexus**, the fifth in the area of the **Pharyngeal** (throat) **Plexus**, the sixth in the area of the head called the **Cavernous Plexus**, which includes the pituitary gland and the nerves related to vision, and the seventh is in the area of the **Carotid Plexus**, which is related to the pineal (master) gland.

The story found in **The Revelation** tells of the rewards to be gained when each level of consciousness is mastered, or when the light is lit and each Chakra is activated. This, of course, occurs when the Kundalini rises from its place at the base of the spine and awakens the fire of higher, spiritual awareness in each of them. It appears that the seven cities named in The Revelation describe, not only the locations of the "Churches" or Chakras, but their characteristics as well. There can be no doubt that the cities named refer to the seven centers since the rewards mentioned are appropriate to the physical functions of each.

Ephesus, it is clear, represents the **coccygeal chakra**. For it says that those who overcome the negative pull of this level "shall eat of the tree of life ... in paradise."

The coccygeal, of course, is related to the digestive tract. This level at the base of the spine is, therefore, related to the basic instincts of survival and concerned with both the acquisition of food and the preservation of the body. Thus, with this very first Chakra, we are reminded of our true nature, which is eternal. We are, when perfected, able to partake of the spiritual food from the tree of life in eternity.

Smyrna represents the ethereal body located in the area of the sacral (sex) **chakra**. Those who overcome the power of attraction to the passions, or who learn to bring them under the control of the Higher Mind, will not taste the second death ... the death of the soul. On the physical level, this center deals with self-preservation and propagation, or survival of the race. But awareness on this level brings with it the understanding that there is no need to fear death because there is no death of the spirit.

Pergamos is the next city mentioned and is related to the **Solar Plexus** or emotional center. It is the seat of the lower emotions and the Sub-conscious Mind.

Evolution of Consciousness

Those who gain control of the negative emotions at this center "shall eat of the hidden manna" and be given a "white (pure) stone (eternal truth)." The stomach lies in the Solar Plexus and therefore has to do with the digestion of food. Symbolically, it is where we digest the ideas and attitudes encountered in relationship with others. There are times when one finds it difficult to "stomach" the treatment and attitudes of others.

It will also be recalled that it is on the negative side of this level that a person feels alienated and at odds with others. He or she resents the success of others, interpreting it as a threat to their own success. This competitive stance brings out the negative attitudes which destroy the soul and alienate one from others.

Thyatira is related to the **Cardiac Plexus**, the point of transition between the three lower (physical) Chakras and the three higher (spiritual/mental) Chakras. Or, between heaven and earth. The symbol of the cross, universally known for thousands of years, relates to the separation of the upper and lower levels of consciousness (Chakras) at the Cardiac Plexus. It is called the "Cross of Matter" or, sometimes, the "Cross of Light" and is the point at which the lower appetites are sublimated (crucified) to the higher levels of consciousness. This is what is known as "the birth of the spirit." It is at this level that the soul makes the choice between marriage to the physical passions of Anteros and the spiritual, creative awareness of Eros. When the latter course is taken, this becomes the center of compassion.

Sardis represents the **Pharyngeal Plexus**. The thyroid gland is located in this plexus and regulates the metabolism or assimilation of food in the body. On the spiritual side, it is at this point one learns how to utilize one's experiences in life. When it draws from the next higher center, the intuitive, it becomes a higher creative center able to foster spiritual growth. For, as the universe was created by the spoken word, so we also create from this center by the thoughts we express in both word and deed. We create our own private universes in this manner, whether or not we are aware of what we are doing.

The names of those who master the art of consciously and positively creating shall have their names "confessed before the father (universal creator) and his angels" or messengers. In other words, those who no longer miscreate but create according to the plan of the master builder, shall become co-creators with him/her (god).

Philadelphia is at the **Cavernous Plexus**, the place of the pituitary gland and the optical nerves and, therefore, the home of the "third eye" or intuition. Philadelphia, of course, means "brotherly love," or "agape." It is love without an object or without possessiveness. Combined with understanding which comes from the knowledge derived from other levels above and below, it is also **Wisdom**. With wisdom comes an understanding that all of life is one and love of all is the glue which holds it all together. This is the level of true creativity. Those who master or learn to trust and live according to the wisdom of the intuitive mind "shall be made a pillar" (a permanent fixture) "of God" (the creative source) "and shall go no more out" (will not need to reincarnate).

Laodocia is located at the **Carotid Plexus**, the home of the pineal (master) gland. Those who become conscious on this level (cosmic consciousness) will sit with the supreme creator on his throne. Or, as we learn

Evolution of Consciousness

from the study of Yoga, they will become fully aware and have the power to control the forces of nature as well as their own lower levels of consciousness (the physical, ego levels). At this level, which many Yogis attain, one is able to control the autonomic nervous system, to control the blood pressure and heartbeat, etc.

Thus it can be seen that the aspirant who has an understanding of the Chakras or seven levels of consciousness and their meaning to the spiritual/mental path, has a standard by which to measure his or her progress toward enlightenment or to wholeness and control over his or her own destiny.

♦

PLEXUS		SEVEN LEVELS OF CONSCIOUSNESS
CAROTID	**VII**	**SUPRA-CONSCIOUSNESS** (Cosmic): Rooted in Cosmic Source (God)—Spiritual Energy (Inspiration)
CAVERNOUS	**VI**	**SUPER-CONSCIOUSNESS** (Intuitive): Creative Wisdom—Transmitter of Higher Knowledge
PHARYNGEAL	**V**	**ABSTRACT CONSCIOUSNESS:** Repository of All Experience (All Lives) Creative Expression (Genius)
CARDIAC	**IV**	**CONCRETE CONSCIOUSNESS:** Will (Pilot)—Choice
SOLAR	**III**	**SUB-CONSCIOUS** (Psyche): Animal Instinct (Emotions) or Animal Mind A. Positive – ESP Clairvoyance, Clairaudience, Psychometry, Divining (witching) B. Negative—Need to Control Others: Competition: 1. Greed (Aquisition) a. Need to be right b. Need to have more than c. Need to be better than 2. Discontent 3. Jealousy/Envy 4. Resentfulness Hostility/Vengefulness
SACRAL	**II**	**UNCONSCIOUS** (Reactive) Instinct (Physical) A. Stimulus-response: Desire/Appetite 1. Gratification: Contentment 2. Frustration: Rage, anger, panic, fear, hysteria, despair, hopelessness, violence B. Creative (Reproduction, Race Survival)
COCCYGEAL **figure 11**	**I**	**UNCONSCIOUS** (Latent) Physical Survival (Individual) A. Body Organs B. Body Cells

The Politics Of Sex

XI

The Politics Of Sex

In all of Nature the procreative act is controlled by the female and occurs when the season and conditions are right for the birth of new life. The human animal is the only exception to this rule. While we take pride in our superiority over all other animals, our breeding practices are the most haphazard, irresponsible, irrational, and destructive on the planet earth. This deplorable condition stems from the fact that, contrary to nature, the male of our species is in control of the act of procreation. Instead of an act of creation, sex has been turned into a form of recreation without regard for the consequences. In order to justify this misuse of the sacred act of human procreation, the male, aided and abetted by the priesthood of male-dominated religions, has for several thousand years propagated the myth that the sex act was created for the pleasure of the male.

In a previous chapter it was shown that the blame for most of the violence and bloodshed in the past several thousand years can be traced to the doorstep of organized religion. It can also be seen that the basis for this violence and bloodshed can be traced to the old, distorted view of the procreative act which religion has fostered. This attitude has bred conflict between men and women, which has in turn infected all other aspects of our lives.

But in order to correct this condition we must cease blaming one another and realize that neither men nor women are to blame for the chaotic state in which we find our world today. We are victims of the conditions which we inherited from past ages when the consciousness of our ancestors was at its lowest level. These present conditions were created in an environment of superstitious beliefs, bred from ignorance.

We have accepted the inherited conditions of past ages as right and proper (rooted in God's law) for so long that we have failed to see how irrational they really are. When one pauses to examine the end results of these conditions, however, it becomes obvious that something is drastically wrong. Rather than rearrange the facts to fit our beliefs, as organized religion has done, perhaps we should reverse the order and make our beliefs conform to the facts.

We go to great lengths to make ourselves appear rational, yet our attitude toward sex and male and female relationships is the most antiquated and irrational attitude one could possibly imagine. It is so ridiculous that, if the consequences were not so serious, the drama of our collective lives would be hilariously funny. It would be a farce.

Let us examine some of our logic regarding sex which we have accepted as divine truth. In fact, we have accepted it for so long that it never occurs to us to question its validity. We act as though it were the unadulterated, ultimate truth delivered directly from God himself. But, if the rules by which we live are mandated by God, then he must be a MAD MAN!

One common attitude that has only recently come into question (by women) is one expressed by men. To wit, sexual arousal is a painful affliction for the male. Since the condition is brought about by women (because they exist), it is their responsibility to relieve it, regardless of how casual the relationship may be. Even going to dinner and the theater with a woman frequently causes this affliction to overtake the male. The only cure, according to the victims of this malady, is sexual intercourse.

This, of course, is in conflict with the old male game of competition in which the woman becomes his private property and no other man has a right to touch her. But never mind the contradiction, male logic simply makes women responsible for whatever happens, whichever way it goes.

Simply stated, the rules of our male-dominated society, which the male-dominated court system follows, say that any female who refuses a male this means of relieving himself of his pain is cruel and unfeeling. Furthermore, her failure to accommodate him of her own free will is justification for rape. On the other hand, the female who succumbs to the above arguments is branded and condemned as a "whore." Although he is free to have contact with as many women as he chooses, as the sole property of her husband, the wife must have intercourse with no other man.

If a woman is raped, it is her fault because she asked

for it either by the way she was dressed or because she has had sexual intercourse before and therefore, being a whore, has no right to refuse her services to any man who lusts after her body. She also has no right to be concerned for the safety of her life or for the possibility of being infected by disease or of being made pregnant. Any pregnancy that results from the rape, according to the Father-god religions, is to be regarded as "the Will of God."

In spite of the "Sexual Revolution" of the 1960's, the attitude just described is still prevalent in our judicial system as well as the society as a whole. Like little boys who hate their mothers for not letting them get into the cookie jar any time they please, males of the species have developed a hatred for women for resisting their argument that they have a god-given right to recreational sex ... on demand. But they also hate women for giving into their childish demands.

What they really want is for women to bring dignity and self-respect into a relationship and to place limits upon their behavior toward them and their children. Deep within himself the male knows that his way is destructive and looks to the female to bring him into balance by imposing discipline upon his behavior. When women acquiesce to the male lower nature they do so not only at the cost of their own sense of dignity, they contribute to social chaos. Women must take responsibility for the fact that when they allow their sacred creative center to be desecrated or sacrificed on the altar of the lower human passions they aid and abet destructive behavior.

Because they have been economically dependent upon men, women have not only allowed themselves to be abused by the male sexual appetite and the need for power over others, they have allowed their children to be abused as well. As recent studies have revealed, the abuse of children leads to the anger and resentment which is later expressed in violent behavior toward life and property. It creates the vicious circle of abuse of women and children which can only be stopped when women assert their rights as human beings and regain their self-respect by refusing to allow themselves and their children to be mistreated.

The woman who aggressively seeks recreational sex is as self-destructive as the woman who accepts an inferior, subservient position to the male appetite. The goal should not be to have equal access to sexual gratification. Sex is not the answer to the problems of human relations. It does not overcome loneliness, frustration, or a sense of inadequacy. Instead, it compounds these problems and creates a greater sense of desperation when used to solve these problems.

Furthermore, all jokes about sex are an insult to women and children and, ultimately, to the human race. Women show a lack of self-respect when they joke with men about the desecration of their bodies as though the joke were on someone else. Many women demonstrate that they believe sex is a proper way to express anger and frustration for, like men, they use the words "fuck you" and gesture with the middle finger to express their rage. How, then, can they condemn rape when, by their actions, they show that they believe sexual violence to be acceptable?

As indicated in the chapter on the Astrological Ages, several thousand years ago the idea of the polarity of the male and female principles in nature was abandoned in favor of the polarity of good and evil. As the level of consciousness degenerated, people lost understanding of the importance of balance between the male and female principles in general and between men and women in particular.

When this occurred, perhaps as long as eight thousand years ago, cooperation between the sexes was abandoned in favor of competition. Competition between the sexes soon spread throughout society to include all segments. From there it spread to include competition between different societies. Today, theologians and psychotherapists base their dogma upon the premise that this is the natural state of the human condition.

It is important to recall that this position was introduced first by the priesthood of male-dominated religions. And the confusion which ensued from the disruption of the natural order gave religious leaders an advantage which they still enjoy. From their positions of power, they have passed rules and regulations to enslave people by controlling their conduct, especially their conduct in relation to the act of procreation.

Since this first began, the struggle for power between the sexes as well as within the political, economic and religious arenas has been regarded as a natural, even sacred condition which must not be altered lest the wrath of God be visited upon us. Today, the male-dominated clergy and the medical, scientific, and psychological fields all use their positions of authority to perpetuate the myth of male dominance as a divine mandate operating in accordance with Natural Law.

But it does not take the intelligence of a super-genius to see that the whole idea of male dominance is and always has been a colossal hoax to which women and children have fallen victims. Nor does it require super-intelligence to see that the male-dominated, anti-feminist society under which we live today is programmed to self-destruct. And that zero hour is not far away. Overpopulation, due to our irresponsible breeding practices along with our irresponsible use of the earth's resources, is speeding us toward our demise as a race along with the earth that sustains us. In the past fifty years the pace of destruction has accelerated so that we can see it happening like a horror movie before our eyes.

Competition, which has been glorified by Church and State for ages, is about to destroy us. It seems clear that, if we do not interrupt our headlong rush to destruction by relearning the feminine art of cooperation, we are doomed to obliteration by the machinery which maleness, without the tempering effects of femaleness, has created. At this juncture, perhaps we should review the circumstances which have brought us to the conditions in which we find ourselves today.

In the chapter on the Astrological Ages, it was pointed out that during the ages found on the lower half of the zodiac, religion dominates philosophy, and each age is dominated by the god and goddess religions alternately. But, beginning with the age of Gemini, the understanding of the need for cooperation between the sexes is abandoned and the idea of one sex dominating the other is introduced. During the age of Gemini, not only did a male god religion prevail, but the role of the female principle in Nature was almost completely denied.

This unbalanced state created a feminine backlash in

the age of Taurus and resulted in the goddess religions in which the role of the male was depreciated. Under the goddess religions the economy of the society was also controlled by women. Since women were in control of the economy and held the property in their names, the ancestry of the children was traced through the mother. In many cases, no doubt, the father was unknown.

"Salvation" in the goddess religion was obtained by having sexual intercourse with a priestess. It was perhaps at this time when the sexually transmitted diseases that plagued the Children of Israel began to be spread among the population.

Sometime around 2500 B.C.E., this arrangement was reversed as the male/god religions once again began to emerge in anticipation of the age of Aries. When this occurred, women and children became the chattels (or slaves) of men, a condition that has remained in place to the present time. Under this arrangement, men took control of the procreative act.

Although Moses later passed laws to prohibit promiscuous sexual behavior, the male-dominated Church and State have promoted promiscuity among men while demanding strict monogamous behavior from women. As a part of the economic structure, it became important for men to know that the offspring of their wives was the product of their loins. Fathers arranged marriages for their daughters for political and economic reasons. The daughter's dowry as well as her good looks (or sex appeal) became commodities with which the father bargained to improve his political and/or financial position.

As stated in the chapter on the Gnostics, the early Christians who followed the teachings of Jesus practiced equality between men and women. But Paul, whose teachings supplanted the teachings of Jesus, based his religion upon the Mithraic religion, which excluded women and the Judaic religion, which was also male-dominated. Since it is Paul's religion that has survived to the present time, it is also his teachings on the inferior status of women which have survived. For the past two thousand years we have forced ourselves to live by rules based upon childish beliefs, imposed by religion, which are inappropriate to the consciousness of the mature adults we have become.

However, during the 17th century the old traditions began to change as a result of two events. The first was the "Industrial Revolution," which produced a new class of "self-made men," the Nouveau Riche, who did not owe their wealth to the family. This, then, freed them from the necessity to be bound by the concerns of their father's family finances and made it possible for them to choose wives for their own reasons.

But the catalyst which brought about the first break with tradition was the advent of the new philosophy of Romanticism in which an emphasis was placed upon individual freedom and the need to get back to nature. This was interpreted to mean, in effect, that one should regard the emotions as superior to reason where male and female relations were concerned.

To have a beautiful wife became a status symbol for these successful young men. It was the wife's job to show off his wealth by wearing fine clothes and entertaining in her elegant home. This, in turn, provided the young woman with the means to improve her financial status or to maintain the standard of her father's home.

Now that her marriage was no longer arranged by

her father, it was the woman's responsibility to make herself as sexually appealing as possible in order to attract the man of her choice. But, in order to reach her goal, she must remain chaste. These men would not buy "damaged goods." After all, part of the game of romance was to win her as his sole property in competition with other men who would also like to have her under their exclusive control. So it became a tradition that the woman made herself as sexually attractive as possible and teased and flirted until the man she wanted caught her. She must never appear to be the aggressor, however. After all, it was the male's place to choose the woman, since it was his money that would provide for her needs, and the woman's place to be servile.

But, once married, she became the property of her husband just as in the old days. What property she brought to the marriage became his. She had only as much freedom as her husband would allow her. And it was his conjugal right to have sexual intercourse on demand regardless of the consequences to her or the children.

The husband was the disciplinarian of the home and could do as he pleased with his wife and children. The laws, which were written and interpreted by men, found that violence against women and children was a part of the man's right to control his family in any way he deemed necessary. In some Catholic countries of South America this still includes the right to incest and murder.

While this tradition began in the upper classes, it was adopted by the middle class as it developed in the 19th and 20th centuries. It continued unchallenged until the 1950's when women began to break out of bad marriages. It culminated in the 1960's with the "Sexual Revolution." At that point women became convinced that they had as much right to the pleasures of recreational sex as did men.

But the human race is still the only animal which uses the act of procreation contrary to the Laws of Nature. And, with the exception of an obscure species of spider, the male human is the only animal which rapes the female. It is also the only animal which does not plan for the birth of its young. Even today, with various means of "birth control," most pregnancies in the world are unplanned. Furthermore, with few exceptions, humans are the only animals known to abuse their young. The Tom Cat is one of the exceptions. Because it often kills its young, the mother is obliged to hide them from him.

Those who regard the Judeo/Christian Bible as their authority for moral conduct should take another look at what it says about sex. It is quite clear that the laws which Moses laid down pertaining to the subject were based upon two major considerations. One, the control of sexually transmitted disease, and two, the protection of women and children. To accomplish this, sexual intercourse was prohibited except for procreation. Although it is obvious that these were not arbitrary laws imposed by a capricious God, the male-dominated clergy of the Hebrew and Christian religions has ignored them.

Among the punishments found in the 20th chapter of Leviticus for infractions against the laws governing sexual behavior is death. In the light of what we now know about the dangers that sexually transmitted diseases pose to the well-being of ourselves and future generations, the penalties which Moses imposed on recreational sex and sexual molestation no longer seem extraordinary. Since these diseases are often life-threatening, extreme measures apparently seemed necessary. At that time, due to the promiscuity begun under goddess-religions and accelerated under the god-religions, sexually transmitted diseases had become a serious problem, as they are today.

It may be that the prohibitions against bestiality had as much to do with bestial behavior between humans as with the act of sex with animals. The prohibition against homosexuality may fall into the same category. For there appears to be strong evidence that diseases of the digestive tract are spread from the mouth and anus to the genitals. The fact that certain sexually transmitted diseases may have been altered to some degree to accommodate a different environment, does not preclude their originating in other parts of the body.

The bacteria which causes certain throat infections (strep throat) and the sexually transmitted disease gonorrhea are from the same family: the coccus, whose cells are spherical in form. Herpes is another disease of the mouth and genitals which may not be identical but is, nevertheless, related. Candida, a yeast infection in the digestive tract is called "Clamidia" (Chlamydia) in the genitals. Once the genitals are infected, these diseases are rapidly spread by promiscuous sexual activity.

Even after they seem to have been cured, these diseases may remain dormant for from five to twenty years and recur in the form of a degeneration of the muscles, bones and nervous system. Diseases of the heart, insanity and painful, crippling arthritis are reported to be a frequent result. Nevertheless, since the individual has a right to make his or her own choices, perhaps there would be no need for concern if these diseases were not transmitted to unborn children. But, as Moses said and modern medicine seems reluctant to admit, these diseases are passed on to the third and fourth generations.[1]

The report issued for 1987-88 by the Centers for Disease Control in Atlanta, Georgia, states that, "Sexually transmitted diseases continue one of the nation's public health problems. Not only is HIV infection the most devastating public problem of this century, but also infectious syphilis has continued increases unprecedented since the advent of penicillin therapy." Resistant strains of gonococcal infection are also steadily increasing, but Chlamydial infections are twice as prevalent as gonorrhea. Finally, it has been found that warts, which are caused by a virus, are associated with cervical tumors.

The report further states that "Women and children bear an inordinate share of the physical and emotional burden of non-AIDS STD." After death, the most serious complications caused by STD are: infertility. ectopic (displaced) pregnancy, and other adverse conditions resulting in negative results to the newborn: infant pneumonia, infant death, mental retardation, immune deficiencies, and tumors. Furthermore, at least seven cancers have been associated with different sexually transmitted diseases. Five of them are associated with the papilloma virus (warts): anal carcinoma, carcinoma of the cervix, cervical tumors, penile carcinoma, and vulvar carcinoma. At least one is associated with Hepatitus B and others with HIV infection.

The saddest part of this report is the fact that 63% of

all new cases of sexually transmitted diseases occur among persons under 25 years of age (parents and potential parents of babies put at risk). Of that number, 2.5 million teenagers are infected each year.

This should give civilized people reason to pause and reflect upon the manner in which the procreative act is used. Even if we do not care about ourselves, do we really want these diseases passed on to our children? When we consider that sexually transmitted diseases are among the most serious problems facing us today, it would seem that any reasonable person would see the logic in at least avoiding sexual contact with strangers or those who have been indiscriminate in their sexual liaisons.

Many modern women are under the illusion that they were freed by the sexual revolution of the 1960's. But this idea is just more male propaganda based upon distorted facts. With the invention of birth control devices, women have been led to believe that, after 4,500 years of being the objects of male sexual appetites, they have been given the right and privilege to experience pleasure from the act as well. But the facts reveal that the needs of women and children continue to be sacrificed to the male attitude.

Male medical doctors and scientists have led women down the primrose path with a promise of pleasure in exchange for allowing their bodies to be mutilated to allow for recreational sex without the nuisance of unwanted pregnancies. Very little was said about the protection of women from sexually transmitted disease, at least not until the AIDS epidemic became an issue. And, while reducing them in number, the devices do not prevent all unwanted pregnancies.

The Politics Of Sex

Nevertheless, in compliance with the male demand for more unconditional access to recreational sex, women have submitted to the surgical procedures of tubal ligations, unnecessary hysterectomies and the implantation of intrauterine devices. And, like a herd of sheep, they have willingly swallowed "the pill" that plays Russian Roulette with their lives. All of this because they are afraid of losing their man or of not catching one at all. This belief that they are nothing without a penis in their bed is the direct result of male control over the politics and economics of society which makes women dependent on them for their survival.

Disease is not the only problem the unborn face. Unplanned pregnancies have resulted in the birth of babies whose lives are as haphazard as their conception. Because proper planning and care are not made for them before they are born, they are not given the care and education necessary for them to grow and express the highest and best that is in them.

But never mind. Our male-dominated society has a plan for these disenfranchised members of our society. The fittest of them are lured into the military forces and sent off to fight and be killed for the glory of God and Country. The rest are cared for in our expanding prison and mental institutions. Or, they are placed on "Welfare" and treated as mindless, second-class citizens.

The overcrowding that has resulted from the reckless breeding practices of the human race has led to competition for survival on the lowest level. This, in turn, has led to the violence and destruction which civilized people profess to abhor.

Reason indicates that sex was created for the

purpose of perpetuating the race. In all of Nature it is not the male but the female who determines when conditions are right for reproduction to take place. This, of course, is for the protection of the young.

Most new born animals require constant care from their parents to survive. But human young are one of the most helpless. And, while in most animals this care is needed for only a matter of weeks or months, the human child requires care for many years. Yet, while the human child demands a long term commitment of care and nurturing in order to produce a healthy adult, human breeding is the most haphazard and irresponsible of all the animals on the planet.

The chaotic, irrational conditions under which we now live can be traced directly to the doorstep of organized religion which continues to put men and women at odds with one another by the persistent demand that the old superstitious beliefs regarding human nature continue to be accepted. For thousands of years it has manipulated us by appealing to our lowest nature, our physical appetites, and the desire for power over others.

Were it not for the distortion of the facts regarding the procreative act, the question of whether or not women should be allowed to have abortions on demand would not be an issue today. So it seems that if we are to get at the root of the problems which face us we must change our way of thinking. We must cease thinking with our emotions and begin to base our conclusions on reason.

For several thousand years organized religion has focused on the physical universe and the relationship of our physical selves to a physical creator. We have long lived as though what we see is all there is, or that we are our bodies. So, while paying lip service to the spiritual side of life, we find the Christian religion, in the tradition of the ancient Pagans, teaching that the ultimate goal of mankind is a life after death in resurrected physical bodies.

Therefore, in keeping with religious tradition, when modern psychology was born it looked for the motivating force of our lives in the physical body. By reducing us to our lowest and most basic impulses, it has decided that we are "sexual beings." Since this conclusion was reached about a hundred years ago it has been regarded as a foundation for self-understanding or a truism without which no other truth can be discovered. Today, people regard their "sexuality" to be their most precious asset because they believe that without sexuality they might as well be dead!

But using this as a measure, instead of becoming more enlightened, we seem to have become more confused than ever. We are no more free than we were before. Since we have become convinced that we are sexual beings, we have simply added to the repression of religion the obsessions of psychology. Both of them have made slaves of us.

Although psychology has contributed much toward our self-understanding, it has also done us a great disservice in perpetuating the myth of the male-god religions that sex was created for the pleasure of the male. Although psychologists have broadened their position to allow that women are human too and should therefore be allowed to enjoy sex, there is a catch clause which says that this is true so long as they remember that, in the process, their first responsibility is to give pleasure to the male.

The View From Olympus

But its greatest sin lies in the fact that it has propagated the myth that the problems of the psyche (soul) can be cured by a "healthy sex life." And, finally, it continues to insist that all "normal sex" must culminate in coitus, or penis penetration of the vagina. Incidentally, it still refuses to state categorically that masturbation is not a cause of insanity. Ordinary logic should have laid that to rest long ago.

In the first century of the Current Era, when the Gnostic Christian teachings began to be made public, they opposed the idea of the domination of one sex over another. Instead they instituted a balanced attitude toward the body and an attitude of respect and equality between the sexes. The Gnostic Gospels clearly indicate that this was the attitude which Jesus fostered.

But even today many Christians make reference to Jesus' stand on monogamy as an endorsement of Paul's repressive position on the issue of sex and the relationship between men and women. By omitting those parts of the scriptures of the early Christians which showed a healthy attitude toward the body, the Church was able to perpetuate the old Hebrew idea of the male superiority and their right to recreational sex.

These omissions were brought to light with the discovery and publication of the early Christian scriptures hidden in the deserts of Egypt and Palestine for hundreds of years. It is clear now why they had to be hidden away. It was necessary to wait until a time when it was safe for them to be revealed once more. In the Gospel of Philip, Jesus says, "Fear not the flesh nor love it. If you fear it, it will gain mastery over you. If you love it, it will swallow you and paralyze you."[2] This, as has been shown, is contrary to the teachings of the Pauline Church.

By hanging onto the outmoded Mosaic and Mithraic laws, the Church has been able to keep women subjugated and demoralized and men enslaved as its pawns. One of the major tools of repression it has used has been the denial of birth control while, at the same time, whetting the male appetite and giving men complete control over the act of procreation. This, coupled with the denial of the right to information, has insured the Church hierarchy its position of power.

Getting back to the Bible, we discover that there is only one form of sexual behavior, apart from intercourse (coitus) between married or committed couples, which is not prohibited. In fact, it is not even mentioned. It is difficult to imagine that **Masturbation** was not prevalent in the time of Moses since it is obviously a natural activity from childhood throughout adulthood when there are no deterrents in the form of taboos. The fact that it is not mentioned would seem to be an indication that it was not considered harmful.

Yet the idea of masturbation as evil has been a part of Western culture for hundreds, if not thousands, of years. The idea has its beginnings in the Hebrew religion, which has fostered this belief regardless of the fact that there is nothing in its literature against it. Even today, the elders of Judaism and Christianity point to the sin of Onan as an example to deter the practice. In both cases, it seems more likely that the reason for the prohibition has been to insure an increased population among the respective membership which, in turn, equates with greater political power.

But one would have to stretch the imagination a

very long way to be able to interpret the story of Onan as a prohibition against masturbation. The true interpretation is based upon a Hebrew tradition which is unrelated to the issue. The Hebrews of Biblical times had a tradition which said that if a man died and left no children, it was his brother's duty to impregnate the widow. The child, however, would be considered the offspring of the deceased brother.

But Onan's deceased brother had been "wicked in the sight of God," and Onan resented the requirement. So he went through the motions of doing his duty but withdrew before ejaculation and "spilled the semen on the ground, lest he should give offspring to his brother."[3] This brought the wrath of his people down upon him because he had failed to fulfill his duty according to their tradition.

It is clear, therefore, that the sin of Onan was not masturbation, unless of course one considers that all sexual activity, even intercourse between husband and wife, is masturbation. And a case might be made for this point of view since the dictionary definition says that it is "to manipulate one's genitals or the genitals of another for sexual gratification."[4] When this definition is considered in the light of the history of the past 4,500 years, it is clear that what has occurred between men and women has not been intercourse (which implies some active participation between both parties), but masturbation. The man manipulated the genitals of both parties until he had an orgasm. The woman was not supposed to enjoy it. In fact, any woman who dared to show any sign of deriving pleasure from the act was regarded as evil.

When St. Augustine was converted to Christianity, the religion of his mother, he had a lot of unkind things to say about Manichaeism, a Gnostic religion to which he had belonged for a time. He was particularly displeased with their sex practices, which he never really described. He only referred to them in terms of disgust. But what he did imply was that, whatever these disgusting practices were, the women were brazen enough to enjoy it. We may, however, be able to discover what these practices were by piecing together some of what we know about the Gnostics on one hand and Augustine on the other.

Jesus, as previously indicated, is quoted in the Gnostic Gospel of Philip as stating a balanced position in his attitude toward the body. He said that, although one should not be obsessed with it, neither should he or she be afraid of it. We have learned through the study of the human mind, fear is caused by ignorance and repression. Therefore, it can be assumed that Jesus did not advocate repression of the sexual impulses.

We also know that the Manichaeans, a Gnostic sect, believed that sexual intercourse was to be limited to the purpose of procreation. This position was regarded as heresy by the Church. How then can we accept Augustine's report of abhorrent sexual practices among these people in the light of these facts? The truth seems quite likely to be that the Manichaeans practiced masturbation which may have included mutual masturbation.

This seems more likely when we consider that Augustine was a male chauvinist who fathered at least one illegitimate child and believed that women were inherently inferior to men. The Church adopted his belief that the mother contributed nothing to the genetic heritage of the child. She simply provided the "soil" for the male seed which contained the soul.[5]

The View From Olympus

Since the soul was in the seed of the man, he was to be the sole proprietor of the child. Therefore, the male was to be in control of the act of procreation; the woman was to have no say in the matter of birth control.

Sociological tests and surveys, as well as common sense, tell us that our failure to discuss the truth about sex openly and honestly is a major cause of the serious sex related problems which confront us today. Nevertheless, organized religion is engaged in an all-out effort to prevent this openness.[6] The loss of control over our sex lives would be a major blow to the power of the Church and, therefore, must be stopped. But those who succeed in becoming free of the oppression of religion as well as the obsession of psychology and their propaganda about sex, find that the sexual appetites have little to do with biological or physiological needs. They are, instead, artificially bred into us through acculturation or brainwashing by the established authorities in our society.

There is an old parlor game which demonstrates the power of suggestion over the mind. If someone tells you not to think about ice cream, suddenly you cannot get ice cream out of your mind. This is exactly what organized religion has done, especially the Roman Catholic Christian religion which is run by unmarried priests. Because they were told not to think about sex, they became obsessed with it and passed the obsession on to their parishioners. Because they have had no wives of their own, they have used the confessional and other devious means to seduce the women and girls of the Church.[7] Nor have they confined their activities to the female sex. They have also molested little boys.[8] Finally, so as not to neglect anyone, they have had liaisons with other men as well.

When properly understood, much of what is perceived as a need for sexual expression is found to be a psychological need to be validated by another person. But the psyche seldom finds the satisfaction it seeks in sex. However, because we are led to believe that we are supposed to derive satisfaction from this source, we keep trying. One of the reasons so little satisfaction is derived from sexual intercourse is the fact that there is so much exploitation built into our consciousness regarding the act. It has been used so often by those who have a need to control others or express their anger and frustrations that there is no love or trust involved.

First of all, we are told not to think about sex. Then we are told that the only legitimate sexual outlet is between husband and wife. Then the priesthood, which has made the rules in the first place, breaks them by exploiting their position of authority to gain sexual gratification for themselves from those who are dependent upon them as examples and guides for moral/ethical living. This condition has encouraged others in positions of power to take the position that, if it is all right for the clergy to sexually exploit those under their control, why not psychotherapists, fathers, uncles, brothers, cousins, and anyone else who has a need to have power over others?

With all of these different categories of people who feel justified in exploiting the weak and defenseless, who is left to be trusted? Since those who have been abused abuse in turn, the answer to this last question is that there are very few trustworthy people left. Since so many of us have been victims of this kind of abuse, a large segment of our population has had its self-respect so badly damaged that it is unable to trust anyone.

When our bodies were separated into two sexes (millions of years ago), our psyches remained androgynous and, therefore, self-sufficient. Therefore it seems only logical to conclude that it is only the illusion of dependency upon others for our psychic well-being which causes us to have problems with the psyche. Because we have been taught that we are sexual beings, when we feel the need to be validated by others, we believe that our problem stems from sexual deprivation.

But when the Creator, through the medium of Natural Law, made us free-will agents, he/she made us responsible for the way in which we relate to the material world. When given physical bodies to use as vehicles through which to experience the phenomenal world, we were also made their masters. We were not intended to be their slaves. As machines, our bodies, like our automobiles, have needs to which we must give attention. But while they need food, water, clothing, and shelter for survival, sexual intercourse is not the imperative we have made of it. Since it was created for the purpose of perpetuating the race, it has little or nothing to do with our personal well-being.

Other animals confine the sex act to the propagation of their species. There is absolutely no logical reason to assume that a human being could not live an entirely normal, healthy lifetime without having had sexual intercourse. It is therefore apparent that the need for sexual gratification is an artificial quotient which has been imposed upon our psychic life through the process of socialization. Consequently, it is possible that many people in the modern world have developed psychological problems who might otherwise have been perfectly healthy and happy had not the necessity for being "sexually active" been imposed upon them. Their problems are the result of a failure to live up to the expectations of society rather than because of a lack of sexual stimulation from another body.

It is now clear that the insatiable appetite for sexual gratification which has our society in its grip is the result of an artificially implanted idea. Freudian psychology and its off-shoots have rationalized that abstinence from sexual activity is equivalent to repression. Repression, they have concluded, is a negative attitude which must be eliminated since it is the cause of psychological illness. Therefore, one can only prove to the world that he or she is not psychologically maladjusted by becoming "sexually active." There is no alternative in this rational trap.

But history reveals that each time a society becomes obsessed with sex there is an increase in sexually transmitted diseases. From descriptions given, it seems that gonorrhea was the disease which plagued the Children of Israel. During the Middle Ages, when sexual promiscuity was common, syphilis raised its ugly head to become the scourge of the day. Today, AIDS, Herpes, Warts, Clamidia and other diseases have been added. The unfortunate side of it is that they all have serious consequences for the off-spring of infected parents.

Perhaps it is time we stopped to examine the situation and ask ourselves what we really want from life. Could it be that, like little children, we are in trouble with Mother Nature because we have been trying to fool her by trying to get around her Laws? If so, it is obvious that we have failed. The question now raised is, do we want things to continue as they are or do we want something better? Are we going to go on messing up our lives and those of our children or are we going to look for more satisfactory alternatives?

After due consideration of the facts before us, it begins to look as though the safest form of sexual activity is that of masturbation. It is certainly the most effective way to avoid unwanted pregnancies as well as sexually transmitted disease. Furthermore, if we can take the reports of sexologists seriously, it is also consistently the most pleasurable and therefore the most satisfactory form of sexual expression. This seems to be true for both men and women.

In recent years some women have begun to free themselves from the sense of shame and guilt which religion and a male-dominated society have imposed upon them regarding their "sexuality." Many have attained freedom because they have dared to seek sexual release without benefit of the male penis. In general, although modern psychology has regarded masturbation in the male as acceptable (if not ideal), it has regarded the same practice in women to be a sign of psychological maladjustment.

Recent reports, however, seem to prove the contrary to be true. It has been found that the anxiety level of those women who rely solely upon **vaginal stimulation by the penis** is much higher than for those women who are, "self-sufficient."[9] According to the *Kinsey Report*, "The techniques of masturbation and petting are more specifically calculated to effect orgasm than the techniques of coitus itself.[10]

Ninety-five percent of the women who responded to the questions circulated for the *Hite Report* stated that they had been raised with the idea that sex was bad. Some reported that they had specifically been warned against masturbation on the grounds that it would cause them to go insane. Nevertheless, 82-percent said that they masturbated. Of these, 95-percent reported that they were able to achieve orgasm easily. In overcoming the inhibitions surrounding "self-love," many women have found a sense of fulfillment they had not known before. Some expressed it as a sense of "self-determination," of "human dignity," or of "power and liberation," and "of control over her own life." [11]

It is interesting to note that these are the same conditions needed in embarking on the path to enlightenment. When Jesus said that we should love our neighbor as ourselves, it is obvious that he believed self-love to be of primary importance. We now know that it is, psychologically speaking, impossible to love another until we are able to love ourselves. Furthermore, love and respect for ourselves cannot exclude our bodies, which are an integral part of the way in which we express ourselves. Therefore, those men and women who wish to become whole, integrated and self-controlled individuals must first free themselves from their dependency upon others for a sense of well-being. Or, to put it as a Buddhist would, he or she must be free from emotional attachments.

This does not mean that one cannot have relationships. The most successful relationships are those which are contracted between persons who are complete within themselves. Without the psychological hang-ups which interfere with healthy relationships, there is freedom to enjoy one another completely.

The View From Olympus

When one finally discovers the facts about sexual frustrations and psychological hang-ups, he or she inevitably finds that the real concerns are not with sex at all, but with how we feel about ourselves and the way in which we relate to others. This, after all, is the test which determines the level of consciousness we have attained as spiritual beings.

For nearly a hundred years the theme of Freudian psychology has been that, once women overcame their reluctance to having sex on demand by the male, the psychological problems which debilitate us would disappear. But this has not been the case. If anything, our problems have gotten worse. In spite of modern methods of birth control, theoretically giving women the freedom to be as promiscuous as men, we are only becoming more acutely aware of them. Gradually we seem to be coming to the realization that sexual freedom does not equate with psycho/spiritual freedom. It cannot ease the pain of mental anguish.

At last, like the Prodigal Son, we seem to be coming to the awareness that we are not our bodies after all. And that, because we are not our bodies, we cannot be sexual beings. We are instead psycho/spiritual beings inhabiting physical bodies. Therefore, the true satisfactions in life can only be found in the realm of the Mind. There is no substitute for self-understanding or awareness of the soul (psyche) and spirit within us.

When one's consciousness has been raised, one becomes a different person. The higher the level of consciousness and the longer it remains at a high level, the less one is in need of sex as a means of releasing the tensions of pent-up emotional stress. When this goal has been reached, as the Ancient Wisdom says, one has crossed over from a life of the physical world of darkness and ignorance into the world of spiritual/mental enlightenment. This is the meaning of the ancient "Cross of Light" which Constantine redesignated the "Cross of Christ" ... the Pauline Christian sacrificial god.

The male chauvinists (as opposed to modern enlightened men) have long seen something ludicrous in what they have called "women's intuition." They have been of the opinion that logic is superior to the emotions, which they have imagined are the basis of intuition. Therefore, they have perceived themselves to be superior to women since they believed themselves to be logical. But this is now found to have been an illusion. The problem is that they have confused insensitivity with logic.

When the mists have cleared and male logic is seen in the light of reason, it becomes apparent that men are no more logical than women and that intuition is as much masculine as it is feminine. It is feminine because it requires passiveness in order for it to be activated. It is masculine because it is empowering.

What is needed today is recognition that men and women are made of the same stuff: flesh and blood, soul and spirit. We must learn that we were created as partners to share the responsibilities as well as the pleasures of life together in cooperation with one another. There should be no doubt in our minds that because of our biological differences men and women have different ways of perceiving life. But instead of allowing these differences to drive a wedge between us, we should learn to appreciate them and use them to enhance our relationships.

The structure and hormonal differences between us give the male a tendency to be more aggressive than the female. On the other hand, the female tends to be more nurturing than the male. Yet biology confirms what the Ancient Wisdom has always taught: we inhabit androgynous bodies. Bodies, which may be decidedly male or female, also carry the residual characteristics of the opposite sex.

These same characteristics are carried over to the psyche as well. We are both god and goddess, whether we inhabit a male or female body. Therefore, we cannot become psychologically balanced until we allow the characteristics of the opposite sex to be expressed naturally.

The psychological problems which are revealed in therapy, those which seem to be evidenced in our sexual behavior, are only the symptoms of problems in other areas. Reduced to their basic elements, all of our psychological problems can be shown to be related to an inability to fully express either the male aggressiveness or the female nurturing qualities within ourselves. This is true whether we are boys, girls, men or women.

Aggressiveness is a necessary ingredient in determining our self-esteem. It is in the ability to be aggressive or assertive that we establish our integrity as human beings. Our self-respect is determined by our ability to maintain a sense of equality with others by feeling capable of surviving physically, emotionally, and mentally on our own. But, while the masculine quality of assertiveness is needed to establish ourselves as whole persons, the feminine quality of nurturing is necessary to make our relationships with one another work.

We must learn to distinguish between gentleness and weakness. Men and women alike despise weakness but love the gentleness of a mother's touch. Weakness is a lack of control, while gentleness requires discipline. Women have brought the contempt of both men and their children upon themselves because they have lost the ability to make this distinction.

The reason our relationships have failed throughout written history, it is now apparent, is that the masculine and feminine qualities have been separated and exaggerated in the sexes. Men have been expected to be aggressive and not nurturing while women were expected to be nurturing and not aggressive. The twain were never to meet in one individual. However this has created war, not only between the sexes, but within our individual selves as well.

As we begin the healing process, it will be necessary for men to encourage women to be more assertive in establishing their integrity as independently whole persons. Conversely, women must encourage men to express the nurturing side of their natures. This, of course, has begun to happen in some segments of society, but, in order for a real difference to occur, it must become an integral part of our culture.

When this has taken place, it seems possible, we will find that more and more women and men will discover their best friends to be of the opposite sex. Marriage founded upon friendship and the desire to allow each other to express the best that is in him or her is what the male and female relationship is about. And it is this kind of marriage which lasts.

Having children in a marriage of this kind is an experience which is shared as a part of the growth process. Within this framework, families can become what we have always wanted them to be: groups of people who love and support one another so that each becomes the best his or her abilities will allow.

While we are making the transition from the old to the new way of living, we will all tend to have a sense of incompleteness. This sense of lack is an accumulation, not only from the past of this life, but from many past lifetimes. For this reason a great deal of patience and special effort will be required to overcome the effects of the negative input we have all received.

First, adults must seek to heal each other of the wounds which were inflicted upon them by a confused and violent society. Secondly, we must learn to provide for the emotional needs of our children so that they will not reach adulthood with an emotional deficit. Both little boys and little girls need to have their sense of integrity established by being allowed to be assertive while, at the same time, being validated with parental nurturing. The lack of these two elements does not automatically disappear when we reach adulthood. What is lacking in childhood will continue to be lacking in adulthood and must be satisfied before we can become completely whole and able to function at the peak of our potential.

But as long as we continue to believe that the natural order of human beings is different from that of the rest of Nature, we will be trapped in the world of violence which competition creates. If women want to be respected by men they must first have respect for themselves by giving up belief in the myth that without a man they are nothing. They must be willing to take full responsibility for themselves, without competing with men or each other. It is not necessary to be tough in order to be independent.

We live under conditions in which those in power

function on the lowest levels of consciousness. As has been shown, male-dominated religion and psychology recognize only those levels of consciousness which pertain to our animal nature. They deny the existence of our god-consciousness. Therefore, those who are the victims of human animal nature must set a new precedent and take responsibility for their own lives by creating a separate, alternative life. But it must be one based upon a higher way of living ... by cooperation instead of competition.

The first step toward independence and self-respect is to cease competing with one another. The reality of the situation dictates that, before there can be equality in the male-dominated world, women must become economically independent. Since the power in our society is based upon economics, women will never have equality until this is accomplished. It is against human nature to give up an advantage when everything is going one's way. Therefore, the establishment cannot be expected to change of its own free will. Change will only come when women create their own economic base by pooling resources and by working together.

In their own back-handed way, modern men seem to be begging women to assert themselves and set the standards for peaceful cohabitation. They cannot make a complete transition until women take the initiative. Previously women have been powerless to take on this responsibility because they had no economic power. But they do have the resources at their disposal now and, with careful planning and cooperation with one another and with enlightened men, they can build an economic base for themselves separate from the male-dominated, greed-oriented corporate world.

The View From Olympus

Incidentally, what has been proposed for women should also be applied to the problems of the so-called "minority races" and followed by men who see the evils of the dog-eat-dog world of large corporations. The economy of the United States was built by the cooperative efforts of various family and ethnic groups who pooled their resources to accomplish what they could not do alone. Things began to fall apart only when people began to compete with one another.

In order to regain the respect of men, women must develop a new set of values based upon the Laws of nature and their own self-respect. Men are contemptuous of women who sell themselves cheaply by making themselves readily available to be used as sex objects. Although there is no excuse for such behavior, this is the message that is sent when men say that women ask to be raped when they dress in a manner which suggests that they think of themselves as sex objects.

Men are not bad because they exploit women and children. They exploit women and children because they are undisciplined and because women allow them to do so. Like a spoiled child who acts out of selfish desire, men are sending the signal that they want women to impose discipline upon them. They have been contemptuous of women because women have had contempt for themselves. It is their self-contempt, in turn, that causes women to allow themselves and their children to be used.

Women must stand up on their own two feet and take back control of their lives. They must regain their self-respect and demand the right to sit in the councils that determine the destiny of the human race. But, before they can make an impact upon the decision-making processes of government, they must take possession of one-half of all the seats of government through the electoral process. Without the nurturing quality of the feminine principle which women can bring to government, there can be no peace on earth.

✦

The View From Olympus

XII

Keys To The Mystery

We human beings are a curious lot in many ways. But nothing makes us more curious than a good mystery. And the greatest mystery of all is life itself. For many thousand years mankind has expended untold amounts of time and energy in an attempt to solve this mystery. From time to time the veil has been lifted and the pieces of the puzzle assembled to form a complete picture, only to have them scattered and the cloud of ignorance descend once more.

But the race consciousness is now at a point of evolution in which the veil is once more beginning to lift and the pieces of the puzzle beginning to fall into place. Many of these pieces have been hidden in the myths and legends of the past awaiting the time when our consciousness would reach the level at which we could recognize them.

Ever since Western people began to translate the ancient myths into modern languages, they have judged them as literature and failed to recognize the meaning which they conveyed. For the most part, tales of the gods and their escapades have been viewed as the creations of primitive, ignorant people who had little understanding of the nature of the universe or the meaning of life. But the religions in which these myths were created were not called "Mystery Religions" for no reason. They derived their name from the fact that the gods and creatures who populated them were symbolic representations of the Mystery of Life.

Much study has been made into the symbols of the ancients. But the emphasis has been placed upon cataloging and categorizing rather than interpreting them. Since it has been assumed that the ancients were ignorant, the symbols have usually been interpreted in the simplest, most literal way. However, when we give the ancients credit for being intelligent, knowledgeable people, we discover that they may have known more about the nature of the universe and our place in it than we yet know. When interpreted properly, it is discovered that these symbols reveal the story of the creation of the universe as well as mankind's place in the unfolding saga.

They not only explain the details of the over-all plan, but get down to the specifics of who and what we are, where we have been, and where we are going. The roles of the gods and creatures of Mythology are the depictions of the various aspects of our nature and show us what to do about them in order to become perfected beings or gods.

Psychologists were probably the first to recognize the significance of these symbols as a means by which to give us a better understanding of our unconscious minds. But, because they failed to recognize the higher levels of consciousness, they were unable to gain a full understanding and therefore misinterpreted many of the symbols.

As previously mentioned, Odysseus and Hercules are prototypes of mankind. Their adventures are used to describe the journey of the soul on the earth plane. The tales describe the kinds of tasks which must be accomplished as one experiences life under the influence of the vibrations of various houses of the zodiac through many incarnations.

Jesus used this method of teaching in what Christians call the "Parables." The story of the Prodigal Son draws a graphic picture of the state of mankind when it lives on the level of its passions. He describes this state as that of "feeding with the pigs," or appetites.

As mentioned earlier, the Greek myth of Eros and Psyche, which psychotherapists have used to describe the unconscious mind, is a means of describing our nature symbolically. But psychology has painted a distorted picture of our true selves because it has denied the existence of the most important part of our nature, the spiritual/mental or higher self. When the whole myth of Eros and Psyche is told, it reveals a more comprehensive and meaningful story of who we are and what our purpose in life was meant to be.

Aphrodite, the Olympian goddess of love and beauty, was the lover of Ares, the god of war, courage, and strength. They became the parents of Eros, the god of altruistic love. But Eros remained a child because, as Themis, the goddess of law and justice, informed them, he was alone. Soon thereafter Anteros was born, and Eros quickly began to grow and increase in size and strength.

As previously indicated, Anteros is the god of

passions, the antipathy of love. This aspect of the story seems to illustrate the point that we do not grow under ideal conditions. It is the struggle with opposites, or adversity, which creates the conditions of growth.

Psyche is the youngest of three mortal sisters. As a part of the evolution of our consciousness, the two older sisters represent the lower levels of consciousness: the emotions. In her original state, Psyche represents the Conscious Mind.

If we place our three characters Eros, Psyche and Anteros in the context of the three human aspects of body, soul and spirit, we find that Anteros represents the body, Psyche the soul, and Eros the spirit or Higher Mind.

The palace in which they dwell is the human body (the "Temple of God"). At first Psyche lives in the palace content with the nocturnal visits of her husband, Eros (who comes when her mind is not engaged with the mundane affairs of life). But eventually her sisters, Doubt and Suspicion (who are jealous of her), begin to plant suggestions in her mind to make her question what kind of man her husband is. For all she knows, he could be an evil, ugly monster since she has never seen him. But, when fear finally drives her to attempt to get a look at him (examine him with her rational mind), he leaves her saying that "love cannot dwell with suspicion."[1]

After this, Life (Aphrodite) gives her the task of proving herself worthy of her spiritual spouse, the Higher Mind. She is told that she can only be reunited with her husband by "dint of industry and diligence."[2] She is then given the task of sorting out the various aspects of life according to their nature. But because she is overwhelmed by the task, Eros sends her help in the form of little ants, or ideas, which sort them out for her. However, this is not considered satisfactory by Life because we do not learn by thinking. We learn by living through the experiences of life without taking short cuts.

So Aphrodite, or Life, is not satisfied that Psyche has garnered her knowledge legitimately. Therefore, she gives her the task of gathering pieces of golden fleece from the backs of sheep found feeding without a shepherd. Since sheep represent innocence and the golden fleece signifies spirituality or Higher Awareness, her task is to gather spiritual awareness from a state of innocence or unadulterated truth. This time the river (of life) god comes to her aid. She learns her lessons immersed in the stream of life and the experiences accumulated in the process of daily living.

Finally she is sent to Persephone, goddess of the underworld or the subconscious mind, to bring back a box containing beauty. She is instructed not to open the box, but Psyche's curiosity gets the better of her. Thinking that some of the beauty in the box would make her more attractive to her husband, she opens the box and finds nothing but "a Stygian sleep" (subconsciousness) which takes possession of her.

But once again Eros comes to her rescue. This time he goes to the heights of heaven to plead for her life, and the gods give their consent. Eros (Higher Mind) then sends Mercury (Conscious Mind) to bring Psyche up to the heavenly realm to meet with the assembly of the gods. When she arrives, Mercury offers her a cup of ambrosia and tells her to "drink and be immortal." When she drinks of the heavenly ambrosia (Spiritual Water, Soma, Homa, Wine), she becomes permanently wedded to her husband, Eros, or the Higher Mind.

Keys To The Mystery

The Psyche in each of us is in a somnambulistic or subconscious state until we are awakened by our higher consciousness through the help of our Conscious Minds. In the awakened state, the contents of the Sub-conscious Mind are no longer hidden.

The meaning we should get from this mythical tale is that our true self is the soul and our true mate, Higher Consciousness. Life has placed us on earth in physical bodies in order for us to learn from experience. We must earn the right to be united with the Higher Self by overcoming the attraction of the appetites (ruled by Anteros) which are so appealing but are not what they seem. Instead of enhancing our lives, they dull our senses and cause us to fall asleep or to forget who we really are and what our true goal in life is meant to be. But the Higher Self is ever alert and working to make us worthy of godhood. When we turn the Conscious Mind toward the Higher Mind and seek guidance from it, we become carried up to the higher mental/spiritual realms of existence.

This is the mystery which all of the ancient religions contained. When we are once more united with our Higher Self, we become fully aware and as one with the gods of the mental/spiritual world. As such, we become masters of our own fates in the manner of the gods.

About twenty-six hundred years ago, the Hebrew prophet Jeremiah prophesied that there would come a time in which there would be no need for one neighbor to teach another about God or the source of our being. Everyone, he said, would have this knowledge in his or her own heart without the mediation of a spiritual teacher: a priest, rabbi, minister or guru. At about the same time, the Oracle at

The View From Olympus

Delphi proclaimed that everyone should "Know thyself and know God."

Today, it seems to many that the time is not far away in which this prophecy will be fulfilled. Science, in the past four hundred and fifty years since Copernicus reawakened our interest in scientific knowledge, has done much to reveal the nature of the universe. Now, in recent years, we are becoming more acutely aware of our own nature and of our relationship to the Universal Scheme. Recently, the means by which to attain self-awareness has begun to proliferate in various places. In the fields of the physical sciences, philosophy, psychology, economics, politics, and the health professions, as well as in a few religious circles, there are many who have come to recognize the interconnectedness of all things.

It is now seen that we are not only inextricably connected to one another but to the environment in which we live as well. Furthermore, it is also realized that the earth, our home, is integrally connected to all of the other heavenly bodies. More importantly, it is accepted that the energy which motivates all of creation is Universal Mind from which we cannot be separated. As a part of this Universal Mind, we are a part of the essence of the source of all being which some call God. Therefore, by coming to understand ourselves, we automatically arrive at an understanding of God. Thus, it should be evident that self-understanding cannot be fully attained without an understanding of the universe as a whole and that, by the same token, an understanding of the universe is not complete without an understanding of ourselves.

Commenting on the subject of scientific innovations in *The Philosophy of Physics* (1936),[3] Max Planck states that it rarely happens that the old guard is converted to new ideas. The changes occur by accretion as the new generation grows up accepting them as familiar.

For many years a number of Westerners have toyed with the ideas of astrology and reincarnation but have been afraid to commit themselves for fear of being ridiculed or, worse yet, black-balled by the establishment of their chosen professions. But since the revolution of the 1960's this has changed rather quickly. While experimenting with drugs, many young people discovered dimensions in their unconscious minds they did not understand. Since the drug experience only raised questions and did not provide answers, some began to look for answers elsewhere. Many found their way to Eastern religions which have not forgotten their roots in the Ancient Wisdom.

Among the beliefs to be found in these religions are the beliefs in Karma, Reincarnation and Astrology. This eventually led to an increase in the study of these subjects in the West. Since the 1960's there has been a steady increase in the acceptance of the spiritual and psychological implications in these subjects.

In her book, *The Aquarian Conspiracy*,[4] Marilyn Ferguson deals with phenomena which she says constitutes a "paradigm shift." This phenomena represents a change or shift in our attitudes from the old orthodox attitudes which are contrary to the natural order of the universe to a new attitude of harmony with Universal Order. Enumerated are many changes occurring in the way in which we perceive life and deal with its problems. But several changes have occurred since the publication of her book which are of significance.

One of the most recent changes has taken place in

the field of psychology and involves new techniques in psychotherapy. Grounded in an ancient belief still held by at least two billion people, mostly in the East, it seeks to deal with problems in the present life which have their beginnings in past lives. Included in this new approach is the science of astrology which, while dealing with symbols or archetypes, also embraces **Reincarnation**. But because these ideas have been denied for so long, they have been slow to be accepted among the general population.

In his long career, Carl Jung, the Swiss psychiatrist, dared to explore many areas of an occult (hidden) nature. His research eventually led him to the study of religion, both Western and Eastern, as well as the mythology of many cultures. While some of his former students believe he had a strong leaning in favor of the belief in reincarnation and the science of astrology, he did not make this publicly known.

It has been suggested that he failed to give much time and effort to these subjects because of the negative reaction he received from his colleagues. His theories of the "Archetypes" and the "Collective Unconscious"[5] were never really tolerated by them. Had he attempted to incorporate reincarnation and astrology into his system, it might have cost him all of his credibility.

Now, however, his theories are beginning to be vindicated by some of his students who have, without hesitation or embarrassment, added to his theories a third, which they call "Past Life Complex."[6] The tide seems to be changing and the perceptions of many people altering in order to accommodate these ideas. Perhaps this is due to the accretion of which Planck spoke.

Keys To The Mystery

There is a new system of psychotherapy emerging which views the human psyche in a holographic way. The move appears to be away from the old, materialistic, power consciousness and a self-centered perception of reality, toward one which views life in the context of cooperative relationships. The belief in reincarnation and astrology are being taken seriously for the first time in the modern era. This new openness replaces the skepticism of science and the orthodoxy of Western religion in a similar way to which the new physics has replaced Newtonian physics.[7]

In recent years there has been a growing number of therapists who have come to recognize the validity of a variety of approaches to the various levels of consciousness. Among them are: biofeedback, guided fantasy, waking dreams, dream therapy, Zen and Yoga. To them may now be added reincarnation and astrology. Roger Woolger suggests that we are on the verge of making a radical change in our understanding of the human personality. The new psychology may include the soul of mankind as an integral part of the self.[8] Although the idea has long been denied, this has always been the meaning of the term "psyche."

At this juncture in the process of making changes in the way in which we perceive ourselves, there are many who remain skeptical of the new forms of therapy. But Dr. Morris Netherton's experience has proved that "Past Life Therapy" does not depend upon proof of reincarnation. It works effectively whether or not the patient believes in it.[9]

To understand the new therapies, one must be aware that the personality is not a single unit. It is complex. Like the layers of an onion, there are many levels of the self. These layers must be peeled back and examined in the process of self-discovery. While Jung used dream analysis to accomplish this end, the new techniques utilize "stories." These stories are the apparent recollections of events and circumstances of past lives which emerge from the unconscious mind in the process of self-discovery.

Most people who undergo Past Life Therapy soon become convinced of the value of the process. First, because the person has a sense of recognition of the personality(ies) who surfaces(surface) from the past. There is a feeling of dimly knowing that the other self(selves) has(have) always cast a shadow in the background of the unconscious mind. Secondly, it almost always elicits the feeling that the life of the past personality is continued in the present. It is as though one is attempting to finish what was left undone in the other lifetime(s).[10]

From among his patients, Woolger provides examples to illustrate this point. He talks of:

1. *A woman unable to bear children in this life due to guilt over having abandoned an infant in a time of famine in a past life.*

2. *A man who recalls sexual humiliation by older women while a servant in their employ. The result: a withdrawal into homosexual relationships.*

3. *A woman who has severe pre-menstrual cramps recalls a painful death in childbirth in a tribal life.*[11]

Woolger's own first experience with past life recollection is worth mentioning here because of its connection to the history of the Christian Church which, along with Islam, has dominated the Piscean Age worldwide. This recalled past life placed him in the middle of the Albigensian Crusade. The Albigensians were Cathars who lived in the town of Albi in Southern France. The Cathars were a heretical sect which flourished in Italy and France from the thirteenth to the fifteenth centuries. The branch in France was the largest and most prosperous.

The Cathari were very industrious people and, through their industry, had developed the most highly civilized community in all of Europe. It is believed by some scholars that they did not originate within the Christian religion but derived from Manichaeism, which had its beginnings in the Middle East as a branch of Mazdeanism. While they included some of the New Testament in their literature, they regarded Christ to be a spiritual being (or spiritual state of mind) as did most other Gnostics.

They embraced the dualism of Mazdeanism (of good and evil), believed in transmigration of the soul (reincarnation), were vegetarian, practiced celibacy and forbade marriage, except for the few who wished to have children. The ethical teachings were of the highest order, but the asceticism placed it beyond the reach of the average person. However, it has been suggested that the reason the religion grew and spread so rapidly and had such a stronghold on converts was discontent with the corruption and oppression of the Roman Church.[12]

When the Church was unable to persuade the French King and the local Count to suppress the heresy in their region, the Pope organized a crusade (the first) and guaranteed a free pass to heaven without the need to stop off in purgatory to those who participated in the slaughter of the heretics. This was sufficient incentive to amass an army capable of slaughtering more than a half million of these innocent, peace-loving people. The property of the heretics was confiscated by the Church, which eventually came to own a third of all Europe by this and other means.

In his past life recall, Woolger found himself in the midst of the terrible massacre of these people, who were tortured, hacked to pieces and burned on huge pyres. He believes that he participated in the massacres as one of the mercenaries hired by the Church. But after one of the sieges he had a change of heart and deserted the army to join the heretics. Eventually he too was burned at the stake.[13]

Any doubts regarding the validity of the belief in Karma are dispelled in the process of Past Life Therapy. It sometimes appears that not everyone pays for his or her misdeeds in the present lifetime. Most everyone knows of someone who has lived an entire lifetime breaking the rules of morality and ethics and who has died without seeming to have paid for these misdeeds. But as one learns more about reincarnation and past lives, another picture begins to emerge. One of the things discovered by getting in touch with multiple past lives is that there seem to be patterns that alternate between personalities of different types. A spend-thrift becomes a miser; a prostitute becomes a celibate; life as a slave owner is followed by a life as a slave, and an adventurer may become a recluse in another lifetime.[14] Just as we seem to learn by experiencing the opposites in a single lifetime, the same seems to hold true from one lifetime to another. Within this framework, whatever was thrown into imbalance in one life is balanced in another. The slave owner who was cruel to his slaves in one lifetime will find himself on the receiving end of cruelty in another.

It is also found that we seem to travel in groups so that we can work out the Karma created in a past life or lives. The parent in one lifetime may be the child in the next in a reversal of roles. The sexes may also be reversed so that a husband in one lifetime will be the wife in another. There also appear to be large groupings which include friends and business partnerships.

For years psychologists have used hypnosis as a means of getting at things hidden and difficult to bring up from the unconscious mind. But this has some disadvantages. For one, it places the patient under the control of another person and therefore out of control of his or her own mind. Secondly, the hypnotist is in a position to distort the material dredged up by giving inadvertent suggestions which could result in wrong conclusions. As the importance of free will and individual responsibility become more apparent, this method seems less appealing.

Netherton and others use a system which gets at the unconscious mind without disturbing the consciousness. The patient is therefore in control at all times. The method used is to observe the patient's frequently used phrases. These are found, like the Freudian Slip, to be clues to the problems with which the unconscious mind is attempting to deal. By being guided to focus on a frequently used phrase, the patient is able to uncover the source of the problem. This is accomplished by having the patient repeat the phrase and describe the feelings and images which are conjured up in the process. A story gradually evolves which reveals the source of the problem.[15]

The purpose of Past Life Therapy is to get at things which interfere with a patient's ability to live a full and useful life when the cause of the disturbance cannot be found in the present life experience. In the past twenty years, Past Life Therapy has revealed that most therapy is concentrated in three major areas of the life cycle: pre-natal, birth, and death. During these three critical periods in one's life, the record player in the unconscious mind is activated and the traumas of past lives replayed.[16]

The unborn child, although not yet conscious, is greatly affected by the environment surrounding the mother. What she says, thinks, and feels and what is said and done around her have a direct effect upon the unborn child. This includes the circumstances surrounding conception.

The birth trauma is a major event in one's life.[17] The stimulation it produces awakens memories of past life trauma. As soon as the infant is born, therefore, it begins to try to deal with the unfinished business of past lives, the memory of which was stimulated both by pre-natal experience and the birth process.

Many of the traumas with which people must deal are related to the death in a past life and the circumstances surrounding it. When that death came suddenly, the unresolved parts of that life are carried over into the next, and one tries, unconsciously, to solve or complete them in the present. It seems that one of the reasons that death is such an agonizing ordeal for so many people is that, just as birth may trigger memories of past lives or deaths, death may trigger a replay of past deaths and the unfinished business surrounding both the past and the present life which is passing.[18]

Some psychological problems resulting from past life traumas which have responded well to treatment are listed by Woolger. They are: insecurity and fear of abandonment, depression and a lack of energy, phobias or irrational fears, sadomasochism, guilt and martyr complexes, eating disorders and fear of poverty, accident proneness and violent behavior, family conflicts, sexual problems and abuse, marital problems, and chronic physical problems.[19]

The discoveries made in the course of Past Life Therapy should give us reason to pause and consider the manner in which we reproduce our kind. It seems plain from this information that, if we truly wish to have peace on earth, we must begin by taking responsibility for the way in which we bring children into the world and the kinds of environments we provide for them.

Violence has never been the cure for violence, and a child conceived by rape or incest, under maso-sadistic circumstances, or by unwed teenagers should not be forced into the world to deal with further violence from a lack of proper care. It now appears evident that most of us have had to deal with mankind's inhumanity to its own in many past lives as well as in the present life. The result of this inhuman behavior toward one another is the root cause of the problems with which we are saddled and from which we are struggling to be free.

Therefore, it seems obvious that, if we sincerely want to live in peace with one another, we must start by bringing our children into the world in a peaceful environment, one in which the pregnant mother is prepared for her role in a loving, caring and supportive surrounding that has been carefully planned and prepared.

No feeling person would condone abortion as a first line of defense against unwanted pregnancies. But any reasonable person can see that it is far better that a fetus be aborted (within a reasonable period of time) than for it to be brought into the world to face abuse. In this supposed civilized world of ours in which the procreative act has become a form of recreation, pregnancy and child birth are given a low priority. But it is imperative that they be taken seriously and that the child be planned and cared for in a manner to minimize psychological and physical trauma.

Dr. Gladys McGarey of Phoenix, Arizona,[20] co-founder and physician in the A.R.E. Medical Clinic, tells a story of how her mind was changed regarding abortion. The story is really that of a patient who was the mother of a four year old girl. While chatting of this and that during lunch one day, her daughter suddenly announced that the last time she had been a little girl she had had a different mommy. With this announcement, she began to speak in another language.

Before the mother had recovered from the first shock, the child continued by saying that that had not really been the last time. The last time, she said, she was four inches long in the tummy of her present mother. But, she continued, her daddy was not ready to marry her mother, so she went away. But she came back.

What the child had described was an abortion the mother had had earlier. She had gotten pregnant two years before she and the girl's father were ready for marriage and a family. When four months pregnant, the mother decided to get an abortion. What the child had revealed was that the same entity whose first body had been aborted had returned when the parents were prepared to care for a child.

As has been indicated, astrology presupposes the belief in reincarnation. Therefore, a psychological therapy based upon astrology will of necessity occur with the understanding that reincarnation is an integral part of the treatment. As with modern religion, there are two kinds of astrology. They are the exoteric and esoteric, or the outer and inner forms. Exoteric astrology is found in newspaper columns all over the country. It is the kind used to make predictions for those people who prefer to have others do their thinking for them.

Esoteric astrology, on the other hand, is based upon the Ancient Wisdom and acts as a map of one's potential and the kinds of experiences one is likely to encounter in life. This map (horoscope) is utilized by those who understand its true purpose as an aid to self-understanding. By gaining knowledge about oneself in this manner, one is able to take control of his or her life instead of drifting as flotsam and jetsom on the sea of life as others do. Nor is one a pawn at the mercy of the whims of a capricious God.

From an in-depth study of the subject, it is learned that the purpose of astrology is to allow the Sun (lifeforce, Christ or Eros) to come into our consciousness. This is accomplished by the experience we gain through relationships with others on the global, national, family and personal levels.[21] The horoscope may be seen as a mandala of the individual's potential. Its circular form represents wholeness. The twelve "spokes" which radiate from the center signify the qualities (signs) and areas (houses) through which one must pass before one's individual wholeness is realized.[22]

Most astrologers discover that it is not difficult to predict events in the lives of those who are unconscious of who they are but almost impossible to do so for those who are spiritually awake. Thus it can be seen that those who live their lives passively and without direction are at the mercy of outside influences, including that of the stars. The enlightened person, on the other hand, operates under the Law of Free Will and is therefore unpredictable.

Both astrology and psychology are engaged in a similar undertaking: to help others gain self-understanding. Psychotherapy and astrotherapy, when properly handled, are the means by which one can be rid of the mental debris which gets in the way of true self-understanding and enlightenment. But psychology stops short of understanding the spiritual side of our nature which is revealed in those who have become enlightened.[23]

Alice Howell, an astrologer, has broadened her skill in astrological counseling by adding Jungian psychology to her interpretations. She believes that the psyche is influenced by universal archetypes in the same way the sun is orbited by and interacts with the planets in the solar system.[24]

Liz Greene and Howard Sasportas, on the other hand, are Jungian psychotherapists who also employ astrotherapy. They too have seen the advantage of incorporating the two systems into one. Furthermore, their findings are in agreement with Past Life Therapy.

This is especially true in regard to past life trauma. But they go one step further to find that, based upon their experience with astrology, these replayings from past lives are the basis for certain expectations which one brings into a new incarnation. These expectations are mapped out in the horoscope. What one expects in the way he or she will relate to the mother will be shown in the placement of the Moon and its aspects. The sign and aspects of the Sun in one's chart indicate the pre-programmed picture of the way in which the relationship with the father will be.[25]

Much of what happens in a lifetime stems from these pre-set expectations which are activated at the time of birth. Thus it can be seen that astrotherapy goes a step further than Past Life Therapy by itself in that it credits the incarnating soul with having the choice or lack of choice in the circumstances of birth. It seems that a soul which has not started on the path of enlightenment is not very choosy about the circumstances of its next life. It will take whatever it can get. On the other hand, one who is on the path will choose the circumstances of the next life very carefully in order to insure having the opportunity for optimal spiritual growth and development.

Traditional psychology has had the tendency to blame the parents for the psychological problems that develop in a child. But psychological astrology places at least some of the blame on the individual. Many of the problems between the child and parent are seen as stemming from the way in which the child interprets the actions of the parent. These interpretations, it is now believed, are perceptions which come from inborn beliefs and/or expectations which are formed at or before birth.[26]

Psychological astrology sees the birth chart as a map which depicts the "archetypal conditioning and expectations" of the child. Since these were formed before birth, it places the inborn nature before that of childhood conditioning. Furthermore, childhood experiences are often found to be replays of past life experiences and a continuance of the cycles of trauma which were begun in past lives.

We are dominated by the things which are hidden in our unconscious minds. The astrological horoscope is seen by the practitioners of astrotherapy as a means by which one can become aware of the occult side of his or her mind and thereby overcome its power.

Our attitudes about life and our relationship are shaped by our experiences. The challenge for both therapist and patient is to learn how to neutralize the karmic residue which has been created by our attitudes both in this life and in our past lives. This requires that we make changes in our attitudes toward ourselves and others who may have precipitated those traumatic experiences.

Recently, the separation between the treatment of body and mind has begun to disappear as we come to understand the connection between physical illness and our mental attitudes. The new alternative systems of treatment are most evident in fields of natural healing such as Homeopathy, Naturopathy, Chiropractic and Therapeutic Massage.

When the idea that an illness could be caused by disturbances in the unconscious mind first began to become a popular belief, it also became the belief that anyone who suffered from this kind of disease was a malingerer. Furthermore, since malingering was considered a contemptible thing to do, they were punished by friends, family and the medical profession alike. They were given a prescription for a placebo by their doctor and ushered out the door with a gesture of contempt. Unfortunately, it still happens sometimes, even today.

But today the enlightened among us know that all illnesses have their beginnings in the mind. This includes those illnesses which are the result of accidents, since accident proneness is a symptom of mental/emotional problems. It is becoming apparent that the way in which we react to the experiences we have in life and the attitudes we hold in their regard are imprinted on the nervous system. From the nervous system, they are passed on to the tissues, muscles and bones and cause either good health or disease.

The negative attitudes which cause us to take a defensive pose not only distort our posture but cut off the nerve supply to the various organs and tissues of the body. This in turn leads to a lack of ease in the body with the eventual deterioration of the affected part. This is the condition which is called "disease." Thus it can be seen that in order to have a healthy body one must have a healthy mind. This means that the traumatic experiences of the past which have caused us to have negative attitudes about ourselves and others must be brought to the light of the conscious mind and neutralized.

In the 1970's, Dr. Ida Rolph was the first in the field of psychology to become noted for the use of massage as a means of locating the physical manifestation of psychological trauma. She was a pioneer in making the connection between the psyche and physical illness.

More recently, the awareness of the connection between physical and emotional disease has resulted in a new kind of treatment in the field of Chiropractic. While its aim is very similar to that of Dr. Rolph, the new treatment, called "Network Chiropractic" and developed by Dr. Donald Epstein, D.C. of New York, is a gentler procedure. The release of tensions, both physical and emotional, which result from the treatment are described by many as being akin to a religious experience.

There is much that we can do for ourselves. Ever since the feminine principle was subordinated to the male principle by organized religion several thousand years ago, mankind has suffered from a sense of alienation. We have been forced to compete with one another for our survival and, in so doing, have lost trust in one another.

Although it is one of the most important ways we have to validate one another, one of our greatest fears is of touching and being touched by each other. Except when men fight or wrestle, touching other than with a handshake or a pat on the back has become equated with sex and is, therefore, taboo between men. Until the sexual revolution of the 1960's women were allowed a little more leeway. They could hold hands, walk arm in arm or with arms around each other's waists. They could even embrace and kiss each other without being labeled "queer." But if a woman touched a man in any way but with a handshake, she was asking to be ravished.

For a long time, in the minds of males, all touching has been meant to be a prelude to sexual intercourse. Before birth control, many wives avoided showing affection to their husbands by means of touching out of fear of arousing their sexual passions at an inopportune time. Now that birth control is widely available, women too have learned to suppress the desire to be touched affectionately. They willingly restrict touching to the purpose of greeting others after long absences and to sexual arousal and intercourse. In using the procreative act as a means by which to experience the touch of another human being, many modern women have lost their gentle, maternal feelings.

Perhaps it is time to give the feminine principle a chance to bring back some balance into our lives. For many years men have laughed at women for expressing a need to be loved for themselves and not just for their bodies. But they have done both sexes an injustice, for they have repressed a part of themselves which has a need to be expressed. We can live without sex, but we cannot live without love!

When the procreative act came under the control of the male, sex became politicized. It became associated with power and eventually became the measure of one's worth. For the man it meant the right to control the lives of others (their wives and children, employees and political constituents). For the woman it meant being able to satisfy her husband's lust, being a good housekeeper and mother. In that order.

Since men have controlled the economy, women's survival has depended upon being able to catch a financially secure husband. Because there has always been more women than men, this has placed women in the position of competing with one another. While their survival depended upon catching a man who could support them financially, their power and prestige (and women need it the same as men) came from catching the richest, most powerful man.

So, in reality, our society consists of men competing

with men, men in control of women and children, and, finally, women competing with one another for their own welfare and that of their children since, until recently, they were unable to compete with men.

Because a male-dominated society worships power through the control of others, it is difficult for men to accept the possibility that there are other ways of expressing emotion besides through sex and violence. But, when one relies upon power over others for a sense of control, one is always at risk of losing control. There is always someone around who is more powerful. However, when we realize that true power is the power which comes from within in the form of self-control, we no longer have a problem with loving others for themselves rather than for what we can get from them.

Once we have come to this realization, it is possible to relate to others as equals and to see that our own well-being is tied to the well-being of others. Therefore, we can help ourselves by helping others. And we can help others by loving and caring for them without the need for exploitation. One way this can be accomplished is to break down the taboo on touching so that we can touch one another to show our love (agape) rather than for sexual arousal.

Our cousins, the apes, create a bonding between themselves by grooming one another. But, since we do not have coats of fur and can bathe and care for our own bodies, we do not need that kind of grooming. What we do need is the reassurance of a gentle touch which conveys the message, "I love you because you are you."

There is something we can do to form bonds between us and overcome the negative attitude which our society has programmed into us about touching. We can start by doing a lot of the right kind of touching, by giving one another massages. Although Therapeutic Massage requires technical training, there is a kind of massage which friends and family members can give each other that does not take training. There is a comforting, gentle, nurturing, mother's touch which I call the "Gentle Touch Technique." It is far more effective as a means of raising the consciousness than Tantric Yoga and has none of the negative side effects.

In the future, if we are serious about wanting a society in which men, women and children love and support each other, every home will have a massage table or pad in the family room. This may be a commercially built table which costs from $300 to $500 or one which can be easily made with a few pieces of lumber and a little padding at a cost of around $50. It might even be just a pad alone which can be put on the floor and would cost about $15.

As the group members (two or more) speak words of kindness, appreciation and encouragement to the person on the table, one or two members should move the finger tips lightly from head to toe in an orderly, non-threatening manner over the body which is either nude under a sheet or lightly dressed. Ideally, for best results, this should take at least one hour for each person. Everyone in the home should receive a massage from the other members of the household at least once a week. This should become a family ritual activity and religiously observed.

Those who embark upon this new way of relating, which fosters respect and caring for one another, discover that it eventually restores their trust in others.

The side effects of a renewed trust eliminates the need to compete with others. Thus it can be seen that when we are able to make this transition, we no longer traumatize each other. This condition on a grand world scale could conceivably lead to a society which one day would be free of psychosomatic illness. This in turn would allow us to live longer, healthier and more fulfilling lives.

When this has been accomplished, the age of Aquarius will have been ushered in in all its glory, and we will live in a world in which there is peace at last. "And, they shall beat their swords into plowshares, and their spears into pruning hooks; nation shall not lift up sword against nation, neither shall they learn war any more."[27]

✦

The Panoramic View

Science and mysticism agree that the nature of the universe is both holistic and cyclic. Beyond these two points they may agree on certain principles but disagree upon their interpretation. Those points upon which they fail to agree coincide with the fact that, while they are concerned with the same universe, each deals with different aspects.

While science deals with the objective/physical side of the universe, mysticism deals with the subjective/spiritual or motivating force behind the phenomenal world. It is only in recent years that a few modern scientists and mystics have been able to meet and compare notes. As they have met and conferred with open minds, they have recognized that each of them represents the opposite side of the same coin. At this point they are also able to agree upon the true nature of the universe and mankind's integral role in the drama of creation.

While full recognition is yet to be given to the meaning of the cycles of the ages, we believe that there is sufficient evidence provided by history and archaeology as well as myth and legend (the history of prehistory) to form an hypothesis regarding the ages and their meaning to mankind.

The View From Olympus

Prehistoric records reveal that the cycles of the Astrological Ages are an important part of the Ancient Wisdom. This wisdom has been preserved throughout the cycles of the ages both through periods of darkness (the low levels of consciousness) and enlightenment (higher levels of consciousness through which the race has passed in the process of evolution).

As was shown in the chapter on the evolution of consciousness, the ages of the race correspond to the ages of the individual from infancy to old age. But the precession of the ages of the race, which is keyed to the movement of the sun through the constellations in the heavens, is backward. Therefore, for the greater part of the 26,000 year cycle, or the solar year, the consciousness of the race is on the decline instead of on the increase as is the case with the individual.

It is as though two parts of ourselves were swimming in opposite directions. One is going down stream with the flow, taking the way of least resistance in the pleasures of the physical appetites, and the other is swimming up stream toward spiritual awareness and self-control. To represent this condition, the symbol of the Piscean age is designated as a pair of fish swimming in opposite directions. The symbol has been well chosen since it is the age of Pisces which acts as a period of transition between the lowest levels of consciousness and the highest. Thus it can be seen why the Piscean age is perceived to represent the point in which the struggle between the Will and Desire (or Love and Passion; Eros and Anteros) is the strongest.

Only those who allow the Higher Mind to triumph over Passion will have earned the right to incarnate during the Golden Age of Aquarius, which it is believed will occur during the thousand years

The Panoramic View

approximately between 2,500 and 3,500 A.C.E. This is the period in which those who have succeeded in gaining control over the passions of their Lower Mind will be officially joined together with their "Soul Mate," the Higher Mind, in a kind of "Holy Wedlock." They will "honeymoon" on earth, the place where they met and slew the dragon of passion together.

But when the honeymoon is over they will take their place among the gods and set up housekeeping in the realm of Higher Consciousness where they will continue to live and work as co-creators with the creative force as a full-time occupation.

This, dear reader, is *The View From Olympus*.

◆◆

Notes

Chapter I

1. Kuhn, Thomas S. *The Structure of Scientific Revolutions.* Chicago: University Press, 1970.   185.

2. Jones, Roger. *Physics As Metaphor.* New York: New American Library, 1982.   5.

3. Jastrow, Robert. *God and the Astronomers.* New York: W. W. Norton & Co. Inc., 1978.   28.

4. Judeo/Christian Bible (Revised Std) Daniel 12:13.

5. Ibid.   Matthew 16:13-17.

6. Smith, George. *Chaldean Account of Genesis.* Minneapolis: Wizards Book Shelf, 1977.   307.

7. Donnelly, Ignatius. Egerton Sykes, (Ed.) *Atlantis, The Antediluvian World.*   New York: Gramercy Pub., 1949.   2.

8. Ibid.   27.

9. Wooley, C. Leonard. *The Sumerians.*   New York: W.W. Norton, 1965.   27.

10. Smith, George.,   Op. Cit.,   27.

Notes

11. Ibid.   38.

12. Ibid.   43.

13. Donnelley, Ignatius.,   Op. Cit.,   299.

14. Ibid.   303.

15. Smith, George.,   Op. Cit.,   86.

16. Judeo/Christian Bible.   Genisis (Rev. Std) 6:4.

17. Ibid.   9:20.

18. Spence, Lewis.   *The History of Atlantis*.
     University Books, 1968.   26.

19. Budge, E.A. Wallis.   *The Gods of the Eqyptians Vol. I*.
     New York: Dover, 1969.   3.

20. Temple, Robert K.G.   *The Sirius Mystery*.   Rochester,
     Vermont: Destiny Books, 1987.   153-174.

21. Ibid.   20.

22. Brandt, John C. and Stephen P. Maran, Ed.
     The New Astronomy and Space Science Reader.
     San Francisco: W.H. Freeman and Co. 1977.   173.

23. Temple, Robert.,   Op. Cit.,   24.

24. Ibid.   28-30.

25. Budge, E.A. Wallis.   *Osiris and the Eqyptian Resurrection*.
     Vol. I.   New York: Dover, 1973.   389-90.

26. Kaufmann, William J. III.   *Black Holes and Warped
     Spacetime*.   San Francisco: W.H. Freeman. 1979.   20.

27. Griaule, Marcel.   *Conversations With Ogotemmeli*.   London:
     Oxford University Press. 1965.

28. Temple, Robert.,   Op. Cit.,   24.

29. Ibid.   95.

30. Ibid.   74.

The View From Olympus

Chapter II

16. Pennick, Nigel. *The Ancient Science of Geomancy.*
    Sebastopol, CA.   CRCS Publications, 1979.   170.

17. Michell, John.,   Op. Cit.,   103.

18. Pennick, Nigel.,   Op. Cit.,   164.

19. Ibid.   166.

20. Ibid.   170 .

21. Michell, John.,   Op. Cit.,   71.

22. Ibid.   70.

23. Ibid.   60 .

24. Caine, Mary. *The Gastonbury Zodiac.*   Kingston Surrey,
    England: Mary Caine, 1978.

Chapter III

1.   George, Llewellyn. *A to Z Horoscope Maker and Delineator.*
     Los Angeles: Llewellyn Pub., 1954.

2.   Pagan, Isabelle M. *From Pioneer to Poet or the Twelve
     Great Gates.*   London: Theosophical Pub., 1969. IX.

3.   Koval, Barbara. *The Lively Circle, Astrology & Science
     In Our Modern Age.*   San Diego:
     Astro Computing Service, 1981.   15.

4.   Meyer, Michael. *A Handbook For the Humanistic Astrologer.*
     Garden City N.Y.: Anchor Books, 1974.   15.

5.   *Bulfinch's Mythology.* Illustrated by Federico Castellon,
     Garden City, N.Y.: Doubleday & Co., 1948.   14-16.

6.   Plato. *Timaeus and Critias.*   Desmond Lee, Trans.
     Middlesex, England: Penguin Books, 1971.

Notes

7. Cooper, J.C. *An Illustrated Encyclopaedia of Traditional Symbols*. London: Thames & Hudson, 1979. 198.

8. Stone, Merlin. *When God Was a Woman*. New York: Harcourt, Brace, Jovanovich, 1976. 154.

Chapter IV

1. Adams, W. Marsham. *The Book of the Master of the Hidden Places*. Wellingborough, Northamptonshire: (1933) 1980. 72.

2. Judeo/Christian Bible (Rev. Std) Ezekiel 8:14.

3. Breasted, James Henry. *The Conquest of Civilization*. New York: Harper & Bros., 1938. 137.

4. Ibid. 144.

5. Hall, Manly P. *Old Testament Wisdom*. Los Angeles: The Philosophical Research Soc., 1957. 57.

6. Ibid. 157.

7. Ibid. 161-166.

8. Judeo/Christian Bible The Pentateuch (First Five Books).

9. Ibid. Kings 29:34.

10. Pfeiffer, Robert H. *History of New Testament Times*. London: Adam & Charles Black. 1954. 7.

11. Waite, A.E. *The Holy Kabbalah*. Secaucus, N.J.: University Books. n.d. XI.

12. Pfeiffer, Robert H., Op. Cit., 7.

The View From Olympus

Chapter V

1. Judeo/Christian Bible, John, 3:5.

2. Ibid. Mark, 6:11.

3. Ibid. Romans, 1:32.

4. Ibid. II Corinthians, 13:2.

5. Ibid. I Corinthians, 14:34.

6. Ibid. I Timothy, 2:11-12.

7. Ibid. Luke, 10:38-42.

8. Robinson, James M., (Gen. Ed.), *The Nag Hammadi Library.* New York: Harper & Row. 1977. 473.

9. Judeo/Christian Bible, I Corinthians, 11:1-5.

10. Ibid. Matt., 15:3-9.

11. Ibid. Romans, 3:21-25 & 7:6.

12. Ibid. Matt., 5:17-18.

13. Ibid. Matt., 7:1-2.

14. Ibid. Matt., 7:12.

15. Ibid. Luke, 15:11-32.

16. Ibid. Matt., 7:7.

17. Ibid. Romans, 12:1.

18. Ibid. Matt., 12:7.

19. Ibid. I Corinthians, 3:23 & 6:20.

20. Ibid. Matt., 6:6.

21. Ibid. Romans, 9:14-18.

Notes

22. Ibid.   Matt.,   1:1-16.

23. Ibid.   23:9.

24. Zweig, Stefan.   *The Right of Heresy.*   New York: Viking Press.   1936.   97 & 237.

25. Pagels, Elaine.   *The Gnostic Gospels.*   New York: Random House.   1979.   34.

26. Ibid.   35.

27. Judeo/Christian Bible, I Corinthians 16:22.

28. Keeler, Bronson C.   *A Short History of the Bible.* New York: Farrell.   Repub. Health Research.   1965.   88.

29. Bridgwater, William & Elizabeth J. Sherwood. (Ed's.) *The Columbia Encyclopedia.*   New York: Columbia University Press. 2nd Ed.   1950, 1961.

30. Bury, J.B.   *The Cambridge Medieval History.* Cambridge, England: Cambridge Univ. Press.   1924.   9.

31. Ibid.   14.

32. Ibid.   10-11.

33. Dudley, Dean.   *History of the First Council of Nice.* New York: Peter Eckler.   1925.   Reprint. Health Research.   1966.   29-35.

34. Bury, J.B.   *History of the Later Roman Empire.* New York: Dover, 1958.   349.

35. Dudley, Dean.   Op. Cit.,,   23-35.

36. Bury, J.B.   Op. Cit.,,   349.

37. McKay, John P. Bennett, D. Hill & John Buchler. *A History of Western Society.*   Boston: Houghton Mifflin, 1979.   187-188.

38. Jaspers, Carl.   *Plato and Augustine.*   New York: Harcourt Brace Jovanovich.   1962.   77.

39. Ibid.   67 & 80.

40. Castellio, Sabastian.   *Concerning Heretics.*
    New York: Octagon Books, 1965.   12.

41. Ibid.   19.

42. Ibid.   24-25.

43. Ibid.   29.

44. Lea, Henry Charles.   *The History of the Inquisition of the
    Middle Ages, Vol. I.*   New York: Russell & Russell, 1955.   5.

45. Ibid.   9 & 13.

46. Ibid.   32.

47. Ibid.   34.

48. Ibid.   9.

49. Ibid.   42.

50. Keeler, Bronson.,   Op. Cit.,   102.

51. Ibid.   124.

Chapter VI

1.   Judeo/Christian Bible.   Matt.,   5:17.

2.   Ibid.   Acts,   7:22.

3.   Chatterji, J.C.   *The Wisdom of the Vedas.*   Wheaton, Ill:
     Theosophical Pub. 1973.   13.

4.   Law, Dr.   Narendra Nath.   *Age of the Vedas.*
     Calcutta, 1965.   i-iii.

5.   Prabhavananda & Christopher Isherwood.
     How to Know God.   Hollywood:
     Vedanta Press.   1953.   7.

Notes

6. Leeming, Joseph. *Yoga and the Bible*. London: George Allen and Unwin. 1963. 26-27.

7. Chaudhuri, Haridas. *Integral Yoga (The Concept of Harmonies and Creative Living.)* Wheaton, Ill: Theosophical Pub. 1965. 13.

8. Judeo/Christian Bible. Matt., 11:30.

9. Ibid. Luke, 17:20-21.

10. Ibid. Matt., 22:32.

11. Ibid. Luke, 20:36.

12. Chatterji, J.C., Op. Cit., 92.

13. Judeo/Christian Bible. John, 14:12.

14. Ibid. Matt., 6:33.

15. Motoyama, Hiroshi. *Theories of the Chakras*. Wheaton: Theosophical Pub. 1981. 30-31.

16. Chaudhuri, Haridas., Op. Cit.,, 53-58.

17. Easwaran, Eknath. *The Mantram Handbook*. Petaluma, Ca: Nilgiri Press. 1977. 4.

18. Govinda, Lama Anagrika. *Foundations of Tibetan Mysticism*. New York: Samuel Weiser, 1977. 19.

19. Lonq, Max Freedom. *The Huna Code In Religion*. Marina Del Rey, Ca: Devorss, 1965. 45-51.

20. Easwaran, Eknath., Op. Cit., 62.

21. Judeo/Christian Bible. Acts, 2:1-37.

22. Krishna, Gopi. *The Awakeninq of Kundalini*. New York: E.P. Dutton, 1975. VII-XII.

23. Judeo/Christian Bible. Matt., 9:17.

The View From Olympus

Chapter VII

1. Goddard, Dwight. *Was Jesus Influenced By Buddhism?* Thetford, Vermont. 1927.

2. Rutherford, Ward. *Pythaqoras, Lover of Wisdom.* Wellingborough, Northamptonshire: The Aquarian Press, 1984. 24-34.

3. Furneaux, Rupert. *The Other Side of the Story.* London: Casell & Co. Ltd., 1953. 20.

4. Judeo/Christian Bible. II Timothy, 2:3.

5. Ibid. Ephesians, 10:13-17.

6. Furneaux, Rupert., Op. Cit., 32.

7. Wilson, Edmund. *The Dead Sea Scrolls.* New York: Oxford University Press, 1969. 58-59.

8. Gaster, Theodor H. *The Dead Sea Scriptures.* Garden City, N.Y.: Anchor Books, 1976. 3.

9. Wison, Edmond., Op. Cit., 81-109.

10. Ibid. 385 & 395.

11. Judeo/Christian Bible. Hebrews , 13:17.

12. Ibid. Romans, 13:1-4.

13. Ibid. Matt., 23:9.

14. Ibid. Matt., 17:20.

15. Ibid. Romans, 3:21-25.

16. Ibid. John, 8:22; 8:22.

17. Ibid. I Thess., 5:9.

18. Ibid. Romans, 14:23.

Notes

19. Robinson, James M., Gen. Ed. *The Naq Hammadi Library.* San Francisco: Harper & Row, 1977. 119

20. Judeo/Christian Bible. Colossians 1:15-17.

21. Judeo/Christian Bible. Luke, 17:21; *Nag Hammadi Library:* Gospel of Thomas, 118; Gospel of Mary, 472; Dialogue of the Savior, 235; Gospel of Philip, 141.

22. Judeo/Christian Bible. Colossians, 1:13.

23. Robinson, James M., Op. Cit., Gospel of Philip, 140.

24. Judeo/Christian Bible. Mark, 12:25.

25. Ibid. I Thessalonians, 4:13-17.

26. Ibid. John, 3:3 & 6 .

27. Ibid. Galations, 4:3-5.

28. Ibid. Romans, 4:6.

29. Ibid. Romans, 8:23.

30. Ibid. I Cor., 6:13 & 18.

31. Robinson, James M., Op. Cit., Gospel of Philip, 139.

Chapter VIII

1. Jones, Roger. *Physics As Metaphor.* New York: New American Library, 1982. 11.

2. Capra, Fritjof. *The Tao of Physics.* Boulder: Shambhala, 1975. 19.

3. Wilber, Ken. *Quantum Questions.* Boulder: Shambhala, 1984. 10.

4. Capra, Fritjof., Op. Cit., 18.

5. Bohm, David. *Wholeness and the Implicate Order.* London: Routledge & Kegan Paul, 1980. XI.

6. Sheldrake, Rupert. *A New Science of Life.*. Los Angeles: J.P. Tarcher, 1981. 206-207.

7. Guthrie, Kenneth Sylvan. *Pythagorean Source Book*. Grand Rapids, Mich: Phanes Press. 1987. 19.

8. Ibid. 137.

9. Ibid. 21.

10. Rutherford, Ward. *Pythagoras, Lover of Wisdom*. Wellingborough, Northamptonshire: Aquarian Press, 1984. 45-53.

11. Nicholson, Shirley, Comp. *Shamanism, An Expanded View of Reality*. Jean Houston. "The Mind and Soul of the Shaman." Wheaton, Ill: Theosophical Pub. 1987. VII.

12. Rutherford, Ward., Op. Cit., 37.

13. Plato. *Dialogues of Plato*. "Phaedo." New York: Pocket Books, 1950. 79.

14. Guthrie, Kenneth Sylvan., Op. Cit., 20.

15. Ibid. 20.

16. McClain, Ernest G. *The Pythaqorean Plato*. Stony Brook, N.Y.: Nicolas Hays, 1978. 3.

17. Michell, John. *The Dimensions of Paradise*. San Francisco: Harper & Row. 1988. 7.

18. Ibid. 7.

19. Ibid. 12.

20. Jones, Roger., Op. Cit., ix.

21. Ibid. 4-5.

22. Ibid. 11.

23. Michell, John., Op. Cit., 14.

24. Cooper, J.C. *An Illustrated Encyclopedea of Traditional Symbols*. London: Thames & Hudson, 1978. 198.

Notes

25. Ibid.   146-151.

26. Ibid.   149.

27. Ibid.   199.

28. Ibid.   60.

29. Ibid.   176.

30. Ibid.   196-197.

31. Ibid.   143.

Chapter IX

1. Robinson, James M., (Gen.   Ed.)   *The Nag Hammadi Library.*
   "Gospel of Philip."   San Francisco:
   Harper & Row 1977.   139.

2. Bennett, John B.   *Rational Thinking.*   Chicago:
   Nelson-Hall.   1980.   18-77.

3. Judeo/Christian Bible.   Genesis,   1:3.

4, Ibid.   1:27.

5. Ibid.   John,   10:34.

6. Ibid.   Galatians,   7:7.

SUGGESTED READING

Barnet, Peter H.   *Tools of Thought.*   Cambridge, Mass:
   Schenkman Pub.   Co.   1981.

Beardsley, Monroe C.   *Thinking Straight.*   Englewood Cliff,
   N.J.: Prentice-Hall.   1950.

Cerminara, Gina.   *Insights For the Age of Aquarius*
   Wheaton, Ill: Theosophical Pub.   1973.

Hayakawa, S.I.   *Symbols, Status and Personality* .
   New York: Harcourt Brace & World.   1963.

The View From Olympus

Chapter X

1. Ouspensky, P.D. *The Psychology of Man's Possible Evolution*. New York: Vantage, 1973. 8-16.

2. Judeo/Christian Bible. Luke, 15:11-32.

3. Young, Arthur. *The Reflexive Universe (Evolution of Consciousness*. New York: Merloyd Lawrence, 1976.

4. Ibid. 37-42.

5. Ibid. 42.

6. Pryse, James. *The Apocalypse Unsealed*. Mokelumne Hill, Ca: Repub. Health Research, 1965.

Chapter XI

1. Judeo/Christian Bible. Exodus, 20:5.

2. Robinson, James M. *The Nag Hammadi Library*, "Gospel of Philip." New York: Harper & Row, 1977. 139.

3. Judeo/Christian Bible. Genesis, 38:9

4. *Webster's New World Dictionary*. David B. Guralnich, (Ed. in Chief.) New York: Prentice Hall, 1984.

5. Walker, Barbara. *The Woman's Encyclopedia* . San Francisco: Harper and Row, 1983. 921.

6. Ibid. 920.

7. Chiniquy. *The Priest, The Woman and the Confessional*. San Diego: National University Press, 1975. 3.

8. Phil Donahue Show. March 15, 1989, Donahue Transcript #031788.

Notes

9. Fisher, Seymour. *Understanding Female Orgasm*. New York: Pocket Books, 1965. 322.

10. Hite, Shere. *The Hite Report*. New York: McMillan Publishing Co., 1976. 137.

11. Ibid. 15-16.

Chapter XII

1. Bulfinch, Thomas. *Bulfinch's Mythology*. New York: Avenel Books. 1979. 86.

2. Ibid. 84.

3. Bartlett, John. *Bartlett's Familiar Quotations*. (Max Plank. *The Philosophy of Physics*. 1936) Boston: Little, Brown & Co., 1980. 686.

4. Ferguson, Marilyn. *The Aquarian Conspiracy*. Los Angeles: J.P. Tarcher. 1980.

5. Jung, Carl, M.D. *Archetypes and the Collective Unconscious*. Princeton: Princeton/Bollingen. 1980.

6. Woolger, Roger, PhD. *Other Lives Other Selves*. New York: Doubleday, 1987. xix.

7 Ibid. 108.

8. Ibid. xviii.

9. Netherton, Morris PhD. *Past Lives Therapy*. New York: William Morrow, 1971. 16.

10. Woolger, Roger., Op. Cit., 16-17.

11. Ibid. 15.

12. Lea, Charles Henry. *A History of the Inquisition of The Middle Ages*. New York: Russell & Russell, (1888) 1955. 92-100.

13. Woolger, Roger., Op. Cit., 8-11.

14. Ibid. 218.

15. Netherton, Morris., Op. Cit., 29.

16. Ibid. 133.

17. Ibid. 126-127.

18. Ibid. 142.

19. Woolger, Roger., Op. Cit., 17-18.

20. McGary, Gladys T. *Born to Live: A Holistic Approach to Child Birth.* Phoenix: Gabriel Press. 1980. 54-55.

21. Hodgson, Joan. *Reincarnation Through the Zodiac.* Reno, Nevada: CRCS Publications. 1973. 25.

22. Koval, Barbara. *The Lively Circle: Astrology and Science In Our Modern Age.* San Diego: Astro Computing Service, 1981. 4.

23. Hodgson, Joan., Op. Cit., 15-22.

24. Howell, Alice O. *Junqian Symbolism in Astroloqy.* Wheaton, Ill.: Theosophical Pub. 1987. 43.

25. Greene, Liz and Howard Sasportas. *The Development of Personality.* York Beach, Maine: Samuel Weiser, 1987. 5.

26. Ibid. 7.

27. Judeo/Christian Bible. Isaiah, 2:4.

SUGGESTED READING

1. Hendrix, Harville. *Getting The Love You Want.* New York: Henry Holt, 1988.

2. Krieger, Dolores PhD., R.N. *The Therapeutic Touch.*

3. Rolf, Ida P. PhD. *Rolfinq—The Inteqration of Human Structure.* New York: Harper & Row, 1977.

4. Thie, John F., D.C. *Touch For Health.* Marina Del Rey: DeVorss. 1973

Bibliography

Bibliography

Adams, W. Marsham. *The Book of the Master of the Hidden Places.*
Wellingborough, Northamptonshire.
Aquarian Press, (1933) 1980.

Alder, Vera Stanley. *The Finding of the Third Eye.*
London:Rider & Co., 1963.

Asher, Maxine, PhD. *The Atlantis Conspiracy.*
Los Angeles: Ancient Mediterranean Research
Assoc. 1974. Rev. 1976.

Barnett, Peter H. *Tools of Thought.*
Cambridge, Mass: Schnekman Pub., 1981.

Beardsley, Monroe C. *Thinking Straight.*
Englewood, N.J.: Prentice Hall, 1975.

Bennett, John B. *Rational Thinking.* Chicago: Nelson-Hall, 1980.

Blavatsky, H.B. *The Voice of the Silence.*
Wheaton, Ill.: Theosophical Pub., 1973.

Bohm, David. *Wholeness and the Implicate Order.*
London: Routledge & Kegan Paul, 1980.

The View From Olympus

Bolen, Jean Shinoda, M.D. *The Tao of Psychology*.
San Francisco: Harper & Row, 1979.

Bord, Janet & Colin. *Earth Rites*. London: Granada Pub., 1983.

Bouquet, A.C. *Hinduism*. London: Hichinson Univ. Lib., 1949.

Braghine, Colonel A. *The Shadow of Atlantis*. Wellingborough,
Northamptonshire, The Aquarian Press, Ltd., 1980.

Brandt, John C. & Stephen P. Maran, Ed. *The New Astronomy and
Science Reader*. San Francisco: W.H. Freeman, 1977.

Breasted, James Henry, PhD. *Ancient Records of Egypt*.
New York: Russell & Russell, 1962.

The Conquest of Civilization.
New York:Harper and Bros., 1938.

Briggs, John P., PhD. & F. David Peat, PhD. *Looking Glass Universe*.
(*The Emerging Science of Wholeness*.)
New York: Simon & Schuster, 1984.

Budge, E.A. Wallis. *The Book of the Dead*. Secaucus,
N.J.: Citadel, 1960.

Dwellers On the Nile. New York: Dover, 1926.

The Gods of the Egyptians. Vol I & II.
New York: Dover, 1969.

Bulfinch, Illus. Federico Castellon. *Bulfinches Mythology*.
Garden City, N.Y.: 1974.

Bury, J.B. M.A., F.B.A. *The Cambridge Medieval History*
Cambridge, England: University Press, 1924.

Bury, J.L. *The History of the Later Roman Empire*.
New York: Dover Publication. 1958.

Caine, Mary. *The Glastonbury Zodiac*.
Kingston, Surrey: Mary Caine, 1978.

Campbell, Anthony. *The Seven States of Consciousness*.

Bibliography

New York: Harper & Row, 1974.
Campbell, Joseph. *Occidental Mythology—The Maskes of God*.
New York: Viking Press. 1964.

Orlental Mythology—The Masks of God.
New York: Penguin Books, 1982.

Capra, Fritjof. *The Tao of Physics*.
Boulder, Colo.: Shambala Pub., 1975.

Carpenter, Edward. *Pagan & Christian Creeds—The Origins and Meaning*. New York: Harcourt Brace & Howe, 1920.

Castello, Sabastian. *Concerning Heretics*.
New York: Octagon Books, 1965.

Cazeau, Charles J. and Stuart D. Scott, Jr. *Exploring the Unknown*.
New York: Plenum Press, 1979.

Cerminara, Gina. *Insights For the Age of Aquarius*.
Wheaton, Ill.: Theosophical Pub., 1973.

Chapman, Sidney, *IGY Year of Discovery*.
Ann Arbor: Universlty of Michigan Press, 1959.

Charlesworth, James H., (Ed.) *The Old Testament Pseudepigrapha*.
Garden City, N.Y.: Doubleday Co., 1983.

Chaudhuri, Haridas. *Integral Yoga*.
Wheaton, Ill.: Theosophical Pub., 1965.

Collin, Rodney. *The Theory of Celestial Influence*.
London: Vincent Stuart Pub., 1954.

Conybeare, Fredrick Cornwallis, M.A. *The Origins of Christianity*.
Evanston, Ill.: Univ. Books, 1958.

Cooper, J.C. *An Illustrated Encyclopedia of Traditional Symbols*.
London: Thames & Hudson, 1978.

Cumont, Franz. *The Mysteries of Mithra*.
Chicago: Open Court Pub., 1910. Reprint
Health Research, Mokelumne Hill, Ca. 1969.

Dames, Michael. *The Silbury Treasure*.

The View From Olympus

London: Thames & Hudson, 1976.

Danielow, Alain. *Shiva & Dionysus*.
New York: Inner Traditions International, 1982.

Davies, Paul. *God and the New Physics*.
New York: Touchstone/Simon & Schuster, 1983.

Devereux, George. *A Study of Abortion in Primitive Societies*.
New York: International University Press, 1976.

Dhiravamsa. *The Dynamic Way of Meditation*.
(The Release and Cure of Pain and Suffering).
Wellingborough, England: Turnstone Press, 1982.

Dikshitar, V.R. *War in Ancient India*. Madras: Ramachandra, 1944.

Doresse, Jean. *The Secret Books of the Egyptian Gnostics*.
Rochester, Vt.: Inner Traditions, Int'l., 1986.

Dudley, Dean. *History of the First Council of Nicea*.
New York: Peter Ekler, 1925. Reprint,
Health Research, Mokelumne Hill, Ca. 1966.

Easwaran, Eknath. *The Mantram Handbook*. (Formulas for
Transformation). Petaluma, Ca: 1977.

Eliade, Mircea. *A History of Religious Ideas, Vol. I*.
Chicago: University Press, 1978.

Evans, Jane. *Twelve Doors to the Soul*.
Wheaton, Ill.: Theosophical Pub., 1979.

Everard, Dr. Trans. *The Divine Pymander of Hermes Mercurius
Trismegistus*. San Diego: Wizards Bookshelf, 1978.

Ferguson, Marilyn. *The Aquarian Coniracy*.
Los Angeles: J.P. Tarcher, 1980.

Finegan, Jack. *Light From the Ancient Past*.
Princeton:Princeton University Press, 1946.

Frazer, Sir James George. *The Golden Bough*.
New York:Mac Millian Pub., 1963.

Bibliography

Furneaux, Rupert. *The Other Side of the Story.*
London: Cassel & Co., Ltd., 1953.

Gardiner, Adelaide. *Meditation—A Practical Study.*
Wheaton, Ill: Theosophical Pub., 1968.

Gaster, Theodor H. *The Dead Sea Scriptures.*
Garden City, N.Y.: Anchor Books, 1976.

George, Llewellyn. *A to Z Horoscope Maker and Delineator.*
Los Angeles: Llewellyn Pub., 1954.

Goddard, Dwight. *Was Jesus Influenced by Buddhism?*
Dwight Goddard, 1927.

Govinda, Lama Anagarika. *Foundations of Tibetan Mysticism.*
New York: Samuel Weiser, 1977.

Graves, Robert. *The Greek Myths Vol. I & II.*
New York: Penguin Books, 1982.

Gray, Louis Herbert, AM, PhD. (Ed.) *Mythology of All Ages.*
New York: Cooper Square Pub., 1964.

Gray, William. *The Talking Tree.*
York Beach, Maine. Samuel Weiser, 1977.

Green, Elmer & Alyce. *Beyond Biofeedback.* New York: Delta, 1977.

Green, Shirely. *The Curious History of Contraception.*
New York: St Martin's Press, 1971.

Greene, Liz & Howard Sasportas. *The Development of the Personality*
(Seminars in Psychological Astrology.)
York Beach, Maine: Samuel Weiser, 1987.

Graiaule, Marcel. *Conersations With Ogotemmeli.*
London: Oxford University Press, 1965.

Grun, Bernard. *Timetables of History.*
New York: Touchstone Books, 1979.

The View From Olympus

Guthrie, Kenneth Sylvan. *The Pythagorean Source Book and Library.* Dexter, Mich.: Phanes Press, 1987.

Hall, Manly P. *Astrological Keywords.* Los Angeles. Philosophical Research Soc., 1958.

Old Testament Wisdom. Los Angeles: Philosophical Research Soc., 1957.

The Story of Astrology. Philadelphia: David McKay, 1943.

Hamalian, Leo & Edmond L. Volpe, (Ed.) *Pulitzer Prize Reader.* New York: Popular Library, 1961.

Hamilton, Edith. *Mythology.* New York: New American Library, 1969.

Hayakawa, S.I. *Symbols, Status and Personality.* New York: Harcourt, Brace & World, 1963.

Hendrix, Harville. *Getting The Love You Want.* New York: Henry Holt, 1988.

Himes, Norman E., PhD. *Medical History of Contraception.* New York: Gamut Press, Inc., 1963.

Hite, Shere. *The Hite Report.* New York: MacMillan Pub. Co., 1976.

Hodgson, Joan. *Reincarnation Through the Zodiac.* Reno, Nevada: CRCS Publications, 1973.

Hoeller, Stephen A. *The Gnostic Jung and the Seven Sermons of the Dead.* Wheaton, Ill., Theosophical Pub., 1982.

Howell, Alice. *Jungian Symbolism in Astrology.* Wheaton Ill: Theosophical Pub., 1987.

Hutchins, Robert Maynard. *Great Books of the Western World.* Chicago: Encyclopedia Britannica, Inc., Vol 16.

Ingalese, Richard. *History and Power of the Mind.*

Bibliography

London: L.N. Fowler & Co. Ltd, 1963.

Iyer, Raghavan. *The Gathas of Zarathustra.* (From the Zend Avesta). Santa Barbara: Concord Grove, 1983.

Jaspers, Carl. *Plato and Augustine.*
New York: Harcourt, Brace and Jovanovich, 1962.

Jastrow, Robert. *God and the Astronomers.*
New York: American Library, 1982.
Until the Sun Dies. New York: Warner, 1977.

Johnson, Dwight. *Spirals of Growth.*
Wheaton, Ill: Theosophical Pub., 1983.

Johnston, Charles. *The Yoga Sutras of Patanjali.*
Albuqerque, N.M.: Brotherhood of Life, 1982.

Jones, Roger. *Physics As Metaphor.*
New York: New American Library, 1982.

Josyer, G.R. *Vimankia Shastra.* (Trans.) Maharishi Baradwaja. Mysore, India, Coronation Press, 1973.

Jung, Carl. *The Archetypes and the Collective Unconscious.*
Princeton: Princeton/Bollingen, 1980.

Man and His Symbols. New York: Dell Pub., 1981.

Memories, Dreams, Reflections.
New York: Pantheon Books, 1963.

Modern Man In Search of a Soul.
New York: Harcourt, Brace & World, 1933.

Kaufmann, William J. III. *Black Holes and Warped Spacetime.*
San Francisco: W.H. Freeman, 1979.

Keeler, Bronson C. *A Short History of the Bible.*
New York: C.P. Farrell (1881)
Reprint Health Research Mokelumne Hill, Ca., 1965.

Kelsey, Denys, MB, M.R.C.P. and Joan Grant. *Many Lifetimes.*
Graden City, N.Y.: Doubleday, 1967.

The View From Olympus

Kennedy, David M. *Birth Control In America.*
　　　　　　New Haven: Yale University Press, 1970.

King, C.W. M.A. *The Gnostics and Their Remains.*
　　　　　　Minneapolis: Wizards Bookshelf, 1973.

Kingsland, William. *The Gnosis and Christianity.*
　　　　　　Wheaton, Ill.: Theosophical Pub., 1975.

Koval, Barbara. *The Lively Circle; Astrology and Science In Our
　　　　　　Modern Age.* San Diego:
　　　　　　Astro Computing Service, 1981.

Krieger, Dolores, PhD, R.N. *The Therapeutic Touch..*
　　　　　　Englewood Cliffs, N.J.: Prentice-Hall, 1979.

Krishna, Gopi. *The Awakening of Kundalini.*
　　　　　　New York: E.P. Dutton. 1975.

　　　　　　Higher Consciousness. New York: Julian Press, 1974.

Kuhn, Thomas S. *The Structure of Scientific Revolution.*
　　　　　　Chicago: University Press, 1970.

Krupp, Dr. E.C. *Echoes of the Ancient Skies.*
　　　　　　(The Astronomy of Lost Civilizations.)
　　　　　　New York: New American Library, 1983.

Larson, Martin A. *The Essene Heritage.*
　　　　　　New York: Philosophical Library, 1967.

　　　　　　The Story of Christian Origins.
　　　　　　Taklequah, Okla.: Village Press, 1977.

Law, Narenda Nath. *Age of the Vedas.*
　　　　　　Calcutta: Firma K.L. Mukhopadhyay, 1965.
Layman's Parallel Bible, The. Grand Rapids, Michigan:
　　　　　　Zondervan Bible Pub., 1973.

Lea, Henry Charles, *The History of the Inquisition of th Middle Ages,*
　　　　　　Vol. I. New York: Russell & Russell, 1955.

Bibliography

Leadbeater, C.W. *The Chakras.*
          Wheaton, Ill.: Theosophical Pub., 1974.

          The Christian Gnosis. London:
          The St. Alban Press, 1983.

Leeming, Joseph. *Yoga and the Bible.*
          London: George Allen and Unwin, 1963.

Leo, Alan. *The Key to Your Own Nativity.*
          Edinburgh: International Pub., 1956.

Lewinson, Richard, M.D. *A History of Sexual Customs.*
          New York: Harper & Bros., 1958.

Lillie, Arthur. *India in Prinitive Christianity.*
          London: Keg an Paul, Trench, Trubover, 1909.

Lissner, Ivar. *The Living Past.* New York: G.P. Putnam's Sons, 1957.

Long, Max Freedom. *The Huna Code In Religion.*
          Marina Del Rey, Ca.: Devorss, 1965.

          The Secret Science Behind Miracles.
          Marina Del Rey, Ca. Devorss, 1954.

Marcus, Irwin M., M.D. & John J. Francis, M.D. *Masturbation From
          Infancy to Senescence.* New York:
          International Universities Press, Inc., 1975.

Marcuse, Herbert. *Reason and Revolution.*
          Boston: Beacon Press, 1960.

Matt, Daniel Chanan, Trans. *Zohar-The Book of Enlightenment.*
          New York: Paulist Press, 1983.

McClain, Ernest G. *The Pythagorean Plato* (Prelude to the Son Itself).
          Stony Brook, N.Y.: Nicolas Hays, 1978.

McGarey, Gladys, M.D. *Born To Live*
          (A Holistic Approach To Childbirth.)
          Phoenix, Az.: Gabriel, 1980.

The View From Olympus

McKay, John P., Bennett D. Hill, and John Buchler.
    A History of Western Society Vol. I.
    Boston: Houghton Mifflin, 1979.

Mead, G.R.S. *Fragments of Faith Forgotten.*
    London: Theosophical Pub., 1900.

Meyer, Marvin W. *The Ancient Mysteries* (A Source Book).
    San Francisco. Harper & Row, 1987.

Meyer, Michael. *A Handbook for the Humanistic Astrologer.*
    Garden City, N.Y.: Anchor, 1974.

Michell, John. *The View Over Atlantis.*
    San Francisco: Harper & Row, 1983.

Moody, Raymond A. Jr., M.D. *Life After Life.*
    New York: Bantom, 1975.

Morrison, Tony. *Pathways To The Gods.* Chicago: Academy, 1988.

Motoyama, Hiroshi. *Theories of the Chakras:*
    Bridge to Higher Consciousness.
    Wheaton, Ill.: Theosophical Pub., 1981.

Netherton, Morris, PhD. *Past Lives Therapy.*
    New York: William Morrow, 1978.

Neusner, Jacob. *Invitation to the Talmud.*
    San Francisco: Harper & Row, 1984.

Noss, John B. *Man's Religions.* New York: MacMillan, 1963.

d'Olivet, Fabre. *The Golden Verses of Pythagoras.*
    New York: Samuel Weiser, 1975.

    The Hebraic Tongue Restored.
    York Beach, Maine: Samuel Welser, 1981.

Ouspensky, P.D. *The Psychology of Man's Possible Evolution.*
    New York: Alfred Knoff, 1954.

Bibliography

Oxford Dictionary of Quotations. Oxford:
        Oxford University Press, 1980.

Pagan, Isabelle M. *From Pioneer to Poet or The Twelve Great Gates.*
        London: Theosophical Pub., 1969.

Pagels, Elaine. *The Gnostic Gospels.*
        New York: Random House, 1979.
Plato. Desmond Lee, (Trans.) *Timaeus and Critias.*
        Middlsex, England: Penguin Books, 1971.

Peters, Edward, (Ed.) *Heresy and Authority in Medieval*
        Europe. Philadelphia: University Press, 1980.

Pfeiffer, Robert H. *History of New Testament Times.*
        London: Adam & Charles Black, 1954.

Le Plongeon, Augustus. *Sacred Mysteries.*
        New York: Macoy Pub., (1909)   Reprint
        Health Research, Mokelumne Hill, Ca., 1976.

Prabhavananda, Swami & Christopher Isherwood.
        How to Know God.
        (The Yoga Aphorisms of Patanjali).
        Hollywood: Vedanta Press, 1953.

Prabhavananda, Swami. *The Sermon on the Mount According to*
        Vedanta. New York: New American Lib., 1963.

Progoff, Ira. *At a Journal Workshop.*
        New York: Dialogue House Lib., 1975.

        The Practice of Process Meditation.
        New York: Dialogue House, 1980.

Pryse, James Morgan. *Prometheus Bound.* Mukelumne Hill, Ca.
        Reprint Health Research, 1967.
Ramacharaka, Yogi. *Science of Breath.*
        Chicago: Yogi Publication Soc., 1905.

Rama, Swami, Rudolph Ballentine, M.E., Swami Ajaya, PhD.
        Yoga and Psychotherapy
        (The Evolution of Consciousness).

The View From Olympus

Honesdale, Penn: Himalayan Int'l. Inst., 1976.

Robinson, James M. (Ed.) *The Nag Hammadi Library*.
San Francisco: Harper & Row, 1977.

Robson, Arthur. *Man and His Seven Principles*.
Madras, India: Theosophical Pub., 1973.

Rolf, Ida P., PhD. *Rolfing—The Integration of Human Structure*.
New York: Harper & Row, 1977.

Rutherford, Ward. *Pythagoras Lover of Wisdom*. Wellingborough,
Northampton: Aquarian Press, 1984.

Sagan, Carl. *The Cosmic Connection*.
Garden City, N.Y.: Anchor Books, 1973.

Cosmos. New York: Random House, 1980.

Sakoian, Frances and Louis Acher. *The Astrologer's Handbook*.
New York: Harper & Row, 1973.

The Zodiac Within Each Sign. (Interpreting the
Horoscope With Decanates & Duads).
New York: Frances Sakoian & Louis Acher, 1975.

Sanger, Margaret. *Woman and the New Race*. Fairview Park
Elmsford, New York: (1920) Reprint 1969.

Satprem. *Sri Aurobindo*. New York: Harper & Row, 1968.

Scholem, Gershom. *Kabbalah*.
New York: New American Library, 1974.

Zohar—The Book of Splendor.
New York: Schocken Books, 1963.

Sheldrake, Rupert. *A New Science of Life*.
San Francisco: J.P. Tarcher, 1981.

Silk, Joseph. *The Big Bang*. San Francisco: W.H. Freeman, 1980.

Sitchin, Zecharia. *The 12th Planet*.
New York: Stein & Day Pub., 1976.

Bibliography

Sjoo, Monica & Barbara Mor. *The Great Cosmic Mother.*
San Francisco: Harper & Row, 1987.

Smith, George. *Chaldean Account of Genesis.*
Minneapolis: Wizards Book Shelf, 1977.

Spence, Lewis. *The History of Atlantis.* University Books, Inc. 1968.

The Problem of Lemuria.
Philadelphia: David McKay, 1933.

Squire, Charles. *Celtic Myth and Legend.*
Newcastle: Newcastle Publishing Co., 1975.

Steiger, Brad. *Worlds Before Our Own.* Berkely-Putnam, 1978.

Steinsaltz, Adin. *The Essential Talmud.*
New York: Harper & Row, 1976.

Stone, Merlin. *When God Was A Woman.*
New York: Harcourt, Brace, Jovanovich, 1976.

Story, Ronald. *The Space Gods Revealed.*
New York: Harper & Rowe, 1977.

Stowe, Lyman E. *Stowe's Bible Astrology.* Mokelumne Hill, Ca.:
Reprint Health Research, 1965.

Suares, Carlo. *The Sepher Yetsira.* Boulder: Shambhala, 1976.

Suzuki, Daisetz Teitara. *The Awakening of Zen.*
Boulder: Prajna Press, 1980.

Suzuki, Shunryu. *Zen Mind, Beginner's Mind.*
New York: Weatherhill, 1980.

Sweet, William Warren. *The Story of Religion in America.*
New York: Harper & Row, 1950.

The Science of Yoga.
Wheaton, Ill: Theosophical Pub., 1981.

Taylor, Thomas. *The Eleusian & Bacchie Mysteries.*

The View From Olympus

San Diego: Wizard's Bookshelf, 1980.
Temple, Robert, K.G. *The Sirius Mystery*.
Rochester, Vt.: Destiny Books, 1987.

Thie, John F., D.C. *Touch For Health*.
Marina Del Rey: DeVorss, 1973.

Three Initiates. *The Kybalion*
Chicago: Yogi Publishing Society, 1940.

Tolstoy, Nikolai. *The Quest for Merlin*.
Boston: Little, Brown, 1985.

Tompkins, Peter, *Mysteries of the Mexican Pyramids*.
New York: Harper & Row, 1976.

Tsui Chi. *A Short History of Chinese Civilization*.
New York G.P. Putnam's, 1943.

Waite, A. *The Holy Kabbalah*.
Secaucus, J.J.: Citadel Press, no date.

Waite, Charles B., A.M. *History of the Christian Religion*.
Chicago: C.B. Waite & Co., 1900.

Wakefield, Walter L. and Austin P. Evans.
Heresies of the High Middle Ages.
New York: Columbia Univ. Press, 1969.

Wambach, Helen, PhD. *Life Before Life*. New York: Bantam, 1979.
Reliving Past Lives. New York: Bantam, 1978.

Watkins, Alfred. *The Ley Hunter's Manual*. Wellingborough,
Northamptonshire: Turnstone, (1927) 1983.

Wilbur, Ken. *The Holographic Paradigm and other Paradoxes*.
Boulder: Shamhala, 1982.

Quantum Questions. Boulder: Shambhala, 1984.

Williamson, W. *The Great Law*.
London: Longmans, Green & Co., 1899.

Bibliography

Wilson, Colon. *The Occult.*
New York: Vintage, Random House, 1973.

Wilson, Edmund. *The Dead Sea Scrolls.*
New York: Oxford University Press, 1969.

Whishaw, Elena. *Atlantis In Andalucia.*
London: Rider & Co., no date.

Whitmont, Edward C. *Return of the Goddess.*
New York: Crossroad, 1984.

Wolf, Fred Alan. *Taking the Quantum Leap.*
San Francisco: Harper & Row, 1981.

Woolger, Roger, PhD. *Other Lives Other Selves.*
New York: Doubleday, 1987.

Wolley, C. Leonard. *The Sumerians.*
New York: W.W. Norton, 1965.

Woods, Ernest. *Seven Schools of Yoga.*
Wheaton, Ill.: Theosophical Pub., 1973.

Womack, David A. *12 Signs 12 Sons—Astrology in the Bible.*
Harper & Row, 1978.

Wynn-Tyson, Esme. *The Fellow With the Yellow Cap.*
London: Rider & Co. , 1958.

Young, Arthur. *The Reflexive Universe.*
(Evolution of Consciousness).
San Francisco: Merloyd, 1976.

Zain, C.C. *Delineating The Horoscope.*
Los Angeles: The Church of Light, 1922.

Zwig, Stephen. *The Right to Heresy.*
New York: Viking Press, 1936.

The View From Olympus

Index

Index

The View From Olympus

Index

The View From Olympus

Index

Index

THE NEW GNOSTIC SOCIETY
A Mystic Philosophy for the New Age
Based upon Universal Law

Providing a communication network
for individuals interested in learning to live
according to Universal Law.

Founded by Donna H. Lloyd, Ph.D.

For information regarding membership
in the Society or to arrange for
seminars and lectures
by Dr. Lloyd,
Call (602) 282-1629 or write to:

The New Gnostic Society
2675 W. Hwy 89A, Suite 410
Sedona, Arizona, 86336